Sandplay and St

The Impact of Imaginative Thinking on Children's Learning and Development

Barbara A. Turner, PhD
Kristín Unnsteinsdóttir, PhD

Foreword by Thomas L. Armstrong, PhD

TEMENOS PRESS®

Sandplay and Storytelling:

The Impact of Imaginative Thinking on
Children's Learning and Development

Back cover photo by Svanlaug D. Thorarensen

Published by

TEMENOS PRESS®
Box 305
Cloverdale, California 95425
USA
www.temenospress.com

1 2 3 4 5 6 7 8 9 10

Library of Congress Cataloging-in-Publication Data

  Turner, Barbara A.
    Sandplay and storytelling : the impact of imaginative
    thinking on children's learning and development /
    Barbara A. Turner, Kristín Unnsteinsdóttir.

    p. cm.
    Includes bibliographical references and index.
    LCCN 2011940684
    ISBN-13: 978-0-9728517-4-9
    ISBN-10: 0-9728517-4-7

    1. Sandplay. 2. Storytelling. 3. Child development.
    I. Unnsteinsdóttir, Kristín. II. Title.

    RJ505.P6T87 2012   618.92'891653
                    QBI11-600204

For the Children...

Table of Contents

Foreword – Thomas L. Armstrong ix

Part I

Overview – Barbara Turner 1
My Way to Sandplay – Kristín Unnsteinsdóttir 3

Part II

Sandplay Therapy
    Introduction to Sandplay Therapy 5
    How Sandplay Therapy Works 7

Part III

Sandplay and Brain Function: How Sandplay Impacts Neurology
    Body Maps in the Brain 11
    The Impact of Images on the Brain 12
    Neuroplasticity 12
    The Neurological Formation of the Sense of Self 13
    The Neurological Components of Psychic Change 15
    The Image in Neural Change 16

The Brain in Relationship: Mirror Neuron Networks
    The Discovery of Mirror Neurons 17
    Interaction and Neural Connectivity 18

Mirror Neuron Networks in Sandplay. 18
Mirror Neuron Networks and Learning 19

Mirror Neuron Networks: The Hands, Learning and Language Formation
Mirror Neurons in the Premotor Cortex 19
Neurological Implications of Hand Movement in Sandplay 20
Neurological Implications of the Visual Image in Sandplay. 21
The Hands and Storytelling. 21

Part IV

The Value of Imaginative Storytelling
The Mind at Work in Imaginative Storytelling and Sandplay 23
Modes of Thinking and Creativity. 24
Play in Development and Learning 25
Creativity and Individuation. 26
The Process of Imaginative Storytelling 27
Characteristics of Children's Imaginative Tales 28

Reflections 31

Part V

The Research Study
Introduction 33

The Outcome of Psychological Tests and Assessments
Scales of Self Assessment. 35
The Achenbach Scale and Attention Deficit/
    Hyperactivity Disorder Rating Scale IV. 36
Wechsler Intelligence Scale for Children. 38
WISC-III 39
WISC-IV 41
Score Improvements on WISC-III and WISC-IV 43

Conclusion 45

Part VI

The Sandplay Cases – Overview

The Sandplay Work of Hanna: Girl 5th Grade – Age 10 49

The Sandplay Work of Ari: Boy 4th Grade – Age 9 105

The Sandplay Work of Alda: Girl 4th Grade – Age 9 143

The Sandplay Work of Filip: Boy 3rd Grade – Age 8 189

Concluding Remarks 231

Resources 233

Glossary of Jungian Terms 235

References 239

Index 247

Foreword

Thomas Armstrong

The field of formal education has had relatively few books dedicated to an exploration of the unconscious and the inner psyche of the child. Neither Freud nor Jung was particularly interested in applying their psychologies to education. Some of Freud's disciples did make important contributions to the field, including Alfred Adler (1978), Bruno Bettelheim (Zelan & Bettelheim, 1982), Rudolf Dreikurs (Dreikurs & Dinkmeyer, 2000), William Glasser (1975) and A.S. Neill (1984). For Jung, there is Frances Wickes' wonderful book *The Inner World of Childhood* (1988) and the more recent work of Clifford Mayes (2005). But by and large, this is a virgin field. That's why it's so refreshing to have a new book applying the Jungian practice of sandplay therapy directly to an educational setting.

This wonderful book, the product of a partnership between Barbara Turner, an American psychotherapist and Kristín Unnsteinsdóttir, an Icelandic learning specialist, integrates an understanding of the school difficulties of four children with their explorations in imaginative storytelling and sandplay work. I don't believe I can express how significant this book is in breaking new ground that hopefully other educators and psychologists will continue to till in the future.

The situation in education these days is grim. Our children sit in classrooms for six hours a day, five days a week, 40 weeks a year, yet only a handful of researchers have bothered to inquire about what is going on beneath the surface of their conscious experience. Many of these children have undergone traumas that they bring with them into the classroom: the death of close ones, divorce, physical or sexual abuse, bullying, and mental or physical illness, among others. And when they begin to experience difficulties in learning, instead of inquiring into the contents of their psyches, educators are too quick to label the child with some convenient term (ADHD, learning disabilities, dyslexia), and then go about "remediating" it with tools that don't reflect in any substantial way their rich inner lives. This book is a wonderful antidote to this overly rational way of approaching the needs of children in school settings.

In the course of reading this book, you will learn about Alda, a nine-year-old girl who struggles with reading, yet sings and dances with ease, and whose "dyslexia" and "ADHD" improve as she begins to tell stories and work with the miniature figures that make up her sandplay worlds. You'll delight in eight-year-old Filip's humorous and playful activities in the sand as he creates worlds with titles like *The Beautiful Jungle and the Dangerous Statue* and *The Secret of the Pirate Funfair*. You'll begin to understand how Filip's wandering mind during class time, which earns him the designation of having attention deficit disorder, is finally able to find in the sand tray a sacred and protected space (the Greeks called it a *temenos*) where his imagination is allowed to move in an organic fashion that is transformational in its healing, and that ultimately leads to a significant amelioration of his symptoms and even to increases in his IQ test results. That, in fact, is one of the great findings of this research – that children actually improve their intelligence test scores by exploring their unconscious. I believe that this is the first time a study has ever revealed this fascinating connection between a child's inner psychodynamic world and intelligence testing. In the field of educational psychology, we have long used IQ tests as an indicator of a child's "potential." Clearly, *Sandplay and Storytelling* shows us how laughable this conception is, and how much more is included in a child's potential when we begin to embrace her unfathomable inner depths. This book also makes a significant contribution to our understanding of how the child's brain is positively impacted by the physical and psychic act of touching the sand and manipulating the archetypal symbols of the inner self. As we learn more about neuroscience and the child's developing brain, we begin to see how important it is that children have the opportunity to engage in rich multi-sensory multiple intelligences activities like storytelling and sandplay to help them integrate right and left hemispheric functions, and limbic and neocortical areas of the brain. I want to congratulate Barbara Turner and Kristín Unnsteinsdóttir, for their marvelous contribution to transformational learning and integral psychology, and I wish them the very best in the success of this book so that more and more children around the world can receive the important benefits of storytelling and sandplay in their lives.

Thomas Armstrong, PhD
October 2011

Part I

Overview

Barbara Turner

Permit me to introduce myself. I am Barbara Turner, a psychotherapist with a specialty in Jungian sandplay therapy. My initial interest in sandplay came after I had seen some remarkable clinical work using this modality. In 1988 in Switzerland I began my studies with Dora Kalff, founder of the sandplay method. I focused my doctoral work on sandplay as a medium of individual, social and global change in the Department of Transformative Learning at the California Institute of Integral Studies in San Francisco. I remained impassioned by the method and was determined to develop an understanding of how sandplay worked to move the psyche. This culminated in writing *The Handbook of Sandplay Therapy* in 2005. Prior to that I was also able to return the classic books in sandplay to print, Dora Kalff's *Sandplay: A Psychotherapeutic Approach to the Psyche*, 2003; Estelle L. Weinrib's *Images of the Self: The Sandplay Therapy Process*, 2004; and H.G. Wells' *Floor Games: A Father's Account of Play and Its Legacy of Healing*, 2004. I used sandplay therapy in my clinical work with adults and children for over twenty years and now devote my energy to training sandplay therapists and writing in the field.

Given the wonders of the internet and technology I had the good fortune of meeting Kristín Unnsteinsdóttir in 2007 through the online curriculum I offer in the theory and foundations of sandplay therapy. I soon noticed that her work was exemplary. Through correspondence I learned about her extensive background in Jungian psychology and her expertise in fairy tale and storytelling. Not long after she completed the sandplay curriculum we began consulting about the sandplay work she had done with children.

I soon discovered that Dr. Unnsteinsdóttir had conducted a remarkable study at the school where she is the Learning Specialist. We will review the study in depth at a later point. Briefly, she had a group of elementary school children who were referred to her office for a number of emotional, behavioral and learning issues. She ran a large battery of pre and posttests that measured many dimensions of the children's emotional well being, behavioral issues, information processing, learning styles and traditional IQ scores. Remarkably, in addition to general improvements in emotional well-being and behavior, the posttests showed substantial increases in the intelligence scores of nearly half of the children.

I was greatly intrigued. While this is just one study, the clinical documentation of this finding is highly significant and has far reaching implications for the use of sandplay as a standard component of the educational setting. Dr. Unnsteinsdóttir comes from the fields of Education and Analytical Psychology. My background is in Religious Studies, Counseling Psychology and Transformative Learning. I have long been a firm believer in interdisciplinary studies, knowing that reaching beyond the limits of our particular disciplines has the advantage of contributing new information, insight, vision and possibility to our work. With the input of specialists from outside our areas of expertise, we increase the possibility of seeing things in new ways in addition to learning a great deal. Thus Dr. Unnsteinsdóttir and I began our collaborative effort to share this information with other educators and mental health clinicians who might have interest in sandplay as an important supplement to education. Perhaps this will inspire a new level of collaboration between teachers and school counselors, art therapists and psychologists who train to practice sandplay.

My Way to Sandplay

Kristín Unnsteinsdóttir

The path leading me to use sandplay and storytelling in my work with children was unforeseen 37 years ago when I started my professional life. However on the way my interests gradually coalesced around children's development. I was particularly concerned with their emotional development, and methods that would allow them to access their inner worlds using imagination and creativity.

I started my professional life as a children's librarian in a public library and soon changed to school libraries where I became interested in education. Both my M.Ed and PhD in education were based on studies of fairy tales from oral tradition. In the doctoral studies I also investigated self-generated fairy tales and how they function as catalysts in children's educational and emotional development. My study drew from theories of analytical psychology and models derived from structuralism. Following the completion of my dissertation I continued my studies in analytical psychology. That is when I first learned of sandplay therapy. I located a sandplay therapist who lived nearby the little town where I was living in England and began my personal sandplay process. Soon after I defended my dissertation and returned home to Iceland. This was in 2002. To this day I continue my sandplay process and studies in sandplay.

When I returned to Reykjavik I began work in a public grade school where I became the director of the Learning Center. From the beginning I was determined to use sandplay and storytelling with my pupils who needed help with learning disabilities, reading competence, attention and/or emotional problems. I was convinced that the best I could offer these children would be drawn from fields I understand well and am profoundly interested in. This led me to the conclusion that the children's strongest tool to tackle problems of all sorts is their imagination. My role was to help them get into touch with this source within themselves. In all of my reading about sandplay I did not find any accounts of the systematic use of the method in the school environment until I came across an inspirational article that described the positive influence of sandplay on reading skills (Noyes, 1981). This supported my own ideas and I was excited by the possibilities this might have at the Learning Center.

I began offering sandplay to the children who visited regularly. Sometimes a child would use the entire time period for work in the sand, and other times we would do additional activities in conjunction with sandplay. At all times I collaborated closely with the School Psychologist and did extensive consultation on my sandplay case work.

I soon realized that I missed doing research and received a grant that allowed me to launch a study that lasted from 2005–2009. This was entitled, *The Influence of Sandplay and Storytelling on the Self-Image and Development of Children's Learning, Mental Wellbeing and Social Skills*. The cases presented in this book are all drawn from this project. I have recently received another grant that has enabled me to resume data collection.

I was professionally isolated during the first few years of my study at the Learning Center. I knew of no one in Iceland who was working with sandplay using Dora Kalff's Jungian approach. After studying abroad for years I did not have the means to take a long break and leave the island for further studies. It was such a welcome revelation when I contacted Barbara Turner in 2007. In 2010, after consulting on a number of the sandplay cases from my study we decided to collaborate on a book that would focus on evaluating the regular use of sandplay and story making in the school context. The opportunity to work with Barbara has been invaluable to me professionally and has put my study into a context that was beyond my imaginings. As a mentor Barbara is not only an extremely experienced and a knowledge-able sandplay therapist and scholar but has also proven to be a generous and open-minded person with a warm sense of humor which makes her so pleasant to work with.

Part II

Sandplay Therapy

Introduction to Sandplay Therapy

Sandplay therapy is a psychotherapeutic modality that was originally developed as a means of doing Jungian analysis with children. Sandplay stems from the pioneering work of Dr. Margaret Lowenfeld, a physician who worked in London in the early twentieth century. Lowenfeld had dual citizenship, having been born in Poland. She visited her native Poland after the ravages of a devastating war and was overcome by the trauma suffered by the children. This experience inspired her determination to find a way to work with children that would allow her to understand their thinking.

Lowenfeld recalled reading a little book written by well-known social critic, H.G. Wells, called *Floor Games* (Turner, 2004). In this delightful book Wells talks about the imaginary worlds his boys built on their nursery floor with wooden blocks and miniature figures. With his inimitable wit and humor Wells describes their endless play and how this was essential to their creative development. He counsels parents, as well as uncles and aunts, about the value of play in childhood. In addition he admonishes shopkeepers for selling only figures of soldiers and having no regular people.

Inspired by this Lowenfeld brought a large variety of miniature figures to her clinic for the children. What she soon discovered was that the children were taking the figures from the cabinet on one side of the clinic and playing with them in the sand box across the room. This motivated her to create a small sand tray in which the individual child could build a miniature world. It was the natural brilliance of the children that created sandplay. Lowenfeld called her method *The World Technique*. Lowenfeld's approach was to ask the child to build a miniature world in the sand tray and then they would talk about it together.

Dora Kalff, who had been displaced from her native Holland by another war, lived in Switzerland very near Carl and Emma Jung. After completing her analysis with Emma Jung, Kalff was pursuing options for a career. Carl Jung said that he had noticed that his grandchildren were always in better condition when they returned from Kalff's house, so he suggested she find a way to do Jungian analysis with children.

Understanding children's abilities and level of development, Kalff knew that any such method would need to be play based, largely non-verbal and not analytical. Kalff then met Dr. Lowenfeld and was intrigued with the possibilities of her World Technique. Kalff studied with Lowenfeld in London and soon recognized that what was taking place in the children's worlds was what Jung had described as the *individuation process*. She also saw that this process of human development was best facilitated when the therapist witnessed the child's work without the interference of questions and dialog used in the Lowenfeld method. Kalff and Lowenfeld discussed their differences in approach to the work and agreed to have two separate schools of practice. Lowenfeld would continue to call her's The World Technique and Kalff called her's *sandplay*.

While sandplay was originally developed for use with children, adults soon became fascinated with the modality and began doing sandplay in their therapy. The sand tray measures 28.5 × 19.5 × 3 inches. It is filled about half full of sand. The tray is painted a sky blue color on the inside so the sandplayer can dig down through the sand to make a lake, river, design, etc. The sandplay therapist has two sand trays, one with wet sand, which can be sculpted and shaped, and the other with dry sand. A *collection* of miniature figures representing all parts of life and fantasy is arranged on shelves nearby. Simple building materials, such as paper, string, sticks and glue, are also in the collection in the event the client is not able to find what is needed for the tray. The therapeutic method is referred to as *sandplay*. The box of sand is the *sand tray*. We interchangeably refer to the individual completed construction as having done a *tray, sand tray* or a *sandplay*. The psychological work done over a series of trays is known as the *sandplay process*, or a *process*.

The therapist encourages the client to make whatever he or she wishes in the tray. As the client works, the therapist observes quietly and makes note of what the client does, uses, and so on. When the client is finished, therapist and client quietly observe the tray together. With a child client we may ask if there is a title or a story to this tray. With the adult we usually ask if he or she had any associations as they did the tray. They can say something or not. The therapist just makes note of it. The therapist photographs the tray for a visual record and disassembles the tray after the client has left.

Sandplay appears very simple on the surface. It is certainly not difficult to put together a collection of toys and a tray of sand. However, what takes place in sandplay work is highly complex and requires that the therapist be very well trained. Sandplay works at a deep level

Sand Trays and the Sandplay Collection

of the psyche and can be profoundly evocative. To keep the process safe, the therapist must understand what is taking place and must be prepared to handle whatever comes up. To do this requires the therapist to have undergone extensive inner work in addition to a proper study of psychology. Training requirements for sandplay are managed by the International Society for Sandplay Therapy – ISST and by its regional branches such as the Sandplay Therapists of America – STA. More information about these organizations can be found in the *Resource Section*.

How Sandplay Therapy Works

Sandplay therapy is an image-based psychotherapeutic modality that works largely in the right of the brain. It is based on C.G. Jung's personality theory, a central tenet of which is that the psyche is naturally inclined to heal and grow to more wholeness. Jungian theory is used in sandplay as a means of understanding how the mind functions and undergoes change. We will refer to Jung's personality theory throughout the text and will attempt to define new terms as they appear. We have also prepared a *Glossary of Terms* for ease of reference.

Jung observed that the psyche is not chaotic, but is characterized by a central ordering principle, he called the *Self*. In the proper conditions this innate disposition to heal and grow toward the wholeness of the Self is activated. Dora Kalff (2003) referred to these conditions in sandplay as the *free and protected space*. Sandplay is free because it offers the client limitless possibilities. It is safe because the tray itself has boundaries and serves as a container. Even more importantly the safe field is created by the presence of the properly trained therapist. The therapist is the most important tool in sandplay.

Early in his work Jung (1976) observed that there were two types of thinking. One is ordinary, *directed thinking*, which is rational and logic based. This form of thinking is sequential and rational and is primarily a function of the left hemisphere in most people. Jung noticed that this form of thought did not stand on its own, but appeared to evolve out of an underlying form of thinking that he called *undirected thinking*. This mode of thinking is non-rational, but has its own form of meaning and is characterized by images and symbols. On the basis of these observations Jung developed his theories of the unconscious and the conscious mind. We will explore directed and undirected thinking later in the text.

Kalff proportioned the sand tray in such a way that it fills the entire field of vision without requiring the client to turn the head from side to side. Standing at the tray thus relaxes our hold on rationality and allows the mind to access the right hemispheric undirected mode of thinking. In this softened or liminal state of awareness, the client enters unconscious mental processing and selects figures that catch his or her attention from the collection. The figures that catch the client's attention are those that bear the symbolic content of his or her inner images. In this way the images or symbols that prefigure new forms of thought assume concrete form. Placing objects in the tray in varying combinations and arrangements, along with the way the client shapes the sand, forms a complex symbolic construction that is visible to both the client and the therapist. Because the psyche is predisposed to heal and develop, the material that appears is that which is on the cutting edge of the client's psychic growth. This symbolic material may carry psychological conflicts that have prevented the client's continued growth, causing an arrest in the development of the personality. It also contains the means to resolve them. The symbolic material may carry new psychic qualities that will enhance and further development toward wholeness. The sandplay process thus provides the conscious personality the means to address conflicts, traumas, losses, etc., as well as the psychic content necessary to further personality development.

Because the images and open possibilities of the right hemisphere precede the precise focus of left hemispheric thinking, the symbolic material in sandplay concretizes and makes evident the next stage in the client's development. The following tray in the series then allows the subsequent phase of the client's healing and development to materialize and be witnessed. Thus, over the course of a series of sandplays, known as a *process*, the client sets in place the steps required for his or her development. The images continue to influence the left hemisphere until they become fully conscious. We will examine this more in depth in the following chapter.

Part III

Sandplay and Brain Function: How Sandplay Impacts Neurology

The creation of a sandplay involves many physical systems. These include movement of the body, the sense of touch, visual capacities, holding and carrying the figures, and so on. As soon as the sandplayer begins to touch the sand and select figures, feelings and memories are generated. Badenoch (2008) observed that the physical sensation of touching the sand facilitates a neural integration that connects the body, limbic system and cerebral cortex in the right hemisphere. Simply said, sandplay activates and moves the neural configuration of the brain.

Body Maps in the Brain

Researchers are now aware that the brain builds mental maps to relate the body to its surrounding space creating a sense of me as an embodied self (Blakeslee & Blakeslee, 2008). We are all familiar with the early brain mapping done by Wilder Penfield at the University of Montreal (1977). Dr. Penfield, a neurosurgeon, who was treating epileptic patients with a mild electric shock to avert seizure, inadvertently discovered that when he applied current to different areas of the brain, the patient experienced sensation in a part of their body, a vivid memory, and so on. Furthermore the sensations were consistent with the location in the brain. That is to say that re-stimulation of the same area of the brain consistently evoked the same response. So he began devising a rigorous map of the human brain by systematically stimulating specific areas and having his nurse record the findings. An interesting tidbit is that Barbara's mother-in-law was the long time nurse for Dr. Penfield during his early research.

A highly interesting discovery is that these mental maps do not stop with the skin, but extend to include the surrounding space (Blakeslee & Blakeslee, 2008). University of California Los Angeles neuroscientist Marco Iacoboni (2008) explained this phenomenon by pointing out that neurons for the visual and tactile-receptive fields are related in a particular area of the brain, creating a map of the space surrounding the body, or a *peripersonal* space. Iacoboni described this space as a map of *potential actions*. This has far-reaching implications in sandplay which involves the focused interaction of the client with the sand

and the symbols in the presence of the therapist. Research findings also demonstrate that these mind maps expand and contract to include objects. What this means is that the act of engaging with the sand and the symbols neurologically incorporates them into the sand-player's mental map of who they are. The sandplayer carries the symbols in this periper-sonal space of potential action where they exert the energetic impetus to be in the world in a different way, stimulating neural growth.

The Impact of Images on the Brain

We know that images have a profound impact on mental functioning. In his early work neu-rological researcher Ralph Haber (1983) demonstrated that subjects have image recogni-tion accuracy of up to 95%. In fact, images are often far more evocative than words. Images activate many dimensions of cortical activity, including imagination, and have been shown to be far more accurate and incisive in generating associations, stimulating creative think-ing and memory. With the more recent research on mind maps we begin to comprehend the power the symbolic images have on the sandplayer long after the individual sand tray is constructed. Recognizing the compelling force of the internalized symbolic images makes it very clear how prematurely interpreting the sand tray or discussing it with the client com-pels a more conscious appraisal of the content. This interferes with the neural modifications the symbolic images are already in the process of effecting on the client's brain.

Along with the incorporation of the symbolic images into the client's neural body map energy of the witnessing therapist is also absorbed and carried neurologically by the sand-player. During sandplay there is a subtle, but very real mutual experience of the client's work between sandplayer and therapist. By virtue of his or her experience, quality of men-tal development and training, the sandplay therapist must be able to sustain a sturdy and caring presence during the client's transformative process. In the shared field of the client's neural body map the strength and clarity of the witnessing therapist provides a stabiliz-ing force while the client undergoes the neural re-structuring fueled by the images. It is important to remember that the subjective experience of neural re-ordering can feel greatly destabilizing and wrought with terror.

Neuroplasticity

Advanced imaging tools and continued research now reveal that these mental maps are flexible and capable of change (Boleyn-Fitzgerald, 2010). As early as 1973, Polish neurophysiologist, Jerzy Konorski (1948) coined the term *neuroplasticity* in his research into how the brain changed through conditioned response. Contemporary work with stroke victims by Norman Doidge (2007) has amply demonstrated that mental maps are highly plastic and capable of reshaping and restructuring. While we cannot directly see the neurological impact of the sandplayer's incorporation of the symbols into his or her mind map, we can certainly infer that the images exert a compelling influence. Given the plasticity of the neurons it is well within reason to deduce that these right hemispheric images are a powerful means of neural change.

The Neurological Formation of the Sense of Self

Now let's examine how this neural plasticity impacts our psychological functioning and our sense of who we are. In order to do this we must first consider how the brain gives rise to a sense of self. Objectively the self is an active function of mental systems, characteristic behaviors and life experiences. Neurologically the subjective sense of self is not a *thing*, but is in fact a complex neural process. While there are a variety of finely nuanced differences of theory and opinion on the subject, for our purposes what is important to understand is that the sense of self is an operation of knowing (Damasio, 2010). This process of knowing concerns our beliefs and what we understand to be true. This is a process that allows us to be aware of our experiences and allows us to reflect on them. Neuroscientist Antonio Damasio (2010) said that the objective sense of self is:

> ...*a dynamic collection of integrated neural processes, centered on the representation of the living body, that finds expression in a dynamic collection of integrated mental processes* (p. 9).

Damasio (2010) went on to say that it is the *feelings* that we associate with our mental impressions, or inner images, that collectively form the subjective sense of self. It is this subjective sense of self that creates conscious awareness, and what we call the *mind* is the organized conglomerate of all of these mental images. Perception is not the passive absorption of incoming information. It is actively constructed out of the disconnected and vague information received through the senses. As the information comes in there is a continual feedback process that compares the input with what the brain customarily expects and believes. As higher brain functions make sense of the input they feed information back to lower brain areas to confirm that what we are experiencing is what we think or believe is happening. Often however we allow what we believe or expect to alter the new input. *Reality* is largely constructed from our expectations and beliefs (Blakeslee & Blakeslee, 2008).

Beliefs are embedded in the connections between neurons. These are organized by experience into networks that fire in accord with our expectations about how the world works. Blakeslee & Blakeslee commented:

> *Beliefs are ultimately as tangible as the cells in your brain, because that is where beliefs are created, stored, and, with new information, updated or reconsolidated* (2008, loc. 699).

Michael Gazzaniga (1998) neuroscientist and director of the SAGE Center for the Study of Mind at the University of California at Santa Barbara correlated these beliefs directly to the subjective sense of self through what he called the *interpreter*. The interpreter is the aspect of brain function that develops stories to explain our behavior. In Gazzaniga's view it is this very mental capacity that generates belief systems and anticipates what is that constitutes the sense of *me*. He likened consciousness to a pipe organ and commented that the self is an emergent property, not a process in and of itself. The self property is the part that thinks it is the organist (Boleyn-Fitzgerald, 2010).

In a similar vein, Harvard psychologist Steven Pinker (2007) said that what we refer to as *consciousness*:

> *…turns out to consist of a maelstrom of events distributed across the brain. These events compete for attention, and as one process out-shouts the others, the brain rationalizes the outcome after the fact and concocts the impression that a single self was in charge all along* (p. 3).

Now that we understand that our sense of self consists of these myriad belief systems and expectations of reality, we begin to have a clearer picture of the components of our psychological functioning. Apart from hereditary neural impairments, our sense of who we are, our place and value in the world, how we unconsciously anticipate other people will react to us, how life treats us, etc., is built from neural connections constructed out of experience. If an individual's early experiences were safe, nurturing and appropriately respectful he or she builds a neural network that anticipates being valued for who they are, respected, and so on. As this person moves through life he or she views the world through a pair of neurological lenses that assumes and expects others to fit these expectations. As a result of this mindset that takes positive supportive relationships for granted, he or she will be attracted to people and circumstances that correspond. If on the other hand the individual experienced abandonments, betrayals, abuse, or other such detrimental experiences, he or she is neurologically wired to be attracted to people and situations that replicate the anticipated experiences. Be it for good or ill, by repeating these patterns of expectation we reinforce and strengthen the neural networks that support them. However, if we have experiences that do not reinforce the habituated patterns, and that actually create new possibilities, new neural pathways are developed. The neuroplastic flexibility of the brain can actually change our perceptions of self and reality (Boleyn-Fitzgerald, 2010). Of course this is the domain of psychotherapy and is in fact, a dimension of what we call *learning*. Damasio (2010) commented that there is growing evidence that over a period of several generations, cultural changes actually result in alterations of the human genome. Over time, the changes we make in the neural pathways of our thinking patterns produce physical modification to our DNA. While changes to the human genome take some time, this fact supports the knowledge that we are changed by what we experience.

The Neurological Components of Psychic Change

The key to making changes to our neural pathways is to somehow step out of our habituated patterns and to have experiences that are entirely different. This is very difficult to do given that we are blindly predisposed to perpetuate the old patterns. Sandplay creates the ideal conditions for the experience of a new and altered reality. We recall Jung's (1981b) observation that the human psyche is characterized by a central ordering principle, which he called the *Self*, and that it has a natural disposition to heal and further its own development. Sandplay softens the left hemisphere's hold on the sandplayer's current reality and facilitates right hemispheric image-based neural activity that triggers the healing of trauma, wounds, losses, or any neural patterns that interfere with healthy mental functioning. The figures or symbols the client is attracted to conform precisely to the pre-rational neural patterns that the individual needs to continue his or her psychic development. The symbolic images that emerge bypass the unhealthy habituated neural firing and give form to the next phase of the client's healing and development. Step by step, over the course of the series of sand trays, faulty or destructive neural pathways are re-ordered to the *Self*. Functioning individually and in groups in the tray, the symbols are then able to create an entirely new neural experience that is in advance of the conscious mind. The more the neural pathways are aligned with the organizing principle of the Self the greater the mental functioning.

Researchers are discovering that the hemispheric division of the brain is not as black and white as was once thought. It is now known that the left brain is not the sole province of reason or language, nor is the right brain the only location of emotion and visual images. Both the right and the left hemispheres are involved in various aspects of reason, language, emotion and visual image perception (Hellige, Laeng & Michimata, 2010). Even so the brain does remain divided by a thick band of nerve fibers known as the corpus callosum, a primary purpose of which is to inhibit signals from the other hemisphere, and the two hemispheres do exhibit characteristic modes of operating. The left hemisphere narrowly focuses attention to what it already knows, whereas the right hemisphere is broadly vigilant to possibility with no commitment to what that might be. When we know that something is important we use our left hemisphere to be precise about it. This requires generalizations and a simplified version of reality. By contrast, the right hemisphere is always on the lookout for things that might be different from our usual expectations. This is a highly creative space where new things emerge that are beyond our expectations. However, the imagination required to develop the new concepts requires the functions of both hemispheres.

The Image in Neural Change

Ronald Finke (1986), sports researcher at Texas State University, observed that forming a mental image primes neural mechanisms in the visual system to anticipate receiving the object as real. The images precipitate change. The mental images in sandplay effect neural changes in the brain that prepare the individual to receive, or accept the content as real. The image changes how we expect, or anticipate our realities to be. Through the neural mechanisms of visual perception the images in sandplay work to alter old perceptions and to activate new ways of perceiving. They prepare us to perceive new things, and new ways of being and doing.

Haber's (1983) image recall research and Finke's (1986) research on the anticipatory characteristics of images underscore the powerful effects of the symbolic imagery of sandplay. The images live on, activating imagination and creative neural activity. In addition, as we discussed above, the symbols used in sandplay are literally incorporated into the individual's being and continue to exert their influence neurologically. When the sand tray is constructed the newly formed neural pathways are in the very beginnings of their development, and they continue to grow as the sandplayer carries the symbols in his or her body map. When the new neural pathways are sufficiently developed the client becomes aware of sometimes subtle and sometimes dramatic transformations in the way he or she experiences and responds to life. The new psychic material, or ways of being, gradually engage the focus of the left hemisphere bringing this content into a meaningful and useful conscious focus. What was formerly more globally generalized in the right hemisphere is organized and categorized by the left hemisphere, effecting a cross-hemispheric integration. The newly matured neural pathways establish new ways of perceiving reality and being in the world that are now known and assumed to be *real*. The psyche is then ready to undergo the same change and developmental process again using the new form of reality, or sense of self, as the starting point. And so the process continues. Of course this is a simplification for purposes of description. In actual sandplay work it is not uncommon to see many levels of psychic change taking place simultaneously. In fact, the complexity of the interacting symbolic images makes it impossible to ever fully understand everything that transpires in a sandplay process.

The Brain in Relationship: Mirror Neuron Networks

The Discovery of Mirror Neurons

Another fascinating field of inquiry in neuropsychology concerns the *mirror neuron networks*. University of California at Los Angeles neuroscientist, Marco Iacoboni (2008) described mirror neurons as neural correlates of the simulation process required to understand other minds. Iacoboni observed that the mirror neuron networks merge information received with our mental faculties of perception, action and cognition (Iacoboni, 2008).

Mirror neurons were first discovered in the early 1990's by researcher Giacomo Rizzolatti and colleagues Fadiga, Gallese, and Fogassi (1992a, 1992b) Working in the neural research laboratory at the University of Parma, Rizzolatti, a colleague of Iacoboni, was studying the effect of motor movement on the brains of macaque monkeys (Iacoboni, 2008). An area of particular focus was a part of the premotor cortex concerned with planning, selecting and executing actions. The remarkable discovery was first made when something the researcher was doing triggered a response in the monkey's brain that matched the neural firing that would occur if the monkey were actually carrying out the action. While there has since been a lot of speculation and debate about what the researcher was actually doing, eating ice cream, peanuts, etc., the main point was that the observing brain fired in the same way as the brain of the person or animal carrying out the action. Motor cells fired at the perception of someone else's actions.

Mirror neurons are bi-hemispheric, located in the premotor cortex, and are important for motor behavior. The activation of a chain of mirror neurons simulates a sequence of simple actions that creates the action in our brains, allowing us to understand the intentions of others (Iacoboni, 2008). In addition the insular cortex has anatomical connections to mirror neurons and limbic areas of the brain, allowing us to understand the emotions of others. This is the area of the brain that is responsible for many bodily regulations, for the evaluation of the extent of pain, and the subjective experience of pain when watching others in pain. In short, we understand the mental states of others by simulating them in our brains via mirror neurons. By coding both for our own actions and our observance of that action in others, we generate a common neural code that results in correspondence between ourselves and others.

Interaction and Neural Connectivity

Boleyn-Fitzgerald (2010) observed that every time we interact we change each other's brains. This raises some fundamental existential questions: *Is there meaning without interpersonal mirroring and the co-generation of a field of shared understanding? Who am I without you? If you do not see me and share my experience, am I really here?* Each time we react to a thought or an emotion, our own cognitive and emotional experience simultaneously changes. Mirror neurons are the biological basis for intersubjectivity. Truly, we are not separate (Iacoboni, 2008). These discoveries about the synchrony between brains play a significant role in sandplay. In the shared experience of sandplay the therapist conjointly shares the client's experience of the sand tray. He or she literally merges with the client through the full internal simulation of the emotional, physical and cognitive impact of the tray. The therapist does not simply watch and record, but *experiences* the sandplayer's physical, emotional and cognitive undergoing throughout the process. The same is true when we examine sandplay case material. Although the motor activity of the client is absent when we are working from photos, we resonate with the sandplayer's psychic intention. As viewers of the symbolic images our neural firing corresponds to the changes in the neural firing patterns of the sandplayer. The mirror neuron networks of the client affirm that his or her sandplay creation is recognized and respected by the therapist as a *reality,* in turn making it a reality for him or her. In this way what has emerged is *set in place* to evolve into conscious awareness.

Mirror Neuron Networks in Sandplay

In sandplay, client and therapist jointly experience the symbolic field in the free and protected space. Because the symbolic content is beyond the client's consciousness he or she experiences a certain amount of psychic stress. This situation is somewhat like *projective identification* wherein the client unconsciously pressures the therapist to experience what he or she cannot contain, thereby vicariously exploring the content and coming to understand it. In the sandplay process the client is subject to psychic tension even when the content is of a very positive nature. The therapist's task is to establish enough equilibrium in the relationship for the client to access the potential space required to accept and integrate the material as a part of his or her reality. This is a right brain to right brain mutually shared experience between client and therapist that allows the client the safety to tolerate the ambiguity and discomfort of the unknown with a sense of wonder. The right hemisphere is also dominant for processing negative emotions and for mediating pain. The client feels safe when he or she senses through the mirror neuron networks that the therapist is both affected by the negative material and is simultaneously able to hold and tolerate it.

Mirror Neuron Networks and Learning

Another fascinating aspect of mirror neuron networks is the role they play in learning and language development. The brain imaging work of neuroscientists Oztop, Kawato, and Arbib, (2006) indicated that the mirror neuron functions of the brain are not individual neurons, but are systems of cross modal neural mirroring. High level brain functions such as action understanding, imitation, and language are attributed to these mirror neurons systems. Neuroscientist V.S. Ramachandran (2002) speculated that the earliest forms of language emerged out of mirroring the motor movements of the lips and tongues of others.

Mirror Neuron Networks: The Hands, Learning and Language Formation

Mirror Neurons in the Premotor Cortex

Early in their work Rizzolatti and Arbib (1998) located a mirror neuron system in the premotor cortex which was interlaced with other motor control neurons responsible for the fine motor skills of the fingers. They hypothesized that the visual input that was necessary for such distal dexterity led to the evolutionary development that begins with recognition of actions and leads to action imitation. Arbib (2002, 2005) expanded the hypothesis into a developmental model that involves seven evolutionary stages: simple grasping; a mirror system for grasping; a simple imitation system for grasping; a complex imitation system for grasping; proto-sign, a hand-based communication system; proto-speech, a vocalization-based communication system; and, language.

Oztop, Kawato and Arbib (2006) posited that Rizzolatti & Arbib's work indicated that mirror neurons are key precursors of neural systems for language. They also said that the mirror neuron system properties in Broca's area of the brain (which figures prominently in language production) provided the evolutionary basis for the shared meaning of language. Neurologist Frank Wilson (1999) agreed that intelligent hand use is linked to language in that hand gestures precede speech. Wilson averred that humans invented language through shared gestural activity. Linguist George Lakoff at the University of California Berkeley observed that in its essence, grammar is spatial (1987). Lakoff described structures of repeating cognitive processes that he called *image schemas*. Understanding and reasoning emerge out of these structural patterns. In their more contemporary research Gallese and Lakoff (2005) demonstrated that the faculties of language are inherent to the body. These researchers concluded that the role mirror neurons play in language is that they bring our private experience into a social context that we share with others. This concept is very like Iacoboni's (2008) concept of embodied semantics, the activation of the bodily areas associated with actions we see, read or hear about through mirror neurons. Evolutionarily the hand contributed the mechanical capacity for refined manipulation and in so doing, the possibility to rearrange the brain's circuitry (Wilson, 1999). Neuroscientists now refer to *embodied cognition*, the understanding that thinking is inseparable from the body and movement, concluding that the most effective techniques for cultivating intelligence aim at uniting mind and body (Gallese, 2007). Oliver Sacks (1990) emphasized that the evolution of the self occurs through the strengthening of connections in neural groups. He called this process *selection*. Sacks asserted that the basis of selection is not mere sensation. It is in fact, movement that is foundational to all perceptual organization. The combination of sensation and movement are the essential components of meaning.

Neurological Implications of Hand Movement in Sandplay

Clearly this research demonstrates that the hands have an essential role in thought and action (Wilson, 1999). The hands are also intimately linked to language skills. With this research as a foundation, it is not difficult to postulate that the movement of the hands in sandplay may have a direct impact on the neural underpinnings of fundamental thought processes and language skills. Of course we do not know the precise neurological correlates of the movement of the hands through the sand, but it is very possible that new neural pathways concerning language and thought are developing and strengthened in the process. The improvements in the children's pre and posttest scores in our study may be directly attributable to the manipulation of the sand and the handling of the sandplay figures.

Neurological Implications of the Visual Image in Sandplay

The visual aspects of sandplay also have bearing on the process of learning and change. The design of the sand tray itself has some interesting neurological benefits. Researchers have identified neurons that respond only to horizontal lines in the visual field, others that code for vertical (Iacoboni, 2008). Visual resolution decreases more slowly along the horizontal axis of the visual field than along the vertical axis. Because sandplay works in the horizontal field of the tray it facilitates focus on the image content.

We have previously explored how the brain maps the body and incorporates the objects around it into this neural map of self, thus carrying the images long after the sandplay is completed. Researchers have discovered that mental images have rich visual properties that may prepare an individual to receive information about the object (Finke, 1986). The internalized images of the symbolic figures in sandplay thus predispose the brain to accept the qualitative content the images carry. This stimulates new neural growth to match the content of the images that bear the precise mental qualities the individual needs to continue his or her development

The Hands and Storytelling

The hands also play an important role in storytelling. Wilson (1999) said that playing with objects with the hands is cognitively paralleled by a story. The movement of objects with the hand demands a representational syntax for the cause and effect of these movements. This is at the root of human language. All things the hands do have a beginning, middle and end. This is the story of what the hands do. Playing with anything to make something is always paralleled in cognition by the creation of a story. The stories created through hand manipulation are elemental cognitive structures that relay the content of the action in words. They are rudimentary, such as front-middle-back; beginning-middle-end and Mary-park-picnic. In sandplay the hands move the sand and symbolic figures, placing them, repositioning them and putting the figures in some form of meaningful relationship to each other. In so doing the framework for a new story of who we are is born. This is the ultimate act of creativity wherein we delineate our perception of the world and our role in it. Neural growth is stimulated and we grow and change. Wilson (1999) captured the essence of the simple, but fundamental role the hands have in defining our sense of self:

> We humans are what we are not only because of our rationality but because of
> our capacity to harness our irrationality....our rationality is nourished by the
> unconscious and animated with playful curiosity (p. 312).

By asking the child if he or she would like to tell a story about a sandplay the child is given the opportunity to extend the creative experience while activating the language centers of the brain. This gives voice to the story that is inherent in the experience of creating the sand tray. It is important to remember that to develop in both content and complexity, the functions of speech, writing and calculation skills need the broader, image-based open perceptions of the right hemisphere. The combined use of sandplay and storytelling bridges the creative process with the ordering functions of language, thus facilitating deep order neural change.

Part IV

The Value of Imaginative Storytelling

I have long held the belief that children's self-generated imaginative storytelling plays a valuable role in their development. As previously mentioned, this was the focus of my doctoral dissertation (Unnsteinsdóttir, 2002). In that study I made an analysis of two traditional Icelandic fairy tales on a narrative and a psychological level. I compared the narrative structure of the tales and the structure of psychic processes identified in them. The investigation also included an analysis of eleven fantasy tales generated during a field study by a group of ten year-old Icelandic children. The study suggested that patterns operating in Jung's process of *individuation* are embedded in the structure of these tales. I argued that these patterns in fairy and fantasy tales embody qualities that invite a creative interaction between the children's conscious and unconscious minds. This simultaneously stimulates their directed and undirected modes of thinking, which is essential for the development of the creative, individual personality. As a result of the analysis of the children's tales I discovered that by making their own fantasy stories the children were engaged in a creative interaction with the unconscious. And through the symbolism that emerged in their stories they addressed emotional concerns thereby contributing to the process of individuation.

The Mind at Work in Imaginative Storytelling and Sandplay

In sandplay and imaginative storytelling children access deeper layers of thinking to find what they need to express their newly developing abilities. Early in his work, Jung (1981b) observed that there was much more to the human mind than was commonly thought. In his prior work with Freud, Jung became aware of the unconscious. However he soon came to doubt Freud's assertion that the unconscious was primarily driven by the desire for pleasure. He theorized that the unconscious constitutes both a *personal unconscious,* containing repressed painful memories, and an impersonal one or what he called a *collective unconscious.* The collective unconscious is composed of *archetypes* that are fundamental and essential patterns that constitute all aspects of human experience.

Modes of Thinking and Creativity

Through his work with schizophrenic patients, Jung saw an image-rich form of thought operating in the unconscious. Jung (1981b) referred to the form of thought that ensues from the unconscious as *fantasy or undirected thinking*. He stated that directed thinking and fantasy thinking coexist as two separate and equal modes of perception, the latter being closer to the archetypal layers of the psyche. Jung described directed thinking as a conscious phenomenon. On the other hand fantasy thinking is either partially conscious or entirely unconscious, and can be inferred only indirectly. Jung observed that through fantasy thinking, directed thinking comes into contact with the

> *...oldest layers of the human mind, long buried beneath the threshold of consciousness* (1967, p. 29).

Directed thinking involves the conscious use of language and concepts and is based on reference to outer reality. It is essentially communicative. It is an instrument of culture and it is the language of the intellect, of scientific exposition and common sense. According to Jung, fantasy thinking, by contrast, employs images, whether singly or in a thematic form, emotions and intuitions. The rules of logic and physics do not apply in fantasy thinking, nor do moral precepts.

Many other psychologists and educators have observed a two-fold division between different or opposite modes of thinking. Dual modes of thinking are found in Freud's concepts of *primary* and *secondary process thinking* (Frazier, 1975). Jean Piaget (1962a), also described dual modes of thought, which he called *autistic* and *intelligent* thought. It is likely, as John R. Suler (1980), clinical psychologist and Rider University professor of psychology, pointed out, that each mode of thinking is an ideal type that never truly exists in a pure form. Consequently he proposed that all cognition processes, everyday thought, fantasy and dreams, involve varying degrees of interaction between primary and secondary process.

When directed thinking is used imaginatively it is comparable to what some scholars call creativity (Kris, 1988; Suler, 1980; Martindale, 1989). What characaterizes creativity is its receptive openness to undirected thought. Colin Martindale (1989), University of Maine professor of psychology, claimed that the major theories concerning the creative process all entail some variation of the principle that creativity involves an oscillation between directed and undirected modes of thinking. Matti Bergström (1998), Finnish professor of physiology, arrived at a similar conclusion concerning creativity. He stated that the human brain has the capacity to draw relationships between material of different origins. On one hand there is material that comes from the environment that is processed by the cerebral cortex. This form of mental processing is characterized by rules and reasoning. On the other hand there is material that has its origin from within the individual. For example, material that is rooted in the brain stem can be characterized by chaos, such as with uncontrolled impulses. The creation of a relationship between these very different types of mental activity occurs in the midbrain and gives rise to an entirely new mental product that is not a derivative of any of its component parts. Very importantly, Bergström (1998) found that this creative assimilation is facilitated foremost during play, in dreams, and while reading or listening to fairy tales or myths.

Play in Development and Learning

There is a wealth of literature and research on the necessity for play in child development and learning, beginning with the early research of Vygotsky (1978), Piaget (1962a; 1962b), Lewin, (1935), Luria, (1932), Huizinga, (1955) and others. As professionals working with children, we know this as fact. Play is the source of creative imagination. It ensues from undirected, fantasy thinking and fulfills many evolutionarily adaptive tasks for the developing child (Singer, 1999; Stewart, 1992 & Chodorow, 1997).

Tufts University professor and play researcher, David Elkind (2007) commented that learning involves self-initiated, pleasurable activities. Fundamentally learning is based upon play and love. Even formal instruction must include these qualities to be successful. In addition children learn through the body and their senses, and both must be engaged for learning to take place. Learning must include movement, handling objects, seeing, hearing, and so on. Elkind further asserted that effective instruction in literacy and mathematics must include children's natural love of stories, rhythm, rhyme, elements of surprise and humor. Learning must include play. The fantasy play of undirected thinking is where children develop their cognitive skills, narrative abilities and capacities for social connection. Children are born storytellers (Paley, 2005). Play with some adult intervention to enhance the activity is particularly helpful to children with educational deficits (Singer, 2004).

Professors , Roberta Michnik Golinkoff, Kathy Hirsh-Pasek and Dorothy G. Singer (2006) affirmed that in the United States, government regulations have seriously impacted the school system and how children are taught. Bush's *No Child Left Behind* program forced teachers away from age appropriate teaching. Now the larger part of the focus is on assessment and assessment preparation. With the global economic crisis we also see this trend in many Western and Asian countries. Children are now being taught skills that were previously considered appropriate for children one or two years older. Children have far less time for play than in previous years. They are under enormous stress, as the increase in obesity rates, depression and behavioral problems attests. Golinkoff, Hirsh-Pasek and Singer observed that modern cultures have moved away from the need for a large labor force and now have industries that demand creative people who are able to access undirected fantasy thinking and to process existing data in inventive, imaginative ways. A great many of our school systems are teaching the children the opposite – how to memorize, perform and get the *right* or expected answers. This is a grave problem.

> *Play and unscheduled down time are central to our emotional well-being throughout our lives* (Golinkoff, Hirsh-Pasek, & Singer 2006, loc. 199).

Psychiatrist and founder of the National Institute for Play, Stuart Brown conducted extensive studies of the play behaviors of a variety of homicidal males and highly successful people. He discovered that the imprisoned population had histories that were seriously play deprived, whereas the successful, creative people had rich play lives that continued into their adulthood. Humans are biologically engineered to play. Play shapes the brain and is a necessity for adaptive and creative thinking, for problem solving and for management of complex tasks. People who have not played are unable to handle situations that call for inventive solutions. Brown succinctly said,

> *Of all animal species, humans are the biggest players of all. We are built to play and built through play. When we play, we are engaged in the purest expression of our humanity, the truest expression of our individuality* (2009, loc. 75).

Creativity and Individuation

English psychiatrist Anthony Storr (1989) related the process of creation to Jung's individuation. Both creativity and individuation processes concern the synthesis of oppositional qualities. Central to the individuation process is what Jung (1981b) referred to as the *transcendent function*. To summarize, Jung theorized that when the conscious position was inadequately prepared for the tasks at hand, or not properly aligned with the Self, the psyche is out of balance. In an attempt to restore psychic balance the unconscious produces what Jung called a *compensatory product*. The compensatory product is the exact opposite of the ego's unbalanced position.

The ego engages in a desperate search for a solution to its current dilemma. It oscillates between the extreme negative and positive poles of the ego's position and the compensatory product. It comes to a standstill when the conscious position simultaneously recognizes the opposition. Psychic pressure builds and is forced down into the unconscious where a symbol is produced. The *symbol* is an entirely new psychic product that bridges the mental stalemate and generates new psychic material that resolves the conflict. The symbol is part conscious (the part we recognize) and part unconscious (the new psychic qualities it carries). It remains active until the new psychic qualities become conscious. In short, the transcendent function, or symbolic process, is a naturally ocurring creative act that results in the formation of entirely new mental capacities. As we can see, creativity cannot be forced but must be permitted to emerge. American psychologist Carl Rogers methaphorically explained:

> *The farmer cannot make the germ develop and sprout from the seed; he can only supply the nurturing conditions which will permit the seed to develop its own potentialities* (1977, pp. 356–357).

The Process of Imaginative Storytelling

The process of imaginative storytelling is similar in many ways to what takes place in sandplay. In storytelling conscious thought might be more predominant than in sandplay but not necessarily so. The ability to access undirected thinking in sandplay or in storytelling varies by individual. My objective with using fantasy storytelling following sandplay was to give the child the opportunity to activate the language systems in the deep psychic level opened by sandplay. The choice to tell a story was always optional. I suggested telling a story following their sandplay and emphasized that the story need not be a traditional story. I let them know that it might just as well be like a dream.

Some children preferred to play in the sand and move objects around while telling the story, while others played quietly and told the story after they finished. I wrote their stories as they told them. Occasionally the children required encouragement with their storytelling but most importantly they needed time and the certitude that I always approved of their stories. When an intervention was necessary for the story it consisted of very gentle questions to put them on the track. I avoided asking leading questions and remained mindful to interfere as little as possible. Most of the children's stories end on a positive note but there is palpable pain in some of them, such as Ari's *The Baby Turtle* in Tray 12, Alda's *The Dark Cave* in Tray 2, and *Rich or Poor* in Tray 9. However Ann Cattanach's reminder in her discussion of play therapy is applicable here to storytelling.

> (It is) …*important not to be impatient for happy endings or comfortable resolutions if the child wants to stay with the sadness and the pain* (1994, p. 32).

Hans Dieckmann (1986), German analytical psychologist, pointed out that from childhood human beings have a need to confront the cruelty and horror in the world, both in the outer world experiences and in intrapsychic processes. He emphasized that on our way to becoming conscious humans we must be able to meet these dark forces, come to terms with them and withstand them.

Allowing the child to recognize and feel his or her losses and pain within the safe therapeutic relationship facilitates his or her tolerance of these experiences. The therapist's safe, holding presence also helps the child develop greater self regulation skills. The sandplay and storytelling was not a singular event, but involved a process with a beginning and ending dates. The children were clear that they had twelve sandplay and storytelling sessions over the course of the school year. Their psyches understood that they were in a process and that they would be able to return and continue their work. There was time and safety enough for their experiences of pain and for healing.

The impact of an adult facilitating the process without pressuring the child was an important factor in the study. Rogers (1977) made the argument that a warm and supportive environment free from pressure fosters and activates the individual's tendency to actualize. Dora Kalff (2003) referred to this as the *free and protected space* in the sandplay aspect of the children's work. The storytelling environment was also designed to be optimally safe and allowing. The effect of my involvement in the children's storytelling might be explained in light of what Soviet psychologist, Lev Vygotsky, called the *zone of proximal development, or ZPD* (1978). Vygotsky defined the ZPD as the difference between the level of problem difficulty that the child can engage in independently and the level that the child can accomplish with the assistance of an adult.

Similar to sandplay, the process of fantasy storytelling generates symbolic material that is in advance of development. Jung stressed the essential role of the symbol in psychological growth when he said:

> *Development of the individual can be brought about only by means of symbols which represent something far in advance of himself and whose intellectual meanings cannot yet be grasped entirely* (1979, p. 293).

Characteristics of Children's Imaginative Tales

Children's self-generated imaginative fantasy tales often parallel traditional fairy tales in their structure and specific manner of communication. Pictorial language and an atmosphere of strangeness are prominent attributes of both. In his analysis of European fairy tales Max Lüthi (1986), professor of European literature at Zurich, identified the central stylistic features observed in fairy tales. These are: *one-dimensionality,* the coexistence of real and magical worlds; an *absence of psychological depth and motivation* in the characters; *abstraction,* the lack of realistic detail and tendency towards extremes, contrasts, and fixed formulas; and, *isolation,* the lack of sustained relationship between characters. I have since identified a similar structure in children's fantasy tales.

The setting and plot of the children's fantasy stories can often be traced to a variety of environmental influences not the least of which are films and videos. Carol Fox (1993), English professor and author on literature, said that children create a new metaphor for their experiences by adapting material from other sources such as books and other media. In his sandplays and stories Filip drew from popular movies. A prime example is his story for Tray 7 entitled *Indiana Jones and the Lost Wicked Robbers from the Wild West.* Another is *The Dragon Warrior and Tai Long* in Tray 9.

Maria Tatar (1987), Chair of Folklore & Mythology at Harvard University, noted that one of the hallmarks of fairy tale is that its various figures reveal their traits through their actions. This is also true of children's tales. Fantasy tale characters are not actual flesh and blood people, nor do they have multi-dimensional psyches like normal human beings. Instead they are one dimensional figures that represent different human characteristics which, if lined up side by side, may characterize a more or less whole picture of a human being. Marie-Louise von Franz (1989), Jungian analyst and prolific author on analytical psychology, also emphasized the importance of looking at the heroes of fairy tales as abstractions. In Jungian terminology they are *archetypes,* or collectively inherited prototypical templates that underlie and give shape to human experience. When we use Jungian theory to analyze a fantasy tale or a sandplay, both are revealed as inner world drama, where all the characters, actions and places carry intrapsychic stirrings, impulses, attitudes, modes of experience and strivings of the individual personality or psyche.

In many ways the trials recounted in fairy tales and children's fantasy tales are reminiscent of initiation rites. Joseph L. Henderson (1990), American analytical psychologist, noted that initiation rites relate to phases of change in the life of an individual. Henderson observed that the initiation process moves through a rite of submission, a period of containment, and culminates in a rite of liberation. All initiations involve the death of inadequate beliefs, mental faculties or ways of being, and the birth of renewed, more adaptive conditions. Examples of the initiation process can be seen in Hanna's story *The Great Spell,* in Tray 5, in her story, *The Great Puzzles,* in Tray 8 and in Ari's story, *The Gold,* in Tray 4. One of the traditional methods human beings employ to obtain understanding of themselves and others is to tell and listen to stories. Thus it is not surprising that the structural characteristics of initiation rites in human development parallel the composition of narratives.

According to von Franz (1989) every fairy tale describes different steps of dealing with the *Self,* the unifying principle within the human psyche. In some tales the emphasis is on confronting archetypes of the *animus or anima,* the contra-sexual aspects within the female and male psyches, respectively. This we see examples of in Filip's story *The Queen and the Chief,* in Tray 11 and in Hanna's stories *The Traveling Conch Shell,* in Tray 10 and in *The Great Labyrinth Contest,* in Tray 11. Others involve confrontations with the *shadow,* those aspects of ourselves that are intolerable to consciousness and are repressed. Violent shadow aspects are often visible in Ari's trays and stories such as *The Big Dinosaur,* Tray 5, in *The Good Soldiers and the Bad Ones,* in Tray 10 and in *The Man with the Dinosaur,* Tray 11. Sometimes we see other archetypes at work in the children's sandplays and stories. A good example is the wise old man in Hanna´s story in Tray 12, *The Intriguing Experience.* All human beings are characterized by diverse qualities - strengths and weaknesses and creative and destructive energies. It is not in the individual's power to discard the negative aspects all together. It is by making the effort to confront the dark sides of ourselves that we are able to transform their harmful influences into something that is manageable and reconcilable. Struggling with these aspects of ourselves is an ongoing process. Like Jung's concept of consciousness growing more in alignment with the Self, the opinion of many narratalogists is that life is a process in constant creation with equilibrium or order as its goal. The Swiss linguist Jean-Michel Adam (1985) asserted that in all narratives there is interplay between a rupture of order and efforts to restore stability. Von Franz (1990) observed:

> *No fairy tale end is a solution forever. It is only as if a positive solution is reached for the moment, but one has the feeling that if life were to go on, trouble might start again* (p. 28).

Reflections

The importance of symbols in development and the valuable role the caring adult can play in this process invites discussion of the tremendous potential value of stimulating imaginative play with sandplay and story making within the educational setting. The prospect of having properly qualified school counselors, art therapists and psychologists working in cooperation with special education teachers in the schools could have a significant impact on the children's learning. Further, we suspect that the incorporation of sandplay and storytelling as a part of the regular K-6 curriculum for all students could greatly affect overall academic and social performance.

Reflections

Part V

The Research Study

This section contains the data, procedures and outcomes of Dr. Unnsteinsdóttir's research into the effect of sandplay and imaginative storytelling on learning and emotional-behavioral development. For ease of reference we have shaded the scores of the four children whose sandplay and stories we include.

All steps have been taken to mask the identities of the children, and all have been given pseudonyms. The study was conducted with full parental permission, and with official sanction from the Icelandic Data Protection Authority.

Introduction

From 2005 to 2009, I conducted a study called, *The Influence of Sandplay and Storytelling on the Self-Image and Development of Children's Learning, Mental Well Being and Social Skills.* The study aimed at investigating and evaluating the regular use of sandplay and storytelling in the Learning Center at a public grade school in Reykjavík Iceland, with concern for any possible influence these methods might have on the children's development.

The primary question of my investigation was: Can sandplay and storytelling on a regular basis affect learning skills, self-image and mental well being of pupils with poor self-image, learning difficulties and/or emotional problems?

Over a period of four years, nineteen children took part in this study. All together there were seven girls and twelve boys, at the rate of four to six children per year. The participants were not chosen at random but shared the common characteristic of belonging to deviation groups with poor learning abilities, reading difficulties, attention and/or emotional problems and social isolation. Each participant attended 12 sandplay sessions.

In Table 1 the participants are put in order of age and are listed by their pseudonyms. The Table includes a short description of each child's temperament, personality and nature of any problems. According to the Table, five boys and one girl suffered from Attention Deficit Disorder (ADD) and there were two boys with Attention Deficit Disorder – Hyperactivity (ADHD) Five girls and three boys were identified as being dyslexic. Two children, a girl and a boy, had limited learning abilities. Three boys were socially isolated, and two boys suffered from emotional difficulties.

Table 1. Presentation of the Participants

Participant	Characteristics
Bjork (F) Grade 2	Creative and emotional. Socially immature. Dyslexia. ADD.
Burkni (M) Gr 2	Very lively and charming. Reading difficulties. ADHD.
Elrir (M) Gr 3	Creative. Dyslexia. ADHD.
Filip (M) Gr 3	Sensitive and delicate. In his own world.
Haukur (M) Gr 3	Kind and calm. Is not doing well at school. ADD.
Alda (F) Gr 4	Gentle but insecure and hesitating. Dyslexia.
Ari (M) Gr 4	Perceptive and inquisitive. Often in his own world. ADD.
Erla (F) Gr 4	Frequent change of mood. Mild mental retardation.
Eyja (F) Gr 5	Quiet. Dyslexia.
Fjola (F) Gr 5	Kind and quiet. Icelandic is not her mother tongue. Ambitious.
Hanna (F) Gr 5	Polite and reserved. Creative. Dyslexia.
Reynir (M) Gr 5	Kind and sincere. Limited learning abilities. ADD.
Smari (M) Gr 6	Reserved and depressed. Language impairments. Isolated.
Valur (M) Gr 6	Bright, creative. Sometimes anxious and unsociable. On medication.
Vidir (M) Gr 6	Quiet and very reserved. Socially isolated. Reading difficulties. ADD.
Orn (M) Gr 6	Socially isolated. Attention deficit and oppositional defiant disorder. Dyslexia.
Orri (M) Gr 7	Good-natured and positive. Dyslexia.
Svala (F) Gr 7	Positive and perky. Popular. Dyslexia.
Torfi (M) Gr 7	Introverted and very unsociable.

At the beginning and at the end of the school year of participation, in collaboration with the school psychologist, we administered a battery of standardized tests, which included: the Wechsler Intelligence Scale for Children – WISC (Wechsler, 1992; Skúlason and Salvarsdóttir, 2006); The Achenbach Scale, Child Behavior Checklist – CBCL (Achenbach, 1991); and the Attention Deficit/Hyperactivity Disorder Rating Scale IV (Barkley, 1990). The CBCL and the ADHD Rating Scales rely on parent and teacher reports. During the first year of the study we used Beck's Youth Inventories of Emotional and Social Impairment (Beck, Jolly and Steer, 2006). Subsequently we used Ouvinen's (1999) scale of self-image *I Think I Am*. The WISC is the most statistically reliable measure we used. The parent, teacher and self report instruments depend on subjective accounts and observations, however they do provide very valuable information and are included in what follows. Additionally there were pre and posttest evaluations of reading and mathematics skills. These tests were not standardized in Iceland. Therefore we have removed them from the study. We do however discuss the children's reading and math performance informally in the case analyses.

The Outcome of Psychological Tests and Assessments

Scales of Self Assessment

During the first year of the study Beck's Youth Inventories of Emotional and Social Impairment (Beck, Jolly and Steer, 2006) which assesses self-image, apprehension, and depression were used. According to this scale the self-image of Ari and Eyja had improved considerably and Torfi's anger had diminished significantly. Hanna's apprehension and depression and Orri's apprehension and anger had lessened. On the other hand Alda's answers implied that her anger and confusing behavior had increased considerably. The possible reasons for this become clear in the analysis of her sandplay work.

The scale, I Think I Am (Ouvinen, 1999) was used the following three years. This assessment considers physical and intellectual attainment, emotional well-being, relationship with parents, family, classmates and teachers. According to this scale three boys, Burkni, Haukur and Valur and one girl, Erla assessed their condition as much improved at the end of the year. Svala considered her condition a little bit better, Bjork and four boys, Elrir, Filip, Reynir and Smari considered it stable. Two participants, Fjola and Orn assessed their condition only once, at the end of the year. While the girl considered that her condition had deteriorated the boy felt it remained average. One boy, Vidir, considered his condition worse at the end of the year and in both assessments his condition was far below average.

Table 2. Self-Image and Mental Condition of the Participants

Participant	Self-Image & Mental Condition Improve	Self-Image & Mental Condition Stable	Self-Image & Mental Condition Deteriorate	Assessment Made Only Once
Bjork (F) Gr 2		x		
Burkni (M) Gr 2	x			
Elrir (M) Gr 3		x		
Filip (M) Gr 3		x		
Haukur (M) Gr 3	x			
Alda (F) Gr 4			x	
Ari (M) Gr 4	x			
Erla (F) Gr 4	x			
Eyja (F) Gr 5	x			
Fjola (F) Gr 5				x
Hanna (F) Gr 5	x			
Reynir (M) Gr 5		x		
Smari (M) Gr 6		x		
Valur (M) Gr 6	x			
Vidir (M) Gr 6			x	
Orn (M) Gr 6				x
Orri (M) Gr 7	x			
Svala (F) Gr 7	x			
Torfi (M) Gr 7	x			

The Achenbach Scale and Attention Deficit/Hyperactivity Disorder Rating Scale IV

These two scales rely on the opinion of parents and teachers. When the findings of the two are compared a relatively complicated and discordant picture appears. We will however attempt to describe the main conclusions.

Table 3. Teachers' and Parents' Assessment of Symtoms of Attention Deficit and Hyperactivity Disorder Among the Participants

Participant			Attention Deficit Teacher		Attention Deficit Parents		Hyperactivity Teacher		Hyperactivity Parents
Bjork	(F)	Gr 2	Pre O	Post O+	Pre O	Post O+	Pre x	Post x–	
Burkni	(M)	Gr 2	Pre O	Post O+			Pre X	Post X+	
Elrir	(M)	Gr 3	Pre O	Post O			Pre X	Post X	
Filip	(M)	Gr 3	Pre o	Post o–	Pre O	Post o–			
Haukur	(M)	Gr 3	Pre O	Post O–					
Alda	(F)	Gr 4	Pre O	Post o–					
Ari	(M)	Gr 4	Pre O	Post O	Pre O	Post O	Pre x	Post x–	
Erla	(F)	Gr 4			Pre O	Post o–			Pre X Post x–
Eyja	(F)	Gr 5							
Fjola	(F)	Gr 5							
Hanna	(F)	Gr 5			Pre O	Post o–			
Reynir	(M)	Gr 5	Pre O	Post O–					
Smari	(M)	Gr 6	Pre O	Post o–					
Valur	(M)	Gr 6							
Vidir	(M)	Gr 6	Pre O	Post O	Pre O		Pre x	Post x–	
Orn	(M)	Gr 6	Pre O	Post o–	Pre O	Post O–			
Orri	(M)	Gr 7	Pre o	Post o			Pre x	Post x–	
Svala	(F)	Gr 7							
Torfi	(M)	Gr 7							

o Attention Deficit; O Attention Deficit Above Clinical Limits; x Hyperactivity; X Hyperactivity Above Clinical Limits; –: Symtoms Diminished; +: Symtoms Increased.

Teachers and parents agreed that the symptoms of attention deficit were much more common than symptoms of hyperactivity. According to the teachers, twelve pupils had the symptoms of attention deficit. Among those were Filip, Alda and Ari, three of the four children whose cases are included in this book. Symptoms had diminished among six of the twelve participants at the end of the year. Among those were Filip and Alda.

According to the parent reports, seven pupils had symptoms of attention deficit at the beginning of the school year and all were over clinical limits. Among those were Filip, Ari and Hanna. Hanna is the fourth child whose sandplay case we include. Parents of four children reported diminished symptoms at year end. These included Filip and Hanna.

According to teacher reports six pupils had symptoms of hyperactivity. Ari was in this group. Teachers reported four had diminished symptoms at year end. According to the parent reports only one pupil had symptoms of hyperactivity and the symptoms had diminished considerably at the end of the year. There were five children with no parent or teacher reports of attention deficit and/or hyperactivity, Eyja, Fjola, Valur, Svala and Torfi.

Teachers reported general improvement or improvements in some areas of emotional well being for seven pupils. Among them was Alda and the girls Bjork and Eyja and the boys Elrir, Orri, Smari and Valur. Teachers reported deteriorated conditions for four pupils, Erla and three boys, Reynir, Torfi and Vidir.

According to the parent assessments the emotional condition improved for nine pupils in general or in some domains. Among those were Filip, Ari and Hanna. Others were two girls Erla and Eyja and four boys, Elrir, Haukur, Orn and Smari. According to the parents the condition of two pupils had deteriorated, Bjork and Vidir. It is interesting that according to Alda's parents her anxiety and depression had increased while teachers reported that symptoms of physical complaints and problems with social skills had diminished significantly. Again, the reasons for this will become clear in the review of her sandplay work.

Wechsler Intelligence Scale for Children

The Wechsler Intelligence Scale for Children, WISC-III was employed the two first years of the study and WISC-IV the two following years. As there are variations in what is measured by WISC-III and WISC-IV we will first review the outcomes of WISC-III followed by those of WISC-IV. In general little variation is expected in WISC-III and WISC-IV scores from test to retest when scores for age corresponding control groups are taken into account. According to Wechsler (1992) there is a question of 7–8 points positive difference in the overall score total if retested within the interval of 12–63 days.

Discrepancies in scores due to practice effects are lower for the Verbal score than for the Performance score on WISC-III. On WISC-IV practice effect scores are lower for Verbal Comprehension and Working Memory than for Perceptual Reasoning and Processing Speed (Gudmundsson et al., 2006). The longer the interval between the tests the smaller the practice effects. In this study there was a seven to eight month period between pre and posttests. Any outcome increases or declines of more than one standard deviation are hardly coincidental. The 95% security boundaries were based on no overlapping of confidence limits from test to retest.

As mentioned the 19 pupils all suffered from one or more of the following: poor learning abilities; reading difficulties; attention or emotional problems; and social isolation. We thus anticipated that the outcome of WISC scores would be lower in this population than in a control group, particularly among those of the 19 children that had learning difficulties of some sort. Research on WISC findings show significantly lower results on all aspects of the tests of children with reading, writing and mathematics difficulties as compared to a control group (Gudmunðsson et al., 2006).

WISC-III

WISC III IQ scores include Verbal IQ, Performance IQ and Full scale IQ. Furthermore the test gives information about Index scores that concern Verbal Comprehension, Perceptual Organization, Freedom from Distractibility and Processing Speed. These scores are standardized to a mean of 100 and a standard deviation of 15.

The full scale IQ of six out of the ten pupils that took WISC III was insignificant since the difference between Verbal IQ and Performance IQ sections was too great. The insignificant numbers have been put in parenthesis.

In the posttest, eight of the ten pupils made improvements in Performance scores. This is clearly visible in the Perceptual Organization scores where Alda improved by 12 points. She also made significant improvement in Freedom from Distractibility. Ari's score declined 6 points in Perceptual Organization but given his very high scores in the pretest, remained exceptionally high. Ari also showed improvement in Verbal Comprehension and Processing Speed and Hanna made some improvements in Perceptual Organization and Freedom from Distractibility.

Table 4. IQ Scores and Index Scores in WISC-III

WIS-III	Verbal IQ	Perform IQ	Full Scale IQ	Verbal Comprehension	Perceptual Organization	Freedom from Distraction	Processing Speed
Bjork (F) Pre Gr 2	80	99	(87)	86	98	77	106
Bjork (F) Post	82	109	(93)	83	105	80	104
Difference	+2	+10	+6	−3	+7	+3	−2
Elrir (M) Pre Gr 3	107	96	102	108	102	94	86
Elrir (M) Post	101	94	97	102	98	91	88
Difference	−6	−2	−5	−6	−4	−3	+2
Alda (F) Pre Gr 4	83	84	81	87	80	71	97
Alda (F) Post	92	94	92	93	92	88	94
Difference	+9	+10	+11	+6	+12	+17	−3
Ari (M) Pre Gr 4	83	119	(99)	82	122	104	106
Ari (M) Post	95	116	(105)	93	116	97	112
Difference	+12	−3	+6	+9	−6	−7	+6
Reynir (M) Pre Gr 4	74	78	73	72	82	80	81
Reynir (M) Post	83	84	81	83	86	86	94
Difference	+9	+6	+8	+11	+4	+6	+13
Eyja (F) Pre Gr 5	96	101	98	97	102	86	97
Eyja (F) Post	103	107	105	108	105	80	109

Table 4. IQ Scores and Index Scores in WISC-III (*cont.*)

WIS-III	Verbal IQ	Perform IQ	Full Scale IQ	Verbal Compre-hension	Perceptual Organization	Freedom from Distraction	Processing Speed
Difference	+7	+6	+7	+11	+3	−6	+12
Hanna (F) Pre Gr 5	101	96	99	102	98	97	104
Hanna (F) Post	101	104	102	98	105	104	106
Difference	0	+8	+3	-4	+7	+7	+2
Vidir (M) Pre Gr 6	86	109	(95)	87	105	83	97
Vidir (M) Post	92	119	(105)	92	116	94	106
Difference	+6	+10	+10	+5	+11	+11	+9
Orri (M) Pre Gr 7	90	123	(105)	93	124	77	106
Orri (M) Post	92	137	(115)	95	139	80	101
Difference	+2	+14	+10	+2	+15	+3	−5
Torfi (M) Pre Gr 7	104	107	106	106	109	91	112
Torfi (M) Post	101	124	(112)	105	124	88	109
Difference	−3	+17	+6	−1	+15	−3	−3
Average Difference	+3.63	+7.3	+5.98	+2.78	+6.05	+3.04	+3.5

WISC-IV

For this part of the study we used an Icelandic standardization of the WISC IV (Gudmundsson et al., 2006). Four factor-based index scores were calculated: Verbal Comprehension, Perceptual Reasoning, Working Memory and Processing Speed. The Verbal Comprehension

Table 5. Full Scale IQ Scores and Scores of the Four Main Indexes of WISC-IV

WISC-IV			Full Scale IQ	Verbal Comprehension	Perceptual Reasoning	Working Memory	Processing Speed
Burkni	(M)	Pre Gr 2	99	98	86	91	128
Burkni	(M)	Post	111	96	104	103	130
Difference			+12	−2	+18	+12	+2
Filip 1	(M)	Pre Gr 3	71	82	77	77	73
Filip 2	(M)	Post	(80)	102	84	74	80
Difference			+9	+20	+7	−3	+7
Haukur	(M)	Pre Gr 3	76	82	89	74	83
Haukur	(M)	Post	(88)	77	113	83	94
Difference			+12	−5	+24	+9	+11
Erla	(F)	Pre Gr 4	70	68	70	74	102
Erla	(F)	Post	(60)	50	86	60	78
Difference			−10	−18	+16	−14	−22
Fjola	(F)	Pre Gr 5	(87)	77	96	83	115
Fjola	(F)	Post	(93)	86	100	86	112
Difference			+6	+9	+4	+3	−3
Smari	(M)	Pre Gr 6	(78)	84	104	77	73
Smari	(M)	Post	(76)	67	107	74	92
Difference			−2	−17	+3	−3	+19
Valur	(M)	Pre Gr 6	(101)	90	115	91	108
Valur	(M)	Post	113	108	115	97	112
Difference			+12	+18	0	+6	+4
Svala	(F)	Pre Gr 7	(78)	69	86	94	100
Svala	(F)	Post	(87)	75	107	86	100
Difference			+9	+6	+21	−8	0

Table 5. Full Scale IQ Scores and Scores of the Four Main Indexes of WISC-IV (*cont.*)

WISC-IV			Full Scale IQ	Verbal Compre-hension	Perceptual Reasoning	Working Memory	Processing Speed
Orn	(M)	Pre Gr 7	85	86	89	83	108
Orn	(M)	Post	(82)	79	102	77	95
Difference			−3	−7	+13	−6	−13
Average Difference			+5.0	+0.65	+11.4	+1.4	+2.2

concept formation and draws upon learned information. The Perceptual Reasoning index assesses non-verbal and fluid reasoning and draws upon visual-motor and visual-spatial skills. The Working Memory index assesses children's ability to memorize new information, hold it in short-term memory and manipulate that information to produce reasoning processes. The Processing Speed index assesses children's abilities to focus attention, scan and order visual information. The child's performance in the four indexes is summarized in the full scale IQ.

The full scale IQ of eight of the nine pupils that took WISC-IV was insignificant since the difference between the Verbal Comprehension index and the Perceptual Reasoning index was too large. The insignificant numbers have been put in parenthesis.

It is notable that the posttest scores on WISC-IV reveal improved Perceptual Reasoning for nine pupils. Of these three made significant improvement, Burkni, Haukur and Svala. Verbal Comprehension improved significantly for one pupil, Filip and considerably for another, Valur.

Score Improvements on WISC-III and WISC-IV

Of the 19 participants eight of them made significant improvements in one of the fields measured by WISC-III and IV (Table 6). This was true for two girls and six boys or half of the boys participating in the study. Among the eight children were Filip and Alda. Filip's field of improvement was Verbal Comprehension and Alda's was Freedom from Distraction. Five participants also made considerable improvement, although statistical significance was not obtained: two in Perceptual organization, two in Perceptual reasoning and one in Verbal Comprehension. On the other hand posttest scores showed that two pupils had regressed. These were Erla (mild mental retardation) who regressed in all areas except Perceptual Reasoning and Smari, diagnosed with language impairments, who regressed in Verbal Comprehension.

Table 6. Review of Significant Improvement on WISC-III and WISC-IV

Participant			Field	Improvement in Scores	
Burkni	(M)	Gr 2	Perceptual Reasoning	18 (86/104)	(WISC IV)
Filip	(M)	Gr 3	Verbal Comprehension	20 (82/102)	(WISC IV)
Haukur	(M)	Gr 3	Perceptual Reasoning	24 (89/113)	(WISC IV)
Alda	(F)	Gr 4	Freedom from Distraction	17 (71/88)	(WISC III)
Smari	(M)	Gr 6	Processing Speed	19 (73/92)	(WISC IV)
Orri	(M)	Gr 7	Perceptual Organization	15 (124/139)	(WISC III)
Svala	(F)	Gr 7	Perceptual Reasoning	21 (86/107)	(WISC IV)
Torfi	(M)	Gr 7	Perceptual Organization	15 (109/124)	(WISC III)

Six pupils made improvement in Verbal Comprehension in both scales (Table 7). The biggest improvement was made by Filip and Valur, who were particularly interested in sandplay. They put a lot of care in the sandplay images and were ambitious with their story making. Their interest in sandplay and story making and the improvements evidenced by the WISC appears to indicate a correlation between the two.

On both scales the improvement on WISC was by far most considerable in Perception (Table 8), where about half of the participants made improvements. This field refers to Perceptual organization on the WISC-III. Four participants made improvements and two

Table 7. Improvement in Verbal Comprehension in WISC-III and WISC-IV

Participant			Verbal Comprehension Improvement in Scores
Filip	(M)	Gr 3	20 (82/102)
Ari	(M)	Gr 4	9 (82/93)
Reynir	(M)	Gr 4	11 (72/83)
Eyja	(F)	Gr 5	11 (97/108)
Fjola	(F)	Gr 5	9 (77/86)
Valur	(M)	Gr 6	18 (90/108)

Table 8. Significant and Considerable Improvement in the Field of
Perception on WISC-III and WISC-IV

Participant	Perception – Improvement in Scores		
Burkni (M) Gr 2	18 (86/104)	Significant	(WISC IV)
Haukur (M) Gr 3	24 (89/113)	Significant	(WISC IV)
Alda (F) Gr 4	12 (80/92)		(WISC III)
Erla (F) Gr 4	16 (70/86)		(WISC IV)
Vidir (M) Gr 6	11 (105/116)		(WISC III)
Orn (M) Gr 6	13 (89/102)		(WISC IV)
Orri (M) Gr 7	15 (124/139)	Significant	(WISC III)
Svala (F) Gr 7	21 (86/107)	Significant	(WISC IV)
Torfi (M) Gr 7	15 (109/124)	Significant	(WISC III)

of them significantly. On the WISC-IV five participants made improvement in Perceptual
reasoning and three of them significantly.

It is also of interest to note that seven additional pupils were strong in the field of Perception
and made better results in this field than in any other field on the WISC, although improvement did not take place between the tests. 14 of 19 participants scored over 100 in this field,
or above average. Two pupils made considerable improvement although not reaching average. It is food for thought how big a role the practicing factor figures in when we consider
that the sand and the three dimensional figures used in sandplay inevitably invite the child
to work with Perception. It is also of interest to reflect on whether there is a correlation
between strength in Perception and reading difficulties. Here it can be mentioned that 11
pupils of the 14 scoring over 100 in Perception suffered from great or considerable reading
difficulties. Six of those were diagnosed with dyslexia. A seventh pupil with dyslexia scored
just below average in the field of Perception.

Conclusion

All the participants in the study made improvements in some fields of learning, development and/or mental condition and behavior. It can therefore be suggested that sandplay

and story making have been influential in this regard. We must re-emphasize that all of the study participants belonged to some form of a deviation group of children with learning disabilities, poor reading competence, attention and/or emotional problems. Even though it can be expected that the outcome of the WISC scores is lower in this study than in a control group, at least among the pupils with learning difficulties, eight of the participants made significant improvement in one of the fields measured. There is a particularly striking result in the field of Perception, where 16 pupils made improvement. Five made significant, four considerable and seven some improvement. It is of interest to reflect on the correlation between strength in Perception and reading difficulties, as 14 participants scored average (100) or better on the posttest. Eleven of them suffered from considerable reading difficulty, and of these six were diagnosed with dyslexia. This outcome is in accordance with the research results of Howard, Japikse and Eden (2006) which reveal that dyslexics are even enhanced on implicit spatial context learning, while they are impaired on implicit higher-order sequence learning. It is also important to point out that six pupils made improvement in Verbal Comprehension.

Any study and assessment of factors that involve development and emotional condition is complicated, and often subjective. It is therefore questionable to interpret the results as absolute for the influence of sandplay and storytelling on children in general. All the same the results give indications of a positive effect as the case studies of Filip, Alda, Ari and Hanna illustrate and support. There is no doubt that it is important to continue to gather data on the influence of sandplay and story making on self image, learning and development of children. Additionally it would be fascinating to further analyze sandplay images and stories for that purpose.

Part VI

The Sandplay Cases: Overview

This section contains the description and analysis of four of the sandplay cases done by the children in the study. We have selected examples from the sandplay processes of two boys, Ari and Filip, and two girls, Hanna and Alda, whose work illustrates a range of presenting issues, process characteristics and outcomes. In all four cases, each sand tray in the series of twelve is presented, along with the child's story. To track the child's psychic changes over the course of the process we analyzed the symbolic material in the child's sandplays and stories and we drew from Jungian personality theory to develop an understanding of what psychic movement the child underwent through the course of the process.

The Sandplay Work of Hanna:
Girl 5th Grade – Age 10

Hanna's Sandplay Work – Overview

Hanna was a reserved and polite girl with a supportive family. Although shy she was extremely creative. She appeared tense, had perfectionist tendencies and seemed emotionally closed off. Hanna was dyslexic and had a long history of anxiety about taking exams. Her records indicated that she has always had difficulty with written comprehension and with mathematics. Over the course of the study she made improvements in reading and spelling and was closer to average by the end of the school year.

On the WISC III, Hanna scored average (102). She made some progress although not significant in Performance (+8) Perceptual Organization (+7) and Freedom from Distraction (+7). According to her self assessment on the Beck Checklist she was average and far from clinical limits (seriously impaired) in all categories. At the end of the year her self-report indicated that her uneasiness, depression and anger had lessened, although not significantly.

Hanna's parents reported that she had symptoms of ADD. They indicated that the symptoms had diminished a little at the end of the year and that Difficulty with Concentration had decreased considerably (–11) on the Achenbach scale. According to her teacher Hanna had no symptoms of ADD. In fact, the teacher's scores were lower by half than the parent's. The teacher's assessment on the Achenbach scale dealing with Difficulty of Thought had increased some (+7).

Hanna was highly imaginative, which is evident in the diversity and wisdom in her sandplays and story making. She always appeared to enjoy coming to sandplay. She was focused on the play. She worked slowly and was meticulous. She gave great consideration to her work, trying things and evaluating. She tended to rearrange figures, move them about, or return them to the shelves. She also worked a lot with the sand but did not use water. She did not use very many figures in her trays and was inclined to vary her choice of figures from one tray to another.

Hanna's sandplay subjects are diverse and the content is rich. In all cases there are themes of opposition and unification. Frequently there are opposing worlds and a location where growth and change can take place. Magic is present in all trays. The protagonists in Hanna's stories are dynamic and are often characterized by independence, courage and joy. Hanna's stories are usually long and she seemed to create them as she worked in the tray. Often her stories describe and explain what is happening in the trays. All of her stories end on a positive note.

Hanna Tray 1

Hanna Tray 1a

Hanna Tray 1b

Hanna's Story
Tray 1

The Desert Pearl or the Beautiful World

The country is divided into two parts. On one side there is an evil world and on the other side a good world where everything is beautiful. The evil ones want to damage the good ones and keep things for themselves. The good ones want to get back the red stone the bat stole from them. If the good ones get back the stone the world becomes good again.

The woman takes care that no harm comes to her animals. A magic mouse that has special eyes can see things far away and can warn when the bad people are coming. The blue stones at the entrance to the good world blink when the bad people arrive and they let the good ones know. They are like a burglar alarm. The starfish found the four blue stones in the water and brought them up to the surface. Before, the red stone was where the ladybug is now because she likes to be there.

The pterodactyl takes things from the good ones and keeps them in the lighthouse.

At last the ladybug found the stone. Because she is so small she went behind the big stone and nobody noticed. When the ladybug got the stone the bat and the pterodactyl changed into good human beings that had been under a spell. And the world became good again and as beautiful as it was before and the animals became happy and the people too.

Discussion

Hanna Tray 1

Hanna begins her work by placing the lighthouse in the near left corner. She then places the large lava stone in center of the tray, but moves it to the far left corner, saying that it is a volcano. She sets the large bat on top of the volcano where he keeps the treasured red stone that he took from the good world. With the red stone on top the volcano appears to have hot lava at its center. This large dark volcano looks ominous at first glance. It is frightening. At the same time it holds tremendous power. Symbolically volcanoes, mountains and stones, as protuberances on the face of the earth, are associated with the sacred qualities of the feminine. Often volcanoes and mountains are considered a manifestation of the divine or the world navel. A mountain or volcano may also be a materialization of the sacred feminine or the perceived dwelling place of the goddess. An example of this is the goddess, Pele, who is said to dwell in the Kilauea volcano in Hawaii (Neumann, 1991). In Japan, the hearth goddess, Fuji, provided the Ainu people with the fire for cooking and warmth. In addition, she was considered a psychopomp, guiding souls to the spirit world and individuals to their own inner truth (Eliade, 1996).

While fire is traditionally considered a masculine energy, the volcano provides a notable exception. In the volcano we see the fiery qualities of the Great Mother, the primal feminine earth energy. In nature the volcano both destroys things in its path and forms new land when it cools in the sea. Intrapsychically this energy can also destroy if not properly appreciated. When we disregard the powers of the dark feminine intrapsychically or in nature, we become overly dependent upon our limited rationality, the masculine energies. Depending on the masculine to guide and direct us puts us in danger of being destroyed by our own arrogance. However when we honor the unknown feminine forces that sustain inner and outer life we are empowered by properly respecting our place in the greater scheme of being.

The first tray in a sandplay process often shows the intrapsychic conflict that will be addressed in the work ahead, the psychic assets the client has available to meet this challenge, and the general direction of the healing and/or transformation that will occur. In Hanna's first tray, the fiery volcano stands directly across from the phallic lighthouse. Because these figures were placed first, are both large and configure the "bad" world, we might presume that Hanna's work ahead in the sandplay process will concern achieving a proper balance between her masculine, rational side and her feminine, creative energies. We know that this is an old problem because a pterodactyl, a dinosaur, sits atop the lighthouse. In addition, because the volcano carries the red hot lava, it is likely that Hanna has a pressing need to discover and harness the strengths of her feminine self, and to supplant the overweening dominance of the masculine. As a female, it is appropriate for this girl to have predominantly feminine energies that are mediated by a small presence of the masculine. Speaking symbolically, over the course of her work we would want to see the lighthouse greatly reduced in size in comparison with the feminine volcano. In addition, we would hope to see a healthy collaboration between these two primal forces.

Hanna tells us that the beautiful Chinese woman in the center back of the tray takes very good care of her animals, and makes certain that no harm comes to them. She is a loving and nourishing presence. Coming from China, which is quite unlike Hanna's native Iceland, this figure carries qualities that are available, yet quite remote in Hanna's psyche. The symbolic construction of Hanna's first tray indicates that the rectification of the relationship of the feminine to the masculine will allow Hanna to develop her own source of internal nurturing as well as her own capacity for self protection and love of self. The caring and nurturing qualities are also mirrored in the brown bear that stands across the tray from the Chinese woman. Bears are known to be fierce mothers who will kill anyone who comes between her and her cubs. The symbolic energies carried by the bear indicate Hanna's need to discover the nurturing aspects of the Chinese maiden and to embody them with the strength and resolve of the mother bear. In the symbolic construction of Hanna's first tray we thus see the nature of the issue to be addressed in the work and the direction of the healing.

Hanna informs us that the "treasure" has been stolen from her and needs to be recovered. Perhaps this is the inner treasure of being uniquely who she is, of being good enough and loveable even with her learning difficulties and differences. Hanna's story reveals that something that was rightfully hers has been separated or taken from her. But it is the littlest animal, the ladybug that is able to spot the treasure. The ladybug or "ladybird" as they are known in the United Kingdom and parts of Europe is a tiny red beetle that is thought to bring luck. The ladybird is associated with the popular English nursery rhyme, called "Ladybird, Ladybird."

Ladybird, ladybird fly away home,
Your house is on fire and your children are gone,
All except one,
And her name is Ann,
And she hid under the baking pan (Opie, 1997, p. 263).

There is also a darker version:

Ladybird, ladybird, fly away home,
Your house is on fire,
Your children shall burn! (Opie, 1997, p. 263).

In both nursery rhymes, it is critical that the mother returns home to her children. Clearly Hanna longs for the warmth of a nurturing mother. In her story it is the ladybug that finds the stolen jewel thus returning it to its rightful place. Again we recognize the need for nurturing in Hanna's symbolic work.

While Hanna's family life was warm and supportive of her, it is always difficult to reconcile being dyslexic. Irrespective of what she does Hanna does not learn in the same ways or at the same pace as her classmates. It is normal for children to compare themselves to their peers and it is painful and confusing to recognize that they are unusual or deficient. Hanna was very fortunate to be loved and accepted by her family. At the same time there remained the task of fully loving and accepting herself and it appears that finding this inner loving mothering was at the core of the work Hanna undertakes in her sandplay and storytelling.

One of the animals the Chinese woman cares for is a tiny mouse with "special eyes." Hanna makes three allusions to vision, or seeing: the mouse with magic eyes, the blinking blue eyes of the gateway; and the tiny ladybug who hides out of sight. Like the bat, who navigates expertly in the dark, the mouse is known to penetrate into places that are unreachable by others. Symbolically the mouse and the bat carry abilities to see in the dark, and to move through the dark places that are otherwise impenetrable. Perhaps the ability to really see, or understand what is and what is not true about her own essence will be another outcome of Hanna's work ahead in her sandplay.

In Hanna's story, we learn that one must first pass through the death-carrying phallic bones before entering the beautiful shell gate. The dramatic contrast between the harsh barrenness of the bones and the rounded holding qualities of the striking white shells reflects a passage out of the masculine and into the feminine. The configuration of this shell gate is womb-like and nurturing. In order to enter this portal to the good world one must pass the approval of the two blue eyes. Only what belongs will make this passage. The rest will be cast away, unneeded, as dead bones. This indicates a capacity to sort things out, to discern what is true from what is false and is a powerful psychic asset that Hanna has available for her work. It is also significant that these gates are centrally positioned in the tray. This psychic strength is at the center of the work ahead in Hanna's sandplay process.

Hanna has already put this psychic quality to work as it appears that the ocelot has just entered the good land. In the pre-Columbian myth of Teotihuacán, the ocelot, or jaguar, was present at the divine hearth onto which the gods had sacrificed themselves (Coe, 1972). In this way, ocelots became symbols of warriors. We know that both wild and domestic cats move gracefully and with determination. Their footsteps are silent, and they know their way around in the dark. As a result of these qualities of sureness and immutable independence, cats are thought to carry special powers. In mythology, cats are considered sacred or demonic, but rarely anything in between (Hausman, G. & Hausman, L., 2000). Here in Hanna's Tray 1, the ocelot makes its journey across the protective eyes and stands between a pair of beautiful roses. This wild cat carries sacred energies and is very powerful. Perhaps the outcome of Hanna's healing will be to embody her own feminine warrior qualities and to carry herself with cat-like surety. This quality of being at home with one's self is mirrored in the snail that sits behind the pond in the near right corner of the tray. In nature the snail carries its home on its back. Symbolically it is always "at home." With the composure and strength of the ocelot Hanna's first tray indicates that she has the potential to be equally at home with her true Self.

Hanna's tray includes much additional psychic strength that is available to her for this journey. The bright green frogs by the pond carry energies of transformation. In nature the frog begins as an egg. It becomes a pollywog, and gradually matures into a frog. There is also a starfish, which is known to re-generate its wounded legs. In addition, as five-pointed, the starfish is considered a symbol of human wholeness. The five points represent the human figure, with two arms two legs and a head, as seen in Leonardo da Vinci's famous drawing of the *Vitruvian Man*. Inspired by the work of architect, Vitruvius, the drawing and accompanying text are considered a standard of proper proportion. Symbolically, this is considered the *anthropos*, or complete human being (Turner, 2005). In Hanna's story it is the starfish that discovers the jewels at the bottom of the pond and brings them to the surface. Symbolically the ponds, rivers, lakes, and other waterways we see in sandplay are openings to the unconscious, to what lies below the surface and is yet unknown. The brilliant blue stones are new psychic qualities that are accessed in the depths of the unconscious.

In sandplay the particular number of certain figures often indicates the phase or current stage of the client's psychic transformation. Hanna's Tray 1 has several groups of two. There are two lakes, two roses, two blue eyes in the gateway, two round red figures and a pair of frogs. Symbolically the number two indicates the emergence of something new. A new psychic quality is emerging out of the wholeness of "one" and splits into a duality. The two halves of the duality reflect, or mirror each other and will continue to develop into conscious manifestation as a new awareness, a new way of being. Two is the first phase of new development. Following two is three. Groupings of three indicate a movement or dynamism. The new quality is growing and continuing its development (Eastwood, 2002). In Hanna's Tray 1 we see two important groupings of three with the bones and the shells. The progression Hanna describes from the bones to the shells is a striking example of movement away from psychic qualities that are no longer needed, the dead bones, toward new qualities that provide a sheltering feminine energy, the shells. As these qualities continue their development and move from three to four they become grounded or anchored in material reality. Once this phase of development is established the new qualities can then be integrated into the wholeness of the personality held by the number five. Importantly in Hanna's tray it is the five-legged starfish that brings the four jewels to the surface.

One indicator of the nature of the problems to be addressed and the resources available to the client often can be seen in the figures that are diagonally opposite each other in the sand tray. While this is not always the case, it is important to examine the nature of the energies that are held in the opposing reaches of the diagonals. The diagonal is the longest distance across the sand tray. Often the figures placed on the diagonal carry psychic qualities that are at the core of the issues being addressed in the process. These can be the new qualities that the psyche needs to integrate into consciousness in order to live a more intact and complete life. The figures on the opposite ends of the diagonal can also carry the energies of a conflict that currently prevents a healthier more evolved level of functioning (Turner, 2005).

In Hanna's tray the volcano-bat-jewel configuration opposes the five-pointed starfish. In this case we might infer that it is necessary to access the strength of her feminine energies (volcano) in order to find her way through the darkness (bat) and to abide in the wholeness of the Self (jewel and starfish.) In Jungian psychology the center of the personality is referred to as the *Self*. The Self is both the source of all being as well as the goal to which it returns. (Jung, 1981; Samuels, 1997). This principal is referred to by countless names across cultures: God, Jesus, Mohammed, Shiva, Brahma, Buddha, the Divine and so on.

The qualities held on the opposing diagonal in Tray 1 are the pterodactyl on top of the lighthouse in one corner and the greenery in the other. Because both diagonals cross in the region of the central gateway we can infer that the very ancient issue of the disproportionate valuation of the masculine, or rationality, will resolve in new growth by "entering into" the feminine. That is to say, by rectifying the valuation of the feminine or creative aspects of the personality in relationship to the masculine.

Clearly Hanna's first sandplay portends the direction of her work and all of the qualities necessary to make the journey she sets about and it will be fascinating to track her progress through the following trays.

Hanna Tray 2

Hanna Tray 2a

Hanna Tray 2b

Hanna's Story

Tray 2

Note: Hanna entered the sandplay room looking downcast, and seemed to be coughing nervously. Her demeanor changed remarkably as she did her sandplay. By the end of the session she was bright and happy and the cough had entirely stopped.

The Little Wooden Village

This little village is all made of wood. The two men are master carpenters. The man and woman with the spoons are bakers and robots that the carpenters made. The little (red) man looks after the statue the two carpenters made. Their tools are in the chest. The green man is searching for some water. The carpenters are finishing building the tower at their side. The (yellow) man is the mayor and a magician too.

From the tower, water rushes underground into the pond where a dolphin that the carpenters made lives. The little red man who is looking after the statue lives in the cone but the windows can't be seen.

It is good to live in this village. The dolphin is always repairing the waterside and makes a pattern on the bank and waves to the people. When it repairs the bank everybody is glad. When the carpenters are building the bakers sing and everybody sings along.

The green man puts the useless dirty water in a bucket and throws it in the corner at the left. Then it changes into clean water, goes to the tower and runs back to the pool.

The mushroom is made of wood and is magical. When the bakers push it out comes cream and flour for cakes. The carpenters had made the mushroom but the mayor put the power into it.

There are no lamp posts in the village but the statue opens its eyes in the evening then all is nice and bright. The watchman goes in circles and the others sing. When everybody is in a good mood they dance. For example the man who collects the water swings his bucket. When the watchman dances his staff goes up and down and his hat blinks.

The old couple likes to be inside but they open the windows when they want to hear other people. When the night comes the carpenters go into their tool chest and under it is a huge house.

Discussion

Hanna Tray 2

As we review the psychic changes undergone over the course of a sandplay process, we often look to see what changes from tray to tray, as well as what remains the same. This provides us a means of forming a meaningful relationship to the psyche's movement that takes place on an unconscious, symbolic level. In Hanna's second tray we see forms of the masculine and feminine, as we did in Tray 1, however their proportions and the relationship between these elemental energies have changed. In this tray we see an abundance of feminine energy in the many circular forms. The large central pool is the most prominent feminine form. It recalls the large rounded volcano from Tray 1, but has here transformed into an opening to the depths of the unconscious. Instead of being fiery and hot it is now a beautiful cool blue pool. We also see circular forms in the pine cone house of the old couple, the larger pine cone, the semi-circle around the bakers and the mushroom. The masculine tower returns from Tray 1 but has transformed from an imposing lighthouse to a colorful and smaller form. With the exception of the baker's wife and the old woman all of the people in the village are males. A major difference from the more threatening and imposing masculine energy in Tray 1 is that these male figures are helpers. It appears that the passage through the central gate in Tray 1 brings some resolution to the relationship of the masculine energy to the feminine. In Tray 2 it is the feminine energy that predominates and the masculine energies are its small helpers, an appropriate balance for a female.

Hanna was noticeably freer with her play as she did this tray. The first figures she placed in the tray are the two dwarfs that stand by the block tower construction in the far right corner. Hanna tells us that these men are carpenters. In fact they are masters of their work. The carpenters made much of what is in this village scene: the tower, the robot-bakers, the dolphin, the mushroom, and the god head. Hanna tells us that they have a large box of tools at their disposal.

The carpenters live underground, much like dwarfs do. Dwarfs work underground and are symbolically considered to have access to the unconscious (von Buchholtz, 2007). Here Hanna accesses the psychic energy that will help her with her work in the unconscious. Of note is that they are *masters* at what they do. In her story Hanna tells us that when the carpenters rest they go underground – beneath the surface – in a big house which is below their tool chest. Symbolically we see that there is communication between inner and outer, the lower and the upper. And when the carpenters build, the villagers play music, sing and dance in celebration. There is joy that new growth and development is taking place.

The wooden couple at the table in the right portion of the tray is a pair of robotic bakers. Bakers provide nourishment by transforming flour, eggs, milk, etc, into bread and cakes. It is troubling that these bakers are wooden robots and it raises the question of what sort of emotional sustenance Hanna has received. The stiff quality of the bakers is also mirrored by the elderly grandparent-like couple directly across the tray. These elders are made of stones. Hanna tells us that they stay inside their house although they will open their windows now and then.

Perhaps these wooden bakers and stone elders reflect the need for the more loving form of nourishment that we saw in Tray 1. However, Hanna has resources to help her even with these issues. Using his magic the mayor transforms the wooden mushroom making it into a rich source of cream and flour for baking. Perhaps Hanna will be able to tap her own inner archetypal form of loving nurture.

Figures made of wood prevail in Hanna's Tray 2. The presence of wood is underscored in the prominent role played by the two carpenters, men who work with wood. Most of the people are made of wood. The tower is wood, as are the two tables, the tool box, the pine cones and the dolphin. Wood is the product of the tree. The symbolism of the tree is vast. In nature the tree is rooted in the earth, the feminine, and has its crown in the heavens, the masculine. Seen this way the tree bears a working harmony between these opposing energies, and is a symbol of wholeness. The *Yggdrasil* from Norse mythology is a well known "world tree" holding all aspects of life, death and transformation (Sturluson, 1984). Wood is the *prima material* of the East (Cooper, 2004). Christ is portrayed as a carpenter, a builder of souls. Trees are associated with the Christian cross, and with the Tree of Knowledge. In the Chinese Taoist tradition wood is one of the five elements, wood, fire, earth, metal and water. The element wood is associated with the qualities of spring and the East (Yang, 1961). It is new growth. As Hanna gains access to her inner resources there is new growth and development.

A beautiful dolphin lives in the central pool and helps define its borders by fashioning a striking mandala-like pattern around its edges. A mandala is a concentric drawing or sculptural form, generally a circle within a square that originates from Hinduism and Buddhism. Mandalas are traditionally used to focus one's attention during meditation and they define a sacred space. As Hanna begins to clarify and move her arrested psychic energies with the assistance of her underground helpers she begins to identify a central point in the personality. While this is not a *constellation of the Self*, the manifestation of the Self archetype in the sandplay, it is a center that gives definition and form to the psychic work she is undergoing in her sandplay process (Kalff, 2003).

The village people wave as the dolphin repairs the banks of the pond. This is a joyful place where access to the depths is maintained. In nature dolphins are highly intelligent sea mammals known to communicate with each other through ultrasonic sounds they transmit. Some dolphins even vocalize to communicate through clicks and whistles. Dolphins are known to help whales that become stranded in shallow waters when birthing, and have assisted swimmers, who run into trouble at sea. In addition, dolphins are very playful (Martin, 2005).

Dolphins figure significantly in mythologies around the world. There are artifacts in Greece depicting a deity riding on a dolphin (De Vries, 1984). Greek sailors considered sighting dolphins as a good portent for their journeys. On Greek vases the dolphin was pictured as an intermediary between the upper and lower worlds, a psychopomp, who guides lost souls and the dead (Gimbutas, 1982). In Hinduism the river dolphin is likened to the holy Mother Ganges, the source of water and life (Singh, 1994). In Christianity the dolphin is pictured with an anchor, signifying the Christian soul or the church guided by Christ (Ferguson, 1966). St. Augustine used the anchor and dolphin figure to illustrate his motto, *Festina lente to,* "make haste slowly" (Ferguson, 1966).

In this beautiful dolphin that is now central to her work in Tray 2, Hanna has the means to draw on new psychic qualities from the unconscious and to bring them up to the surface into consciousness. She is developing the means to communicate with her own inner world. In so doing she will be guided home to the Self.

The last figure Hanna places before telling her story is the man in green with the bucket. This man plays a significant role. He takes useless dirty water and throws it in the left, near corner. There it changes into clean water, goes to the tower and runs back to the central pool. There is lot of healing, cleansing, renewal, repair and construction taking place in Hanna's second tray. Water is being cleansed and re-circulated. Here is a means to transform dirty water into pure. Water is a symbol of the unconscious. Because this water is dirty, Hanna is working to clarify something that has been unclear. In addition, this water is being re-circulated. Perhaps something that has been stuck, that has not 'circled' is now free to move.

Lastly, the carpenters have made a statue of the Buddha, which is carefully watched over by the little man in red. Hanna tells us that at night when things are dark it is the eyes of the Buddha that illuminate the village. Drawing from the depths of the collective unconscious Hanna selects a sublimely powerful and peaceful deity from the Far East to show her the way through the darkness. In Jungian psychology, the collective unconscious is that aspect of existence where we are all connected, sharing in the common and extraordinary qualities that make us human. The collective is the source of similar mythic themes that we see repeated across world cultures. It is the source of the sense of center, of meaning, the organizing principle of our existence (Jung, 1981). Perhaps this unlimited repository of human possibility is encoded in our genetic makeup and takes form in our neural networks. Whatever its composition the collective unconscious is the dimension this little Icelandic girl taps to find a symbol that is completely foreign to her culture and to her conscious knowledge. Wondrously however it carries the precise energies she needs to find her way through the darkness with peace and equanimity.

Hanna Tray 3

Hanna Tray 3a

Hanna Tray 3b

Hanna's Story

Tray 3

The Zoo and the Playground

There are all sorts of animals in this zoo. On one side there are animals and on the other side there is playground equipment. The bird and the hippopotamus (right far corner) *tell us that this is a zoo. The hen has laid multicolored eggs and therefore the fence around it is really pretty, too. The frogs are fountains and spurt water from their mouths. The bird is lying there and takes a bath. When the bird whistles the frogs spurt water up high.*

The woman in red is looking at the animals and the woman with the basket is selling flowers in the garden. The man is buying tickets. Hanna then asks, "Can I fetch something?" (She goes to the shelves and gets a yellow building block and a woman with black hair then places them in the right, near corner.)

A boy stands by the slide. A man turns the globe and if the arrow stops on land he gets something but if it lands in the ocean he gets nothing. The boy on the playground slide makes fun of the kid who lifts up his hands. The monkey moves around in the tree and is watching over the place because he has an overview up there.

Sometimes in the evening the hippopotamus and the starfish become illuminated so that the animals don't become afraid of the dark. A tiny light lights also up on the flowers in the sand. The weather is always good, so the reception desk can stay outside.

Discussion

Hanna Tray 3

There is movement and action in this zoo and amusement park where everyone is busily engaged in their particular activities. Everything seems to be in order and working harmoniously. However the outcome of the globe spinning game is unforeseeable. If the arrow lands on firm ground the player gets a prize but if it lands on an ocean he or she gets nothing. To win something is a matter of chance and not at all certain. Perhaps this reflects Hanna's inner experience of her school work. Because her learning differences greatly interfere with her grasp of the assignments, her random successes are never a certain outcome and seem to occur by chance. The pain of this uncertainty is carried by an intimidating boy who stands on top of the slide that Hanna built using a sea urchin, a flat stone and a bone

He points and makes fun of a little naked child who holds his or her hands up in the air. He torments the child who appears vulnerable and defenseless against this hurtful aspect of the personality. Perhaps this carries the critical aspect of Hanna's unbalanced masculine energy that torments her with disparagement and self judgment.

As Hanna confronts these painful aspects of her psyche a new resource emerges in the form of a monkey poised at the top of the nearby palm tree. The monkey is the only wild animal in the zoo, as well as the only free one. Hanna's story tells us that the monkey has an over-view of the situation from his vantage point in the top of the tree.

The monkey and the green tree bring energy and strength to the painful confrontation between the mean boy and the helpless child. As a result of their agility in moving up and down trees monkeys are symbolically considered the first impulse toward spirituality (Kalff, 1988). Perhaps there is an inner spiritual or religious life that might be awakened in Hanna. On the other hand it may be that the monkey bears the self-tormenting shadow aspect of Hanna's psyche, the part that says there is something wrong with her, or bad. The shadow consists of psychic material that has been in the domain of consciousness, is unacceptable to the ego so is repressed back into the psychic area we call the shadow (Jung, 1977). It is important to remember that the shadow may consist of negative or positive qualities that are unacceptable to the ego. Individuation requires the individual to reduce the separation between consciousness, the collective unconscious and the central archetype of the Self. This is accomplished by integrating the shadow, the personal unconscious, into consciousness. If this monkey energy can facilitate the integration of her judgmental and self-condemning masculine nature Hanna will be free to explore and develop her true personality.

Another source of protection for the defenseless youngster is the dark woman in red, who is moving toward the child and the bully. Her rectitude and intent gaze give the impression that she certainly will not tolerate the cruel behavior. This woman is a powerful feminine force coming through in a mature form. Her dark complexion indicates that these qualities are emerging out of the shadows and are on the move toward consciousness. In addition to the woman in red two other mature women also appear in the tray. One is selling flowers, the other tickets. As Hanna confronts the self defeating aspects of the overbearing masculine position of her psyche, powerful feminine forces emerge to bring stability and balance.

Reinforcing the powerful feminine energies of the three mature women, the beautiful feminine forms that we saw in Trays 1 and 2 reappear here as jeweled fences that protect the animals. Even the base of the slide Hanna constructed is the prominent rounded form of a sea urchin. The sea urchin comes from the bottom of the sea. Its shape is spherical and is reminiscent of the swollen belly of the earth, or of the breast. It is interesting that the cruel misbehaving masculine figure stands on it. It appears that this wounded aspect of Hanna's inner masculine energy is losing its dominant position and is being outnumbered as Hanna accesses the abundant feminine energies that surround it.

This intrapsychic rectification of energies is supported by the merging of feminine and masculine forms that occurs in the balanced combination of circular and squared shapes in the central bird bath. Here the round bird bath sits on a rectangular pedestal in the center of a circular pool. Four frogs sit in a square configuration around the pool. Previously we spoke of rounded forms as carrying feminine energies. This is distinguished from the archetypal shapes of the complete circle and the square, which come together in this special fountain. In their most basic, fundamental shapes, the circle carries masculine, solar qualities and the square the earthly feminine. Archetypally this combination of circles and squares carries the beginnings of a rectification in the relationship of the masculine force, which is now grounded in the more feminine earthly energies of the four-cornered square. Together the circle and the square form an image of completeness, or wholeness (Cooper, 2004).

As we discussed in Hanna's Tray 1, frogs carry transformative energies. In this tray the boy at the top of the slide who taunts and shames the naked child appears to prepare to slide down toward this significant fountain-birdbath configuration. His impending action carries allusions to the transformation of baptism and further corroborates Hanna's intrapsychic movement toward a rectification of the masculine in relationship to the feminine. Hanna's psyche prepares to demote the critical, exacting masculine from its elevated position and to restore it to its proper position as the helper-guide to the feminine through this immersion in the waters.

As Hanna's psyche undergoes this work treasures emerge in the far right corner of the tray. Here Hanna creates a sacred place set apart from the rest of the scene by a delicate chain of five crystal starfish. Inside this special place Hanna placed a crystal hippopotamus, a bird and two feathers. A sacred area such as this that is set apart from ordinary time and space is known as a *temenos*, a Greek word meaning a sacred, protected space. Here it reflects the wholeness carried by the central fountain and is a precursor to the Self, the totality of the personality.

The hippopotamus, starfish and bird are charged with symbolism. The hippopotamus is related to feminine energy. In Egyptian culture the hippopotamus represents the Great

Mother and the hippopotamus goddess, Tau-rt, who signifies bounty and protection (Neumann, 1972).The starfish is a symbol of human wholeness, as we discussed in Tray 1. The bird is believed to be able to carry spirit, to communicate with the gods, and to enter into higher states of consciousness. The white bird here and the dark bird in the center seem to be opposite ends of a polarity that may point to a conflict with which Hanna struggles. In this tray Hanna senses the defenseless child within her and the sources of protection to which she has access. She takes an important step in balancing feminine and masculine energies in her psyche. The beginnings of a polar opposition appear, while we simultaneously see early indications of the emerging Self.

Hanna Tray 4

Hanna Tray 4a

Hanna Tray 4b

Hanna's Story
Tray 4

The Great Time Machine

Indians live in this place and there is an Indian chief who rules. The chief, his wife and son live in the big tent. The Indian chief stands by his throne and watches that nothing evil happens to his land. The elephants look after him.

One time a boy found a time machine. He could travel back and forth in time. He does not tell anybody and the monkey helps him and goes with him in these time travels. When he went for the first time he saw strange animals that wanted to come with him to the land of Indians. These were a ladybug, a zebra, a snail and cats. The boy went everyday to get more animals.

A big statue of a monkey was made and it resembled the little monkey who always had his hand over his mouth. When the little monkey saw something bad coming he went into the statue and did something with its arms. The statue lit up and raised its hands into the air and the enemies were really afraid. In the statue there was a home for the little monkey. Finally the chief became old and tired and the statue replaced him.

Discussion

Hanna Tray 4

In Tray 4 Hanna arrives at the land of the Indians. This land is ruled by a powerful and protective chief, who stands firmly upon a flat rock in the far left corner. He is flanked by two elephants. The chief carries the commanding masculine presence from Tray 1. Here however, he is smaller in stature than the tall lighthouse in the first tray and he stands between two elephants. Elephants are wonderful mothers, who diligently tend their young. Although still very imposing, this masculine energy no longer functions as the one-sided force that drove Hanna's psyche with unachievable expectations and harsh judgments. Here it begins to be tempered by the loving and strong feminine energy of the elephants.

Directly across the tray in the far right corner are a young Indian boy and his monkey companion. In contrast to the omnipotent chief in the opposite corner, this is a new masculine presence that is small and helpful. Sheltered away in a secret and special place, the boy has discovered a time machine that allows him to move beyond the limits of ordinary time and space. Interestingly, Hanna's time machine is a clock. When we see a clock in sandplay we know that time is of the essence. It is urgent to get about the psychic business at hand.

Guided by the healthy animus figure of the young boy, Hanna now has access to different levels of her psyche. In Jungian psychology, the female personality is predominantly characterized by feminine energies, yet must have a healthy masculine component, known as the *animus* (Singer, 1995). It is through the discerning direction of this small masculine element that the feminine personality is able to access the full Self, the center of the personality.

The single monkey from Tray 3 now becomes two monkey helpers in Tray 4, emphasizing Hanna's growing discovery of inner resources. As we have previously discussed, the monkey is symbolically considered an impulse to the spirit. This monkey is quite powerful and functions as a guide and protector. Although Hanna tells us that the little monkey covers his mouth, we see the same gesture in the larger wooden one. These are silent, yet powerful helpers. The little one works quietly with his hand covering his mouth. He is the one who is on the lookout for possible trouble and drives the protective powers of the larger monkey statue. Quite miraculously, given the free and protected space of the sandplay, Hanna's psyche gives birth to helpful masculine energies that will guide her to the center of the personality and her own inner truth.

Hanna makes it clear that these trips in the time machine are a secret. Here, for the first time, this remarkable ten year old girl begins to have her own authentic experience. Now her experience is informed by the Self and is no longer ruled by an exacting masculine authority. In fact Hanna discovers that the unexpected benefits of these time machine travels can be very positive. The little boy brings back some of the wonderful treasures, among which are the ladybug and the snail we first encountered in Tray 1.

In her first tray, the ladybug was the one who was able to find and return the beautiful stone to its rightful place. As a hoped-for development in her psychic growth in Tray 1, here the little Indian boy symbolically realizes her growth. He brings the ladybug to this world as a powerful inner resource that Hanna has available within her own psyche. The ladybug poems we discussed above carry symbolic references to child in need or danger and the mother's return home. In this tray, the land of the Indians, mothering qualities are mirrored by the pair of elephants at the chief's side. As a result of her reordering of the masculine to the feminine energies Hanna is now able to tap into archetypal forces of good mothering, which will feed and nurture her developing personality.

The chief is a strong masculine presence, however we soon learn that he becomes old and tired and is replaced by a statue. The Native Americans are people who live from the earth and who direct their lives in response to the cycles of nature. As the commanding presence of the masculine energy from Tray 1 loses its dominance, Hanna is able to access a more natural, grounded way of being. She is able to draw from inner resources of love and acceptance of herself for who she is.

In addition, the beautiful Chinese lady returns from Tray 1. As the masculine energies are reordered to a proper relationship with the feminine she now assumes a central position. The beautiful feminine energies she carried as a potential development in the first tray now take their rightful center position under the colorful tent. She now has a pink pig at her side. Symbolically the pig is considered fecund for its ability to birth so many piglets (Cooper, 2004). Here in Tray 4 the combined presence of the graceful lady and the pink pig bears promise of an abundance of beautiful feminine qualities in Hanna's continued psychic development.

Hanna Tray 5

Hanna Tray 5a

Hanna Tray 5b

Hanna Tray 5c – *Story Progresses from Right to Left*

Hanna's Story

Tray 5

The Great Spell

This story is about a wonder animal. Once when the wonder animal was a newborn baby its parents left it alone on the mountain and it was there all by itself for many years. It had some wool wrapped around it so it did not feel cold. Later an evil magician changed this animal into an older and different animal. He moved its basket lower down on the hill. Now the wool in the basket was thinner and darker and it felt cold.

Some years later the animal changed again. Now it became an animal that was as big as the houses (spotted dog). *The people in the town were afraid of the animal. But the other animals were not afraid and acted as if they did not even see the big animal.*

One day this animal came into town looking for some food but the people chased it back to the mountain and told it never to come back. The animal was hungry for four months. The little girl who never had been afraid of the animal was playing at the lake and was giving the birds some bread. She liked to play with animals and to help them. The duck that stood by her liked to be patted. This girl heard about the animal. She walked up the mountain without asking her parents' permission. There she saw the animal and spoke to it. The animal was afraid but the girl had food for it and it ate with good appetite. The girl said they should go down the mountain together and that she would help it. The animal was kind to the girl and invited her to sit on its back on their way down. They came down the mountain and she showed the wonder animal to everybody, men and animals, and they played together.

Then the magician came and made some stormy weather. But then the yellow spirit helped and told the magician to go away. The magician said, "I will not go." The yellow spirit became angry and wanted the magician to disappear by spell. But he made the wrong spell and the magician became a good man as he had been before another magician put a spell on him and made him become a magician. (Adds a fisherman with a hat and says that he is the good man.) *Then the yellow spirit put the animal back to the size it was meant to be and that was the animal in the basket in the middle of the hill.*

The little girl was never afraid of the animal and it lived with her and they played together. They had a secret place together and ate together and the animal could help with many things. They often played in the secret place.

Discussion

Hanna Tray 5

In Tray 5 Hanna continues her work with the feminine energies that assumed a central place in the last tray. Here she explores the ability to nurture her intrapsychic wounding through the painful story of a miraculous little creature that was abandoned and left to starve by its parents. The pain and sense of isolation that Hanna suffers is poignantly clear. Even as the animal is transformed and grows through the machinations of a wicked magician, the people in town refuse to feed it and chase it away. However a little girl who loves and understands animals offers it comfort and sustenance. Hanna's story tells us that she did this of her own volition, without the permission of her parents. Through the allegory of her story Hanna reveals that she is able to draw on her own intrapsychic resources to feed the deprived aspects of her personality.

Hanna tells us that the little girl rides on the back of the huge animal as she descends the mountain and returns to ordinary life. She rides the animal as a mount, indicating her mastery of the new psychic qualities and a sound connection to her instincts. Hanna is no longer tormented by an overweening masculine energy, but is now able to nurture it and welcome it into her life. Hanna's feminine energy is much stronger now and is characterized by courage and healing qualities. At the same time she connects to a nonthreatening masculine energy establishing a stable balance between these energies, while both feminine and masculine qualities are sustained by a healthy connection to the instincts.

Following a storm created by an evil magician and the interventions of Buddha, whom she calls the *yellow spirit*, Hanna's psyche reconciles the issues and integrates her newly developed qualities into her personality. The magician is returned to his original status as a nice man and the animal becomes normal size. It is interesting that Hanna selects the fisherman to represent the normal man. Symbolically fish carry profound energies of hope for new life in the spirit. In the Christian faith the Greek word for fish, ΙΧΘΥΣ, is an acronym for what is translated as Jesus Christ, Son of God (Glazier & Hellwing, 2004). In another story from the Indian Hindu tradition Lord Vishnu turns into a large fish and dives to the bottom of the sea to rescue his beloved Parvati, who has been stolen away by a demon. Parvati is Vishnu's consort and feminine counterpart, whom he requires to survive. As with Hanna's rescue of the wonder animal, this tale of Vishnu and Parvati symbolically carries the reordering of the feminine to the masculine.

In the center of the tray there is a little girl feeding the ducks. Ducks flow between sky, earth and water and according to Amerindian culture they mediate between the heavens and the underworld (Cooper, 2004). Thus the duck symbolically carries energies that are capable of accessing new material from the unconscious and the spirit. This is the energy that opens to the creative potential of inner wisdom and facilitates learning about the Self. Hanna's little girl feeds the ducks nurturing the creative and spiritual qualities that they carry.

Hanna Tray 6

Hanna Tray 6a

Hanna Tray 6b

Hanna Tray 6c

Hanna's Story

Tray 6

The Great Race

This is a race. The sleigh with Father Christmas and the little elf also take part in the race. Everybody thinks that the big red car will win and the green car will be the next and that the little red one and the sled will fall out of the race.

The little girl is the referee and the frog has binoculars for following the score and being able to be sure who wins. The audience watches the race and a band is playing. There is man with a drum, sheep are bleating and birds are singing.

When Father Christmas reaches the book it closes and he arrives at his place. The prize is the red diamond.

The race ends with a tie between the little red car and the sleigh. The big red car fell out of the race. It ran out of gas and went out of control. The green one came in next to last. The two that tied became friends and did not quarrel. Father Christmas invited the little red one to come to the land of Father Christmas and then he gave the little car to the referee - in her Christmas shoe. The girl let the little red car compete in all races and it became a master and Father Christmas watched.

Discussion

Hanna Tray 6

Here Hanna creates a race between four different vehicles: a sled, a small red car, a green car and a reddish-violet sports car. As in former trays Hanna puts a lot of care into her work. It is notable how imaginatively she made her sled using a yellow block and a white chair for the driver. The team of seven horses has no real bindings, but for all intents and purposes they appear to be galloping along.

It is interesting that Father Christmas drives the sled. New beginnings take place in this tray like a birth of new light in the darkness at Christmas. The ones whom everyone expected nothing from become the real winners with a tie between Father Christmas and the little red car. They get the prize on the podium, a large red jewel. The fact that the two of them share the prize further supports the symbolism of a new birth. As we have discussed, the number two often relates to the emergence from the unconscious of a new psychic quality (Eastwood, 2002).

There are many witnesses to the triumph of the underdogs. Among them is Mulan, a girl from an ancient Chinese poem, who goes to war to save her elderly father from harm. Mulan is brave and staunchly determined to succeed. In the end she is rewarded for her courage. This tale carries the message that if you love enough and have courage, you can accomplish anything, no matter how impossible it may seem to others (Dong, 2010).

The referee at Hanna's race is a sturdy little girl who holds her own power. She stands alert and aptly carries her own purse. She is no longer a victim as seen in the defenseless child in Tray 4 but a girl who runs the race and makes the decisions. It appears that Hanna has moved out of her disempowered position and is now feeling her capacity to determine what is happening around her and to make decisions on her own. This growing ability is supported by what happens when Father Christmas arrives at the book. It closes and he receives the prize. This is his place, the place where he rightfully belongs. The English saying "They closed the book on it" means that they have completed their business. The fact that the little book is a dictionary, which defines and tells us what things mean, is a testament to Hanna's growing clarity. This victory is celebrated by all. A band is playing, sheep are bleating and the birds are singing. All of nature joins Hanna in the recognition of her developing abilities to take care of herself and to feel empowered.

The colors red and white figure prominently in Tray 6. Red is associated with energy, feeling and passion, all of which is felt in Hanna's race (Cooper, 2004). Father Christmas is both red and white as are his passenger and the sleigh. The cover of the book that defines the winning moment, the small car that shares the victory and the trophy jewel are also all red.

White indicates purity in Western culture (De Vries, 1984). In this tray we see white in the chair that Father Christmas sits on to drive his sleigh, as well as in the two birds and two lambs that stand by the platform. The horse that leads the group is also white. This horse might carry the energies of a psychopomp, a figure that guides the soul at times of initiation and transition (Samuels, 1997). In psychological terms this figure acts as a go-between connecting the ego and unconscious. With this beautiful and graceful animal as a mediator Hanna continues digging deep within her with confidence and refinement.

Hanna Tray 7

Hanna Tray 7a

Hanna Tray 7b

Hanna Tray 7c

Hanna's Story

Tray 7

The Magic Shoes

One time three best friends were on their way home from school. The teddy bear girls were twins. They all went home and prepared some snacks for a picnic. They decided to go up a mountain that was close to the school and they had never been there before. When they got all the way up they had some food and all of a sudden one of the teddy bear girls saw a treasure chest and told her friends. They tried to find out how to open it. The twins' friend succeeded and they thought there was gold in the chest and that they would all become rich. Instead they saw clogs and they tried them on and they all fit into them perfectly, even though they all had different shoe sizes. They called the clogs magical shoes and did not tell anybody about them.

After a few days they went again to fetch the shoes. Two of them put on one shoe and the third was in the middle. Something strange happened. They started to turn in circles and all of a sudden they were in a strange place. Now they knew that the shoes were magic just like they wished. Then they were in the sea and suddenly they became mermaids and played and enjoyed themselves. After they had enough they wanted to go home so asked the magic shoes to bring them home. The shoes did that.

After school the following day they went again to the chest and put on the shoes and now they went to an amazing world where odd people lived in the trees. The people taught the girls to swing in the trees and they had a good time. Then they had enough of that and wanted to return home.

The next day they went up the mountain again, but the shoes had disappeared. They searched for them everywhere. They found a note with the message that the shoes were tired and they needed to rest for a week. It also said that the shoes belonged to them and that nobody could steal them. After that when the shoes were in the chest they went on a voyage and had a good time and learned more and more.

Discussion

Hanna Tray 7

In Tray 7 Hanna takes us on a delightful after school adventure. The capable little girl who refereed the race in Tray 6 returns here with her twin teddy bear friends. Together they climb a mountain and find a very special treasure.

Hanna builds the school herself, using blocks and furniture. She was short one school desk, so creatively turned a bed upside down to make the second one. Throughout her sandplay process Hanna demonstrates a particular cleverness with objects. We recall that she also used the inverted bed as a dais for the Buddha in Tray 2. In Tray 1 she fashioned a gateway out of bones and shells. In addition to the alter table in Tray 2, Hanna built a tower of blocks, encircled the robot bakers with wooden disks and placed a piece of folded screen over the old couple to suggest a roof and a house. In Tray 3 Hanna built a slide out of a bone, a sea urchin and a large flat rock. Tray 4 contained a small tent village that Hanna built with folded screen, a handkerchief and bones used as ridge poles. In Tray 5, Hanna wrapped her transitioning animals with pieces of wool to keep them warm and used a hollow piece of bone as a coffee table.

Although Hanna struggles with reading, she is clearly highly creative in spatial intelligence (Armstrong, 1999). Along with her remarkably imaginative storytelling it is clear that Hanna has great facility with types of thinking apart from reading written language. The freedom of the sandplay method and the openness of the storytelling project provided Hanna a perfect medium to speak in her own language of figures, symbols and imagination. This allowed her to create and to reflect on her own expressions, to give voice to inner conflicts and potentials that were otherwise not so readily accessible to her.

Hanna tells us that the little girl and her friends climb a mountain where they find a pair of magical shoes that transports them to new worlds. The places the children visit while wearing the enchanted clogs are filled with wondrous new experiences. The magical shoes allow her to move through life in a highly original way. Symbolically shoes allude to personal determination to head in a particular direction, and to making the effort to achieve a goal or objective (Cooper, 2004). They are how we carry ourselves through life. Hanna tells us that with these perfectly fitting special shoes the children have new ways to get around that allow them to "learn more and more." It appears that Hanna is beginning to access new ways to learn. It is likely that through her sandplay, Hanna is beginning to build new neural pathways that will open up new channels of learning.

As in prior trays, Hanna's new-found treasure is in a sacred *temenos*, screened from ordinary time and space by a grove of trees. The special nature of this place where they find the treasure chest, and the fact that they must ascend a mountain to locate it, tells us that Hanna has reached new heights. She accesses new levels of the personality and finds inner resources that allow her to move beyond the limits of her current functioning. Because this is a vertical ascent, Hanna's brain may be in the process of forming connections between the different levels of neural experience. Perhaps this is a vertical integration of somatic and sensory brain stem information with higher limbic and cortical functions, which will allow her to better understand and make sense of her learning differences. From this she will develop a more conscious appreciation for her gifts and place less value on the judgments and expectations of others.

The nascent quality of this embryonic development is reflected in the pair of teddy bears. Hanna describes them as twin friends. Pairs of figures in sandplay reflect the number two, which we recall concerns a new psychic quality that is emerging. Something new is beginning to emerge out of the unconscious, the wholeness of number one. As two, the wholeness of one becomes a duality, that will later develop particular qualities, number three, then manifest in the material world, number four (Eastwood, 2002). In Hanna's tray, the twins set out on the adventure with the capable little girl. Together they discover the magical shoes, and new worlds to explore. The twin theme in this sandplay continues the Christmas and new birth themes from the last tray. It has progressed from the promise of the coming of new light in Tray 6 to the pair of identical teddy bears. While the new psychic qualities that Hanna is accessing are beginning to "flesh out," they are still in their infancy. We can anticipate that these new psychic qualities, or budding abilities that allow her to learn more and more, will further develop in the trays ahead.

Hanna's story indicates that she is capable of setting her own internal limits. She is highly practical and reasonable about the proper times to go home and rest, and at the same time, delightfully imaginative. She tells us, "…After they had enough they wanted to go home." She concludes the second adventure by repeating this phrase, and later observes that even the shoes were tired and needed a week off. Clearly she has a mature sense of her own inner needs and the means to address them.

Here in Hanna's school, the teacher sits at her desk in the empty classroom reading the dictionary from Tray 5. Perhaps this teacher aspect of herself is clarifying her relationship to school and learning. Save for the teacher the class is empty of students. The adventure and the learning take place outside the classroom. In the school yard there are colorful jewels and a sandbox for the children's play. The richness of school and learning for Hanna lies in treasures that are located apart from the classroom. Perhaps Hanna is discovering a new appreciation for her own forms of intelligence that aren't necessarily measured and utilized in her school work. Hanna's sandbox is cleverly constructed and occupies a somewhat central position in the tray. Because she makes a special effort to create this sand box in a shell and to place it in a prominent position underscores the personal significance of her sandplay work. It appears that part of Hanna's psyche recognizes that sandplay allows her to explore new aspects of herself that are unavailable to her through ordinary means of learning.

Hanna Tray 8

Hanna Tray 8

Hanna's Story

Tray 8

The Great Puzzles

There was a girl who was asked to solve some puzzles because the world was going to perish. If she succeeded the world was no longer in danger. For the first puzzle she had to reach a blue stone without being pricked by the roses. She succeeded and was able to touch the stone but she just missed getting stuck by one of the roses.

Then she came to puzzle number two. In that one she had to go through a big forest. The trees tried to get her but she used her sword to hit the branches. She succeeded. In the third puzzle she had to jump from one stone to another as they went up and down and get to two blue stones and jump on them.

When she had done that she arrived at the last puzzle. For this one she had to get to three drawers and in them she had to arrange 300 stones, making sure that the right stones were in the right drawer. If she succeeded in that a staircase would appear. With the stairs she could climb to the top of the drawers and open a bottle with an extract. (Hanna fetches a bottle from the shelves) If this goes right everything will be in order in the world.

A leopard and two elephants were on the look-out in front of the drawers. The girl had to pronounce a password for coming in. She reflected and said: "Open up for me because all of the puzzles I have solved and the last one I will unravel."

They let her in and she started to try to put the stones in order but the drawers told her that they were not in the right places. She tried again and learned that two stones were wrongly placed. She sensed that the biggest stones were out of place and changed them around. Then she became frightened because she heard a sound. She saw that the drawers changed into a staircase. She walked up to the bottle with the extract and saw pictures of the people that had tried to solve the puzzles before her. She tried to open the bottle and then a spirit appeared and told her that she had managed to solve all the puzzles and that the world would never be in danger again. Then the spirit took her home and many people were there to welcome her. She was proud and lived a good life to the end of her days.

Discussion

Hanna Tray 8

In Tray 8 Hanna confronts and solves a series of four puzzles. She has no choice in the matter, as the fate of the entire world depends upon her. She is alone in this archetypal journey. There are no helpers and she is totally reliant on her own resources. She must be very brave to undertake this journey. At the same time, the nature of an inner journey of these proportions is such that failure to accept the challenge will result in her extinction. The psyche directly faces the need to access new qualities that will supplant the harmful nature of her overreliance on masculine energies. There are no options now. She must transform or face her own destruction.

In Hanna's last tray, the two bears indicated that something new was beginning to manifest. In this tray these new psychic qualities are on the move in dynamic groups of threes. There are three blue stones, three shells on each side of the central temenos, three animals at the gate, three trees, three hundred stones, six roses and three rose petals. Here Hanna actively works to solve the puzzles, puts things in order, and goes to the center of the Self. Mulan reappears here as the protagonist. Hanna's choice of Mulan is a fitting allegory for her own inner struggles. In spite of the dangers and the many obstacles, here she demonstrates her determination to sort things out and to put them in order.

In this tray, Hanna journeys to the underworld. She is deep in the unconscious. This is a difficult undergoing, and she encounters numerous obstacles. The path to the Self is not an easy one. It requires unremitting attention and single minded purpose. Hanna's passage assumes mythic qualities. It is somewhat similar to the ancient Sumerian tale of Inanna, the fertility goddess, who journeys to the underworld to bring her young husband back to life. Over the course of her descent, Inanna undergoes several trials, and is stripped bare of all vestiges of her worldly power. When she finally reaches her destination she dies and all earthly vegetation withers. She recovers and returns to earth when the gods sprinkle her with the water of life (Campbell, 2008). Like Inanna perhaps Hanna will be transformed and reborn.

Hanna must find her way through a prickly rose garden to succeed at her first task. Narrowly avoiding the danger, she is able to obtain the single blue stone. Rose thorns are rich in symbolism. In Christendom they are considered the suffering Mary undergoes as the mother of Christ. Some say that Christ's crown of thorns at his crucifixion was made of rose briars. Muslim belief holds that the rose grew from a drop of perspiration that fell to the ground from the forehead of the prophet, Mohammed. Both Muslim and Christian literature alludes to the beautiful flowers growing amidst the bush of thorns as God's mercy emerging from his wrath (Gothein, 1928). In the Mexican region of Tarascan, the wedding ceremony ends with the couple lightly scratching each other's face with rose thorns. This blood ritual symbolizes the union of the families and kinship (Friedrich, 2006).

Applying this symbolism to Hanna's sandplay it is clear that the first puzzle concerns making a passage of suffering to obtain something precious. To suffer is to undergo, literally *to carry under*, from the Latin roots *su* and *fer*. To find her way home to the center of the Self, Hanna must undergo, or bear responsibility for herself and for the quality of her life. On a profound level Hanna's psyche strives to find an inner integrity that honors the truth of who she is.

In her second challenge Hanna's heroine must pass through a very dangerous forest where trees "…tried to get her." She manages this crossing by slashing at the grasping branches with a sword. Foreboding forests figure prominently in many fairy tales. We recall that Little Red Riding Hood encounters a Big Bad Wolf, who wants to eat her on the way through the woods to her grandmother's house (Schart, 1982). In another tale, Hansel and Gretel's wicked stepmother casts them out of the house, instructing their father to take them deep into the woods and to abandon them there. After the children use several clever means to return home, and more failed parental attempts to leave them in the woods to die, they are eventually lost. After much hopeless wandering, they come upon a house made of cakes and candies. But it is occupied by a cannibalistic witch, who traps children and devours them (Opie & Opie, 1972).

In Hanna's tray, as in these fairy tales, a venture into the forest is a descent into the darkness of the unconscious. It is terribly frightening because we cannot see what is there. It is unknown and terrifying. Hanna's heroine manages to fend off the threatening trees with a sword. Symbolically, swords and blades are associated with sun gods and are likened to sunbeams and rays of sunlight. Swords are associated with divine cutting power and the decisive action of severing one thing from another (Cooper, 2004). Thus they bring order by sorting things out. A journey to the center of the Self necessarily requires the strength and acuity to discern what is aligned with the Self from that which is not. Fortunately our brave heroine successfully navigates her way through the terrifying forest.

In Hanna's third trial, she must walk on a course of moving rocks in order to stand upon two precious blue stones. This is reminiscent of Odysseus's harrowing passage through the clashing rocks known as the *Symplegades,* on his long return home after the fall of Troy (Homer's Odyssey, 2000). In Hanna's tray the moving stones are dangerous just as they are in Homer's epic. Intrapsychically the treacherous stones are an ordeal that Hanna must confront before she is able to go home. Symbolically managing her way through the moving rocks is an initiation into a new way of being, which brings her closer to her goal.

Significantly, Hanna's heroine encounters blue stones in two of the four puzzles. While color symbolism varies by culture and context, there are interesting references to blue stones. For example, in the Buddhist tradition, one of the Buddha's refuges from suffering is a land paved with blue stones (Birnbaum, 1979). The color blue has a calming effect on many people, and has been shown to lower respiration rate and blood pressure (Birren, 1950). Blue is the color of water and is associated with the water-like qualities of femininity, life and purity. In the Catholic tradition, the color blue is associated with the Virgin Mary (Glazier & Hellwing, 2004). In the Tantric tradition, blue is associated with the throat chakra, the psychic energy center that voices the truth, and opens to spiritual communication (Vedfelt, 1992). In order to arrive at the center of the personality Hanna must develop qualities of inner peace and quietude. She must embrace her feminine nature and she must exercise the clarity and strength to speak her own truth.

Hanna's fourth and final trial requires passing through a gate guarded by a leopard and two elephants. Before she can enter this place, she must provide a password. She must demonstrate her right to enter and offer evidence that she has earned her way. Once inside this sacred center, she must arrange 300 stones in order. This is a daunting, if not impossible, task. However, with a deep instinctual knowing she senses those that are out of order and how they should be arranged. In her first three trials, Hanna's heroine tackles nature using her instincts, which brings her to this central place where she undergoes a profound archetypal re-ordering. Here she draws from the center of the Self to know the proper order of things. To succeed at this task requires that she use her mind in a new and different way. Her ordinary, habituated patterns of thinking will no longer work, and certainly will fail to gain entrance to the center. Instead of the customary black or white, right or wrong patterns of her habituated rational masculine thinking patterns, she now combines wise logic with a deep intuitive, non-rational form of thinking. In her story, Hanna draws from a deep inner wisdom, saying, "Open up for me because all of the puzzles I have solved and the last one I will unravel."

Both the non-rational inner knowing that allows her to detect the misplaced stones and the wise voice she draws upon to address the leopard and elephants, demonstrate a newly developed level of neural integration. Neurologically it appears that Hanna makes a cross hemispheric connection between the focused attention of the left brain and the more globally perceptive awareness of the right. This intrapsychic integration now informs Hanna's thinking with rich, new content from the right hemisphere. In psychological terms we can say that Hanna's psyche now has access to information from the unconscious, which she can put into action in her conscious outer life. She is aligning the conscious ego to the Self.

The dresser was the first object Hanna placed in this sand tray and it plays a significant role. Not only does it hold the stones that need to be sorted, when the heroine climbs to the top she sees photos of the many others who tried and failed. The task and the trials she has undertaken are enormously difficult. The photos are relics of the fruitless attempts of her predecessors. While many people may undertake the journey, few are successful. It demands singularity of purpose and great courage. We are reminded of Lord Krishna's response to Arjuna in the seventh chapter of the Bhagavad Gita,

> *Of many thousand mortals, one, perchance,*
> *Striveth for Truth; and of those few that strive-*

Nay, and rise high- one only – here and there-
Knoweth Me, as I am, the very Truth.
(Arnold, 1970).

As she puts the stones in their proper places a terrible sound rumbles the earth. Nothing will be the same again. The dresser transforms into a stairway leading up to a bottle containing a magic elixir. Hanna tells us that the spirit is on high, sitting on top of the dresser.

While animus possessed at the beginning Hanna now turns to a fitting animus through the character of Mulan, a beautiful Chinese maiden robed in the clothes of a man. This animus acts courageously to save her and leads her to the spirit. Hanna tells us that the spirit "takes her home." And in her touching conclusion, the sentiment of which the reader shares, Hanna tells us, "...she was proud." After suffering her trials, Hanna experiences a centering in the Self, the center of the personality. Hanna now has access to deep psychic resources that will support and enhance her continued growth and development.

Hanna Tray 9

Hanna Tray 9a

Hanna Tray 9b

Hanna's Story
Tray 9

The Great Mirror

This happens on an island and there were only animals and a woman who ruled the country. The mirror was like a god. It helped the animals and taught them how to cope.

One day an evil man arrived and said that he was going to take all the animals and put them into prison. Shortly after he came with some elves to try to take the animals, but they all hid. The man said that he was going to leave and that he would never come again. But the woman sensed that he would come back. In the night he came and took all the animals. The woman searched for them everywhere but could not find them.

She had searched for them for half a year. By then the animals had made a plan and dug a tunnel. The mirror heard this and helped them with it. When the woman woke up she saw the animals coming out of the mirror and she became very glad and hugged them. The animals told her that the man was planning to take her too.

The next day the man and the elves were hurrying so much to go and fetch the woman that they forgot to check for the prison cell where they kept the animals. The elves went to look for the woman and could not find her. The woman asked the mirror to chase the elves and the man away, to make them kind and ask them to never come back.

After the elves had searched for a long time they heard thunder. A bolt of lightning threw a strong light on them so they got scared and ran home and became good. The animals became glad and gave a party.

The men returned and the animals got scared and then they saw that the men had become good. They came often for a visit after that and helped the animals and the woman.

Discussion

Hanna Tray 9

In her last tray to unravel the most intricate puzzles that took her to the center of the Self, Hanna called upon Mulan, the courageous and confident maiden. To accomplish this task she relied upon a healthy masculine energy to guide her. Now, as she begins the process of integrating her new insight into consciousness, she also becomes aware that a real danger exists in allowing the animus to get out of control. Here Hanna sees that it will destroy the animals, her instinctual wisdom. In addition it poses a threat to her feminine self, carried by the elegant Asian woman in a flowing silk gown who stands on a fan in the center of the tray. Hanna places her on a piece of screen with four corners. While not a true square, the squared form indicates that she begins to ground her newly discovered value of the feminine energy. She begins to align the ego, consciousness, with the center of the Self.

Hanna places a fish and a baby turtle hatching out of an egg in the round pond in the far right corner. The open round pond gives Hanna ready access to the unconscious, while the fish and turtle further reflect the proximity of the wholeness of the spirit. We know that turtles carry the archetypal shapes of wholeness in the circular shell and the square underbelly. This little turtle is just arriving, which seems to carry energies of Hanna's newly discovered completeness in the Self. The fish is often seen as a symbol of the spirit. As we have seen previously, the early Christians used a diagram of a fish to indicate their places of worship. In Siberian and Inner Asian shamanism the fish often serves as one of the shaman's spirit helpers. The shaman might travel to the spirit world in the form of the fish, or the fish might accompany him as an assistant (Eliade, 1974).

Paralleling the two mirrors, the woman in the center of the tray is flanked by masks of two shamans. The mirrors function as the god and the shamans connect this world to the world of the gods. They communicate with the gods and are the connection between the earth and the heavens. Shamans are medicine men and women, who go to higher places to contact the spirit. Across cultures shamans frequently use symbols of trees or ladders to access the higher realms. Some shamans actually climb a sacred tree or ladder to do their work, while others carry small images of trees and ladders with them or on their boats (Eliade, 1974). Not unlike the shamans, in her last tray, we recall that Hanna climbed up the magic drawers that transformed into a ladder in order to access the spirit that carries her home.

Hanna titles her tray "The Great Mirror." The mirror, which was the first figure she put in the tray, is the god of the land. In the mirror she sees and reflects on herself for good and for bad. With Hanna's new clarity of vision the threat of the overly valued masculine qualities within her become visible in the huge and threatening man. He carries a rake held in a menacing gesture and appears to move toward the beautiful feminine figure in the center. His helpers, which Hanna calls elves, are weapon-bearing soldiers. Hanna tells us that lightning strikes suddenly throwing a great light upon these qualities that used to be in the darkness - the dangers of her over valuation of masculine energies. Simultaneously, these formerly dangerous figures and the symbolic qualities they carry become not only harmless but supportive. As Hanna becomes conscious of, or "sees," the threat of the overly valued masculine she is able to remain centered in the feminine. As she becomes conscious of it the authority of the masculine force loses the power it once held over her and becomes a helpmate.

The animals captured by the dangerous man return through the mirrors. The animals work underground to dig a tunnel back home. They function like dwarfs working below the surface in the unconscious to bring Hanna back to her center. The mirrors (god) assist the animals with their work. Hanna's instinctual functioning knows where her proper center is. Here Hanna symbolically recognizes the value of the feminine. As she integrates these new psychic qualities into consciousness, Hanna acknowledges that by paying attention to her instincts she will not get off track and become possessed by the demands of the animus. She will remain centered in the feminine and guided by the spirit, or Self.

Hanna Tray 10

Hanna Tray 10a

Hanna Tray 10b

Hanna's Story
Tray 10

The Traveling Conch Shell

This is a beach. There is a lane marked with shells for going to the shore. You should not leave the lane because outside of it are snakes and they can be dangerous. The people are on the shore. Nobody should go to the right corner either, because the legend says that elves can come out of the shell. The trees are supposed to be a fence against the snakes so that they don't go to the beach where the people are.

This boy is called Tom and he went to the beach and was playing with his dog. He really wanted to look at the conch shell and the snakes but he knew that he was not supposed to do that. When the beach had been closed and everybody had left, Tom, who lived close to the beach, was playing with a ball in the garden. He threw the ball too far and it landed by the shell.

Tom couldn't take the lane to the beach because the gate was closed. The only way to take was where the snakes lived. The dog and Tom walked calmly in the sand and then they heard the purple snake say, "We snakes are good but we are very hungry because we have no food left and we would very much like the people to throw breadcrumbs to us when they pass by."

The snake said also to Tom, "If you tell the people that then I will tell you what is behind the conch shell." Tom was going to do that the next day. The snake told Tom to be careful when going to the shell. He said that there were no elves in the shell – that was a trick. The snake also said that when he looked at it from behind Tom would see a face on the shell. Tom went and saw a face and was a little bit scared but then he realized that this was a good face. The face asked if he would like to have some adventures on the sea. The boy and the dog wanted that. The face said: "Lift me up and bring me to the sea and then I will take you to some animals that will play with you and do everything for you."

They went out to sea on the shell and could breathe in the sea. Then they saw many animals and they played together and had a good time.

Then the boy said that he needed to go home and they went into the shell and came back. Next day they told the people that the snakes were good but hungry

and needed some breadcrumbs. The guard on the shore asked how he knew that
and the boy said that he had dropped the ball by the snakes and they told him. He
told nobody about the shell but he visited every day and they went to sea together.

Discussion

Hanna Tray 10

In Tray 10, Hanna visits the beach, the place where land and water meet. In the intrapsychic dimension this is the boundary between consciousness and the unconscious. Having touched the center of the personality in Tray 8, and beginning the process of acknowledging the shadowy aspects of the masculine Hanna is now ready to initiate a more conscious relationship to the unconscious.

The commonplace pathway to the beach is clearly marked with shells. The little figure with the black handbag leading the way to the shore along the shell-marked path is known as "Moominmamma." She is from a Finnish children's story family, the Moomins, and is described as a calm mother, who is always kind, helpful and ready to console. She respects everyone's uniqueness and firmly believes that we learn from our mistakes. Moominmamma always maintains a kindly disposition and only gets rattled when she misplaces her handbag, which contains her emergency supplies. She is not quite herself until her handbag is restored to her side. Perhaps this delightful little figure carries new qualities of mothering for Hanna. It appears that as a part of her journey Hanna has tapped inner sources of a gentle form of loving that can nurture her and fully accept her as she is. Moominmamma is followed by the lovely dark woman in red. Perhaps this figure carries Hanna's developing power and strengths as a girl grounded in the feminine.

Symbolically Tom carries the energy of Hanna's developing animus and the dog her instinctual knowing. This new healthy animus gives her access to the wholeness of the Self and new possibilities for continued development. The shell is sheltered away in a tree-lined temenos. It is in a sacred area and is not a part of ordinary time and space. In addition Tom and his dog are at the periphery of the tray. They are not in the center of everyday life but are the inner guides. Like the shell they are not of the ordinary world.

Hanna confides that Tom, "…really wanted to look at the conch shell and the snakes." Tom and his dog will find the way to the special shell although this task is not easy. It is not accomplished by ordinary habituated means. Importantly they do it not by accident, but by intent. Here Hanna begins to form a more conscious relationship to her inner world. Through her symbolic work in the sand tray Hanna has resolved the issues of her sole dependence on the animus to the exclusion of the feminine. No longer is the animus the dictator of her self-recrimination. Hanna has discovered and respects the new animus as a helper and inner world guide. She needs the discerning power of a healthy animus to find her way through the sea of the feminine unconscious, while at the same time remaining grounded in her primarily feminine nature.

Hanna tells us that straying off of the common path is fraught with dangers. Tom must take risks to visit this mysterious shell. He must confront the snakes. In order to intentionally go deeper into the unconscious it is necessary to pierce through the plane that marks the boundary between what is already known and what is unknown. It is necessary to face the darkness. If an individual is to develop psychologically, to become more than he or she currently is, he or she must enter new and unknown regions of possibility. In her story Hanna comments that Tom lives near the beach. He lives at the boundary between consciousness and the unconscious, and serves as the messenger between the two planes of being. In the story we learn that, because the gate was closed, Tom had to walk through the snakes. However, once he meets them he discovers that they are not as dangerous as was believed. As Hanna begins her explorations into the unconscious she casts light upon, or becomes conscious of what lies in the shadows, and it loses its power over her. In fact, these snakes are actually hungry. In her inner wisdom Hanna recognizes that these are aspects of her personality that need attention and need to be nurtured. Once the snakes are confronted and given what they need they become helpers on the journey.

The snakes tell Tom that there is a face on the back side of the shell. It is animated, alive and vital. As he was with the snakes, Hanna's protagonist is initially frightened by the face. However he soon discovers that it is actually friendly. The face asks him if he would like to have "…some adventures on the sea." Tom quickly agrees and begins his exploits in the sea. Here the animus communicates with the inner world and has a way to explore the unconscious.

Due to its configuration, symbolically the conch shell is associated with the female genitalia. In many primitive cultures the conch shell is the symbol of feminine generativity. It is the portal to the Great Mother, the archetypal feminine energy that gives birth to all of being and consumes all in death (Neumann, 1991). This is the cycle of life and death. The conch shell is also used as a trumpet that is sounded to mark special times or occasions. In South Asian cultures, sounding the conch shell marks the beginning and the end of sacred rituals (Eliade, 1996). It is often sounded from the temple door or gateway to define the border between what is sacred and ordinary time and space. In the Buddhist tradition, Buddha declares his commitment to the salvation of all beings by blowing a conch shell. This mirrors the initiatory theme of Hanna's newly discovered relationship with the unconscious. Now she is able to access new aspects of the personality and her life will never again be as it was prior to this profound personal journey.

In her adventure Hanna pairs snakes and conch, masculine and feminine. As a female child this healthy balance of masculine and feminine energies working together will facilitate her continued development. When out at sea Hanna tells us that they were able to breathe underwater, delightfully confirming her newly developing ability to navigate her way in her inner world. Tom feels joy as he rides the conch out to sea and when he plays with the animals. He dives down into the water and is able to breathe. The animus is a good and vital guide in the depths.

In addition, there are limits to these explorations. Like the three friends in Tray 7, the boy knows when it is time to return home. There is a way to access her inner resources and a way to return to the outer world. In her symbolic work in the sand tray Hanna recognizes that she must enter and exit the inner world with intention and discretion and that she must remain grounded in outer reality.

Hanna concludes her story with Tom telling the guard how he knew about the snakes, but he tells no one about his adventures on the conch. This is a private sacred inner space and it is not appropriate to share it with anyone at this point.

Hanna Tray 11

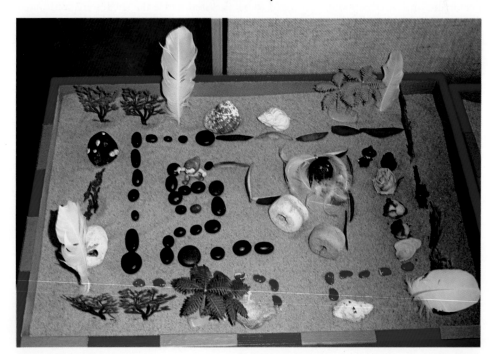

Hanna Tray 11a

Hanna Tray 11b

Hanna's Story

Tray 11

The Great Labyrinth Contest

School was over and two boys were walking home when suddenly they saw a labyrinth, a very strange labyrinth. They decided to compete to see who could find the middle where the magic egg was supposed to be. The winner would become the master of finding the way in labyrinths.

Then they started and Lalli who is very naughty and unkind to others was always losing his way and taking passages that led to nowhere. Snudur who was helpful found the right path and saw the flowers that were supposed to grab the boys. Stones moved and tried to mislead them. The feathers turned around incredibly fast. And they became confused looking at them. The trees made a heavy wind. Suddenly Lalli became stuck in the flowers and tried to call Snudur for help. Snudur did not know whether he should help or try to find the egg. He decided to help him first and then find the egg.

They kept walking and suddenly saw some cork discs rolling back and forth. Snudur decided to jump over them. Lalli also tried to do that. When they had succeeded to jump they saw many feathers. Then the egg they were looking for rose up. They tried to push each other because both of them wanted to get it. Then Snudur said, "Wouldn't it be better if both of us touched it because we are both close to it?" So they jumped and touched the egg. When they came out of the labyrinth many people were there applauding them. They were masters of labyrinths. From now on Snudur and Lalli became the best of friends and discovered that there was magic in the labyrinth.

Discussion

Hanna Tray 11

In Tray 11 two schoolboys walk home from school and venture into a labyrinth. These two boys are dissimilar in character. On one hand there is Lalli, an unkind bully, whom we met making fun of a defenseless child in Tray 3. On the other hand there is the boy Hanna calls "Snudur." This figure is Snufkin, a character from the Moomin stories, Finnish children's stories with a very human message. Snufkin is a philosophical vagabond and meets every new person and event with curiosity and a warm heart. In Hanna's story Snudur is wise and helpful and sees to it that both he and Lalli are able to find their way around the labyrinth. With these two very different boys on a shared quest Hanna is symbolically working to reconcile different sides of her animus.

As we discussed in Tray 3, one of the key concepts of Jung's theories is the individuation process, having as its goal the development of the individual personality. This process demands that the individual differentiate the emerging archetypal content by distinguishing it as separate from the unconscious. In addition the individual must reintegrate the personal and archetypal experience through symbolization. Archetypal content is integrated when both its positive and negative characteristics become conscious. This leads to further development of the ego-self axis wherein the conscious position aligns with the Self. Between the steps of differentiation and integration is an interim, preparatory phase of psychic transformation. During this part of the process the individual is in a liminal state between the conscious and the unconscious (Turner, 1990). In Hanna's Tray 11 the protagonists find themselves in a labyrinth, a liminal region where they undergo tests of initiation. The challenges they encounter are rites of passage into a new way of being in the world. In a liminal state anything can happen and here the boys struggle with moving stones, grasping flowers, turning feathers and rolling corks. These repeated tests remind us of the tests in Tray 8. In this tray the tests are set in a labyrinth, a place where you cannot see what lies ahead. In a labyrinth one must find the center and find the way out again. Only those who are qualified and equipped with the necessary knowledge, or quality of being, can find the center. Those who undertake the venture without this knowledge are lost. In the center lies an egg, a whole that symbolically comprises endless possibilities of the Self.

In this symbolic journey to the center and the return to the outer world, Hanna takes a confident step in her individuation process. She makes sure that both boys are able to find their way out and thereby manages to integrate the oppositional qualities of her animus. It is a healthy and well-rounded animus that emerges from the labyrinth. It is transformed. The two boys "...became the best of friends and discovered that there was magic in the labyrinth." Hanna intuitively understands the necessity of connecting to the unforeseen and illogical places within her in order to unite and reconcile opposing forces of her personality.

In Jung's view, individuation is not an elimination of conflict. It is rather, an increased consciousness of conflict and its potential for further development of the personality. Jung considered the optimum relationship between the ego and the rest of the psyche to be a continuous dialogue (Salman, 1997). As this is a never-ending process it is the nature of the conversation that develops and changes. The prospect of Hanna developing into a mature and healthy individual seems to be good indeed.

Hanna Tray 12

Hanna Tray 12a

Hanna Tray 12b

Hanna Tray 12c

Hanna's Story
Tray 12

The Intriguing Experience

This is a little village where a man was cultivating vegetables in a kitchen garden. The people in the village looked forward to having the vegetables grow so they could buy them. The vegetables started to grow and grow. It was reported in the newspapers because this was the only village where vegetables were cultivated.

One day the vegetables had grown a little bit. A little kid had a look at them and touched them. When he came home he had become seriously ill and had hives all over. They asked what he had been doing and he said that he had a look at the gardener's vegetables.

Some weeks later all the small kids had hives. The people complained and told the gardener to destroy the vegetables. He said that he could not do that. Then a month later there were three pumpkins that had become gigantic while the rest of the vegetables were tiny. The pumpkins had the appearance of being poisonous and having fungus. Now an adult man had hives. The people and animals became afraid and ran in all directions.

Then a detective came with his dog to arrest the gardener. He said that they should not arrest him because in a few days something very important would happen. The people agreed that if nothing amazing happened within a week he would be arrested.

A week passed and the time was four o'clock and the people were prepared to arrest him. Nothing happened and nothing moved. One minute was left to this day. Then suddenly something started to move and everybody watched and cameras were all over. Then a hole opened in the pumpkins and suddenly the most beautiful butterflies the people had ever seen flew out.

The medical doctor in the village said that the hives resulted from the fact that the kids had chicken pox and the grownup man had never had chicken pox. The people were so happy with the butterflies and because there were never such big and beautiful butterflies in the village. The people asked the gardener how he had done this. He said that he had rubbed a cream from the green bucket on the pumpkins and that the pumpkins had first been disgusting but they changed and something beautiful came out of them.

The butterflies flew around every day. The people were no longer afraid of the events. The gardener became famous for his work and the vegetables he grew.

Discussion

Hanna Tray 12

Unlike many of Hanna's more aesthetically pleasing trays Tray 12 is rather commonplace. It is a simple village dotted with stone houses where people and animals move about. This is the marketplace, or ordinary life. She has explored the depths and here returns to the surface to ground her newly developed understanding into consciousness. This is reflected in Hanna's comment that it is "…four o'clock… and there was only one minute left to this day." Symbolically the number four is the number of the earth and manifest reality. Time has come and her journey comes to a close. Now the new psychic strengths that Hanna has tapped can become conscious and become a part of her everyday life.

Hanna's respect for her sandplay work is caringly reflected in the tiny green bucket, sitting by the vase next to the garden gate. This is the little bucket that first appeared along with the rake in the mini sand tray Hanna made in a shell and placed in a central position in Tray 7. In Tray 12 the rake stands quietly by in the umbrella stand and the farmer uses the contents of the green bucket to transform his pumpkins into bearers of wondrous butterflies.

In this tray the stones from the labyrinth in Tray 11 become the boundary of an amazing garden where intriguing things take place. In Hanna's story the villagers are delighted with the garden and anticipate buying many beautiful vegetables. However when a child falls ill after touching one of the vegetables the people turn against the gardener saying his crop is poisonous and dangerous. The gardener is the wise part of Hanna's animus. This is the part of her that knows she has been misunderstood by her family and teachers. This is the aspect of her personality that can now identify such a misjudgment if it occurs again. This is the part of her that truly values her inner beauty and unique gifts even though they may not serve her that well in her school work. The gardener also carries Hanna's positive transference to the sandplay process where she has been lovingly held and allowed to heal her wounds. Through her sandplay work Hanna has been able to tap inner, undeveloped resources that now serve her as a more whole human being.

Interestingly, the village is populated by many of the people who have figured into her prior trays, particularly Trays 2 and 5. Trays 2 and 5 were especially significant in Hanna's work. In Tray 2 we recall being among master carpenter-dwarfs, who lived underground, and had developed a re-circulating water system that turned dirty water into pure. Hanna began her healing and clarifying process in Tray 2. A helper dolphin maintained the banks of the central pond assuring access to the unconscious and providing additional help in the underworld. The little fisherman Hanna identified as the village mayor returns in here in her final tray as the wise gardener. Tray 2 introduced the question of the quality of nurturing that Hanna experienced in the form of robot bakers and the stone grandparents. In this tray these figures now walk about freely in the village square, no longer restricted to their confining house.

In Tray 5 Hanna confronts a feeling of parental abandonment, of having been misunderstood and feared. Much like the gardener who truly values the ugly looking pumpkins everyone else fears in Tray 12, a helpful spirit in Tray 5 was able to see through the common misjudgments and to restore things to proper order. In Tray 12 Hanna opens a small pond in the near left corner. Even in her ordinary life she has access to the unconscious. In addition, the three cows that roam the village reflect the new form of internal nurturing she now brings to her everyday life by tapping an archetypal source of mothering in her sandplay.

Even though the villagers are convinced that the pumpkins cause serious illness and threaten to have him arrested, the gardener knows that they are incubating magnificent butterflies. He waits and attends to them until it is time for the butterflies to come forth. Symbolically butterflies carry the transformation process. Just like the butterfly that changes from a lowly caterpillar into an entirely new and beautiful flying creature, so is the process of psychic transformation. It is not possible to move directly from the former way of being to a new level of psychic functioning, because what is new is qualitatively different from what preceded it. It does not evolve out of what was before. Instead, the psyche undergoes a radical process of transformative reorganization that results in entirely new capacities. We have tracked Hanna's transformation through her symbolic process in the sand tray, and infer that a parallel process of change was taking place neurologically with the formation of new levels of neural integration, both vertically through lower to higher levels of brain function, and horizontally linking right and left hemispheric functions.

In addition to the familiar figures already mentioned, the soldier-elves appear again in Tray 12 as does the little monkey. These characters and themes return in Hanna's final tray as if to say good-bye. This is a final curtain call for this piece of Hanna's development, where all of the issues Hanna has addressed in her sandplay process revisit the remarkable transformation that takes place in the garden. Now they stand as witnesses to Hanna's proud new appreciation for her own inner gifts and unique qualities that she was able to access through her symbolic work in her sandplay and they admire the courage it took this amazing ten year-old child to face her painful losses and wounding.

The Sandplay Work of Ari:
Boy 4th Grade – Age 9

Ari's Sandplay Work – Overview

Ari was a perceptive and creative boy. He was eager to learn about things that interested him. However his parents' divorce the preceding year had a devastating effect on him, resulting in his retreat into his own solitary inner world. He stopped making progress in school and had basically shut down. Even his physical development was arrested.

His work began to improve when he started his sandplay. During the year of the study Ari did much better at school and made good progress. He was a little below average in reading speed at the end of the school year but above average in reading comprehension and spelling.

On the WISC III Ari scored exceptionally well in Performance (122/116). There was a difference of 36 points between Performance and the Verbal part in the pretest and 21 points in the posttest. He had improved considerably in the Verbal part. He also showed some improvement in Processing Speed.

According to the Beck Depression Inventory Ari's self-portrait was average. However his scores were below average for Anxiety, Depression, Resentment and Disturbing Content. Ari was still socially withdrawn following the study. According to the teacher and his mother Ari had symptoms of ADHD. The teacher reported that they had diminished significantly at the end of the year and the mother reported some attenuation of symptoms. On the Achenbach Scale, Difficulty with Concentration had decreased considerably (–10) according to the mother and some according to the teacher.

Ari was eager about coming to sandplay. He worked rapidly with determination and seldom changed anything in the tray. He frequently used the same or similar figures from one tray to another and used dinosaurs and crocodiles most often. A big strong man appeared eight times and soldiers seven times. It is noticeable that males appeared in all the trays but there were never any females. He did not work much with the sand and used water only three times to anchor figures in the sand. There is a lot of conflict between men and animals in Ari's trays. Ari was also quick to make his stories. All his stories ended with the victory of men, often soldiers, and getting the treasure when fighting with animals.

Ari Tray 1

Ari Tray 1

Ari's Story
Tray 1

> ### War

> *There is a war going on. Dinosaurs and men are fighting.*

> *A soldier went on an airplane and landed on a bridge between two islands. Dinosaurs came and wanted to attack him but he hid himself on the island where there weren't any dinosaurs. He phoned his friends and they came.*

> *Pirates and a magician came on a ship. The magician was searching for three magic books on the island. He found a book, made a fire on the skull and examined whether it was a magic book. And it was one of these three magic books!*

Magic powder in a brown bottle fell from an airplane. The magician and the man with the rake tried to get it but they didn't make it. In the meantime the vampire that was helping the dinosaurs showed up.

One of the soldiers found a treasure, some monsters and a golden statue that was owned by a vampire. The vampire lived in a big shell. The soldier started shooting at the dinosaurs. At the same time there was an eruption. The commander arrived at the island. He opened the golden chest and saw lots of gold. The vampire tried to get him but the commander-in-chief who had come with the airplane shot the vampire. And one of the soldiers threw bombs at the dinosaurs. Then the dinosaurs tried to attack him and he climbed up a statue (Buddha). The pterodactyl tried to eat him but the soldier shot it.

Then the Vikings tried to take their ship and sail to the desert island but the crocodile arrived and sank the ship. They tried to swim to the island. The pirates wanted to shoot the crocodile but a scorpion showed up and tried to bite them. Then a soldier shot the scorpion.

A gigantic egg with gold fell on the skull. Soldiers tried to drive over the bridge to the desert island but they couldn't make it. The soldier on the statue threw the magic powder over to the other island. When the magician saw that he threw it on the dinosaurs and they all died. Then all of the soldiers went to the desert island and gathered the gold.

Discussion

Ari Tray 1

In his first sandplay Ari divides the tray into two parts, with a furious battle taking place between the soldiers on one side and a variety of threatening forces on the other. In our experience the trays of children whose parents have divorced are frequently split or divided like Ari's. To the child the parents are not two autonomous people, but function in the child's psyche as a singular unit whose job is to protect and care for the children. When parents separate, the children struggle to divide what is essentially an archetypal unit into two discrete and different roles.

The first figure Ari placed in the tray is a bridge between the two sides. The story tells us that a plane comes in and lands on the bridge, right in the middle of the two warring factions. Just as he is torn between his loyalties and disappointments with mother and father in his outer life, so his intrapsychic conflict places him at the very center of the battle raging in his own psyche.

The enemies consist of a primitive array of dinosaurs, reptiles, insects and a vampire. Dinosaurs are monstrous animals that are now extinct. Because they are so ancient, the presence of the dinosaurs indicates that the issues that Ari addresses in his sandplay are deeply-rooted in his psychic structure and may have a long family history. The reptiles and insects are lower forms of life that symbolically carry psychic threats of a primitive nature. In addition, the vampire poses the formidable threat of having the life blood sucked from his neck in the darkness of the night. The story tells us that when the soldier began firing at the dinosaurs there was a terrible eruption. Everything was shaken up in Ari's world. In his first sandplay, Ari dives directly to the heart of the confusing and highly threatening inner turmoil that threatens his very stability.

Ari's story tells us that the soldiers faced many different enemies, but are victorious in the end. He has many assets available to him here: a treasure; a magician; magic books; an owl and other birds; red vehicles; a gas truck; a beautiful egg; the Buddha; and a horseshoe. Ari's story tells us that when the soldier needed help he called his friends, who responded immediately. It is highly interesting that most of the assets or treasures are located with the enemies on the right portion of the trays. This repeats a theme that we have seen in several of the children's stories, where the treasure has been stolen, or is in the hands of the wrong people and must be recovered.

Even with all of the available psychic strengths, nothing about this struggle is easy. Enemy attacks reoccur. The enemies must be fought again and again. There are many dangers and the effort is Herculean. Even with all of his vehicles, passage to the treasures is fraught with danger. The struggles that Ari faces resulting from the schism in his family structure demand all of his energies, however in his sandplay he forges ahead and addresses them head on with determination and tenacity.

Ari's anger is evident in the many battles he faces. The wonder of the sandplay is that it allows this very introverted boy to address and express his rage in an immediate and non-threatening manner. In terms of his work ahead in his sandplay series we would hope to see the numbers of the conflicts he faces clarified and reduced, restoring a sense of inner peace and wholeness to a psyche that has been ruptured to the point of functional paralysis.

Ari Tray 2

Ari Tray 2

Ari's Story
Tray 2

The Gold and the Books

The soldiers are trying to take the gold from the dinosaurs. The leader of the monsters is standing on the lighthouse and he has a soldier in his mouth.

All the soldiers are killed except the brown one on the Buddha statue. The soldiers do not see the lizards and the crocodiles that bite them. The dinosaurs and the animals also die. Only the monster and the soldier are left.

The man hits the monster and it falls from the lighthouse and into the sea. It tries to find animals in the sea to help attack the soldier. The soldier tries to shoot. The monster found a crocodile that was going to dig through the sand and eat the soldier. The soldier saw it and shot it. Then he shot at the monster but it did not die. The soldier threw a bomb on the monster but it did not die. Then the monster took the bomb and threw it at the soldier but did not hit him because the soldier hid behind the statue. Then the soldier shot and the monster died.

Discussion
Ari Tray 2

In Tray 2 the battle from the prior tray continues and is reduced to one soldier against an enemy monster. Everyone is dead, save the two remaining enemies. This is a battlefield that is strewn with the ravages of war. However as the two distinct sides of Tray 1 become more consolidated around the central lighthouse green trees emerge in the landscape indicating growth and potential.

The house sits on top of the sheep's skull. It is not on a firm foundation, but stands on something that is long dead. The foundations of both his outer world home as well as the firmament of his inner psychic home are gone and will never be the same as he once knew them. The tilted house sits on a diagonal across the tray from a second sheep's skull, which houses a dead seahorse. Directly adjacent to this skull is an old stone house. Ari said that both houses were very old. There are two additional slain seahorses in the central part of the tray. In nature the male seahorses carry the eggs while the babies gestate (Indiviglio, 2001). Based on their roles in nature, symbolically the seahorse is said to carry qualities of a loving, protective fathering. Ari has lost his father. Through the symbols Ari here begins to grieve the loss of his father and his stable home.

The opposite diagonal corners hold the Buddha in the near left and the treasure chest and books in the far right. All of these figures have dinosaurs standing on top of them. It appears that his spirit has been heavily impacted by these old family issues. The diagonals cross in the center at the tall lighthouse, perhaps indicating that healing will come through his ability to shed light on, or better understand the losses he has suffered in his broken home. It is interesting that the lighthouse emerges out of the central water area indicating that this new vision will emerge from the depths of his psyche.

The monster sits on top of the lighthouse with his great big eyes, and has the greatest view of the carnage. Although the story tells us that the monster is the enemy we wonder if Ari doesn't feel like a monster with his deeply felt injuries and his confusing, internalized anger.

Ari Tray 3

Ari Tray 3a

Ari Tray 3b

Ari's Story

Tray 3

The Treasure

This man is searching for gold and he is going to write about what gold he sees and finds in the book. He sees frogs standing around a mushroom. On top of the mushroom is an arrow. He takes the arrow with him and writes in the book that he sees a golden statue.

Then he sees a bridge leading up to the statue and he tries to get to it. He sees birds standing around an egg. He tries to open the egg with his pen. It breaks open and there is gold in it! He sees a book nearby and reads in it that the monster owns all the gold.

Next he goes up to the statue. The monster comes out of the mouth of the statue, so he runs away to another island. There is plenty of silver and gold there. There is also a book. He reads the book and it says that the monster owns the gold and the silver. He takes the book and all the silver. Then he sees still another island. There is a ship and there are dogs standing around a golden chest. He goes and opens the chest. One of the dogs bites him but he bangs the dog with the pen and opens the chest. It was full of gold. Then he sailed home on the boat with all the gold.

Discussion

Ari Tray 3

The structure of this tray is similar to that of the last tray with a central figure on a blue opening and four corners where a lot of things are happening. However the tone and content is quite different. This tray is much more cheerful and promising.

Here Buddha stands in the central waterway surrounded by four corner islands. On each island there is a red book. The far left island is a beautiful verdant landscape that is laden with silver. There are three dogs in the far right corner, perhaps indicating some development in his instincts. The dogs stand in front of and protect a little golden chest full of treasure. The near left corner is rich with the potential of the many birds and the beautiful cloisonné egg, which was the first object he put in the tray.

It is interesting that this island connects to the Buddha with a bridge constructed of a seed pod. Like the egg the seedpod is a container of potential and possibility for future growth. The near right island is covered with frogs, which carry transformative qualities. They surround a big mushroom with a magic arrow on its crown. From their functions in nature we know that birds, frogs and eggs carry energies of potential growth and transformation. Birds are born from eggs, and frogs develop through a number of transformative stages from eggs to pollywogs, and eventually to mature frogs.

The protagonist is a thinking man, who observes things carefully and takes notes in his book Perhaps this is a part of Ari's psyche that is beginning to understand his conflicts in a new way. In the other three red books the man learns that the monster owns the treasure. It is striking how the books are so highly regarded in Ari's Tray 3. Ari who is eager to learn but has difficulties with his reading clearly understands the importance of books. In addition the man has a pen that is a powerful tool. The man opens the egg with it to reveal treasure; he controls the mean dog with it; and he uses it to record his observations. In his previous trays, Ari battled numerous enemies. Here he sorts out his resources and anchors them in the central figure of the Buddha.

In this tray Ari uses softer, more feminine, rounded shapes. The treasures on the far left island are draped in semicircular patterns; the birds and the egg in the near left are similarly positioned; and in the right corner, the frogs form a circle around the dome-shaped mushroom. The last figure Ari added was the large, beautiful shell in the near center. Once the home of a sea creature, the shell is from the depths of the sea and also carries the feminine energies of the unconscious. In Jungian psychology the unconscious is characterized as feminine, whereas the sky or heavens are said to be masculine in nature (Jung, 1980).

The monster issues from the mouth of the Buddha, a divine figure. Symbolically it appears that, instead of being an enemy force, this monster is actually a part of what is central to his Self. Perhaps Ari acknowledges his own inner monster that has fueled his anger and withdrawal. Ari's story tells us that the monster owns all of the gold. It is highly interesting that when the monster appears it no longer poses a threat and the man is able to take the entire treasure home. Here he acknowledges the monster not only as a part of the world, but one that is replete with riches. It appears that as he is able to acknowledge this shadow aspect of himself, he is able to access his inner resources.

Ari Tray 4

Ari Tray 4a

Ari Tray 4b

Ari's Story
Tray 4

The Gold

Once there was a man on an island where there was a lot of gold. He was going to get some gold but bears showed up and killed him. Then they went away. The Vikings came and buried him in a chest and killed the big bear. They also found lots of gold.

Then they saw monsters, gigantic ants that were going to attack them. The ants were crossing the bridge. The Viking with the gold helmet threw a sword at the ant but it did not die. Then he stabbed it with his helmet. He took a bone and stuck the other ant, too, and they both died.

Then the Vikings went up to the nest with the egg. A gigantic baby bird came and ate the Viking who did not have the gold helmet. The other Viking killed the young bird with his helmet. He took all the gold and closed the chest and went home.

Discussion

Ari Tray 4

Having integrated some shadow material in Tray 3 Ari now moves to a place of transformation. In the near left portion of the tray, the Buddha stands next to a coffin bearing the body of a dead man. This is a graveyard, strewn with bones and jewels. Something has died and is being buried. Perhaps here this young boy is able to surrender his idealized father archetype and let him go. It is very touching that Ari ritually placed a single jewel over the heart of the dead man. This is a caring gesture that releases his father with a loving kindness that shows a deep wisdom beyond his years.

Across the waterway from the grave yard is an altar upon which Ari places a beautiful green egg. Six green frogs stand as attendants at the altar's base. As we discussed in the previous tray, the frogs and the egg are symbols of transformation and new growth. This transformation is also mirrored in the striking presence of the color green, which symbolically carries life, renewal and growth (De Vries, 1984). In addition, there is a single green fish in the tiny pond to the right of the altar. As we have discussed, fish are frequently associated with the spirit. Perhaps this green fish in Ari's tray carries new qualities that are emerging from the depths of the Self. It is interesting that the psyche makes ready for something new to come at the same time the man is buried. This is the process of individuation we first encountered in Hanna's work. We recall that the psyche surrenders what it no longer needs - the psychic content that is not aligned with the central archetype of the Self. Doing this allows the psyche to access new qualities that are more aligned with the center of the personality, resulting in intrapsychic growth and development.

Between the graveyard and the altar are five small bridges. Perhaps resolution of this part of the conflict will lead to the wholeness implied in the number five. As we discussed in Hanna's Tray 1, the number five is called the *anthropos*, the whole man, with two arms, two legs and one head, like a five-pointed star, the number five symbolically carries the possibility for a fully functioning human being (Eastwood, 2002; Weinrib, 2004).

To the right of the altar is a family of three owls and a tiny duckling that appear to look on as the transformation begins to take place. There is a second family grouping with the mother bear and her two cubs along the near right of the tray. Although the story tells us that the big bear killed the man and was slain in return, the image of the fiercely protective nature of the mother bear leading her children away from the dead man is striking. Perhaps Ari's psyche is able to acknowledge his place with his mother and the sacrifice she has made to keep life safe for him. Curiously, the bears head in the direction of the baby Krishna with the butter ball. This little figure portrays the mischievous side of the Hindu incarnation of the god Vishnu, who got into the butter churn when his mother was not looking, and helped himself to the luscious creamy butter (Reyna, 1993). Perhaps there is hope for some playful mischief for Ari now that he begins to resolve some of his conflicts.

As all of this takes place in the construction of the sand tray, Ari's story tells of the repeated "stabbing" of adversaries carried out by the Viking with his splendidly horned golden helmet. Ari begins to tentatively act out his anger in the tray. At the same time, his gestures are clearly phallic in nature. It appears that Ari's healing and transformation gives rise to new masculine potency. He is finding his power. Ari tells us that he closes the chest and takes all of the gold home, restoring a sense of order to his psyche and marshalling his inner treasures.

Ari Tray 5

Ari Tray 5a

Ari Tray 5b

Ari's Story
Tray 5

The Big Dinosaur

Once there was a man who was going to Spain. The airplane fell down in Egypt with lots of soldiers. The dinosaurs arrived and ate some of the men. The soldiers grabbed some guns. Lots of dinosaurs crossed over the bridge. The dinosaurs and warriors fought.

Then an Indian came to attack the soldiers with his knife. He sat on a dinosaur and cut one of the men. A knight came and killed the (blue) Indian. The warriors gave the (yellow) knight some guns, armor and bombs. Then the commander flew down in a parachute.

All of a sudden a gigantic club hit the best soldier. The club was a time bomb and had 3 hours and 39 seconds left on the clock. Another soldier arrived. He had been living on the island without being eaten up. (At this point Ari stopped the story and talked a little about fish that eat dead bodies). *When 2 hours and 50 seconds had passed the golden chest hit the tail of the chef dinosaur.*

The soldiers killed all the dinosaurs with bombs and went to check and see if some were still alive. One was alive and ate one of the soldiers. The soldiers killed it and took all the gold. They made an airplane and left the island. One dinosaur was good so they did not kill it and took it with them.

Discussion

Ari Tray 5

The expression of anger and hostility that began to emerge in Tray 4 reappears here, exploding with brutality. All the soldiers Ari could find in the collection are put on the battlefield to fight with the dinosaurs.

Many of the figures in this tray come from the sky: the soldiers tumble down to Egypt as their plane crashes; their commander arrives by parachute; and the gigantic club seems to drop out of thin air. After the victory of the soldiers over the dinosaurs, order is restored. Cleverly, they make an airplane and leave with one good dinosaur and all the treasure. Things coming from the sky have interesting symbolic implications. In the Native

American traditions sky gods are considered to be guardians of the law (Cajete, 1999). The task of the soldiers in Ari's story is to do away with the brutal, primitive forces and to clear the way to the treasure chest. They come from above to restore order to what is out of control.

Time is also important to what transpires here. There is a ticking time bomb in the guise of a huge club. When it is first mentioned, 3 hours and 39 seconds remain on the clock before it explodes. With only 46 minutes remaining on the clock, the golden chest strikes the tail of the chief dinosaur ending the war. Perhaps this time bomb signifies that it is time for Ari to express his pent up anger and take action, with the aim of freeing his precious Self, the treasure chest, from the grips of these primitive, archetypal forces, the dinosaurs. We recall that Ari was so withdrawn when he began his work he was described as "shut down." Through the symbolic play in his sandplay process Ari has been able to experience his anger in a safe way. He accesses and expresses these feelings that were previously so overpowering that he had retreated from life. With the intervention of the resources from above, he rectifies what had been seriously disordered and his life energies can once again begin to flow.

Ari Tray 6

Ari Tray 6a

Ari Tray 6b

Ari's Story
Tray 6

The Small Globes

Once there was a man who was going on a trip to Africa. When he got to the airport he drove to a hotel and there were lots of animals in the neighborhood. He also saw a small globe and rolled it. Then he got some gold and the treasure chest opened a little bit.

He wanted to roll another globe but a man with a gun came and was going to shoot him. He said: "Look at that bird," and then the gunman looked in the air. Then the man took the gun and shot the gunman. He rolled another globe. Dinosaurs arrived and the chest opened more. He shot five dinosaurs and he still had more shots left.

Then a path appeared on the water and he walked across it, where two big dinosaurs stood. He threw the gunman's gun on the island and the dinosaurs followed him.

The man ran and rolled the third globe and the chest opened completely. He signed the guest book and took all the gold with him on his way back. On his way he saw a bird on a nest. He chased the bird from the nest and saw that there were two golden pearls. He took them and put eggs in their place.

Discussion

Ari Tray 6

In this tray the focus is on one primary protagonist. He goes on a trip by air to Africa where he fights with dinosaurs and a gunman whom he tricks. Ari uses the same sturdy man that he buried in Tray 4. Here he is a conqueror who rotates the three globes, passes behind the black feathers, signs his name in the guest book and takes all the treasure with him on his way back. This man is a man of action and courage and the place is his domain. It appears that there is important development taking place in Ari's sense of masculine capability.

The three identical globes play an important role. By spinning the globes the treasure chest gradually opens and eventually the man obtains all the treasure. The three incidents with the three globes remind us of traditional fairy tales where action is taken in three steps. Following this there is an additional step that discloses the solution (von Franz, 1986; Unnsteinsdottir, 2002). In Ari's story the fourth step is taken when the man replaces the pearls with eggs in the bird´s nest. This is consistent with the significance of the numbers three and four as found in mythological texts. The number three stands for the active creation appearing in birth, life and death or past, present and future; while the number four stands for the stability appearing in the four seasons and the four corners of the world (Eastwood, 2002).

The globe shares the symbolism of the sphere as wholeness, the mystical center, for power and what is self-contained (De Vries, 1984). The act of spinning or rotating the globes resembles the rotation of prayer wheels in the Tibetan Buddhist tradition. Prayer wheels are either hand-held or stationary cylindrical chambers that have prayers written on their outer surface and contain prayers written on paper. When spun they are thought to send the prayers out into the universe. Prayer wheels are used to accumulate wisdom and good karma and to purify any negativities, or bad karma (Sherab & Tsewang, 2010). Reflecting this Eastern theme Ari positions a prominent Buddha statue in the far right corner of the tray. Symbolically it appears that Ari's repeated reference to spinning the globes in his story serves as a purification ritual to becoming whole and self-reliant, for it is by rotating the globes that the adventurer accesses the treasure.

In the far left corner Ari forms a screen to protect the treasure chest with five prominent black feathers. The five feathers are reminiscent of the five bridges in Tray 4 that connected the death of the man to the sacred altar. We recall from our discussion the significance of the number five as the *anthropos*, the whole person. The five feathers, three globes and the treasure, which consists of multicolored round stones and eggs, indicate that Ari is now joining what were formerly disconnected intrapsychic forces to make them an integrated whole. As a part of his effort to bring these disparate energies together, Ari releases his aggression and anger through the prominent presence of the primitive animals scattered around the tray. Reflecting this new freedom, Ari places the Statue of Liberty and three colorful frogs behind the story's protagonist. The statue supports his new autonomy and the three frogs carry transformative energies needed to bring these new psychic qualities to consciousness.

Ari Tray 7

Ari Tray 7a

Ari Tray 7b

Ari's Story
Tray 7

The Island of the Dinosaurs

Once there was a man who had two swords and he was going on a boat to an island. He saw that the ship crashed against a stone and all the men fell overboard. The man passed out and when he woke up they were on an unknown island. They saw two Vikings and lots of soldiers, but he knew all the soldiers. He also saw some dinosaurs and attacked them. Then a big dinosaur arrived and killed him.

A man standing on the back of a camel came. He was going to attack but he stopped because the commander in the chair threw bottles with poison on the monsters (dinosaurs). The commander saw that more dinosaurs were coming and all but three soldiers died.

The chief dinosaur arrived with his little boy and two other dinosaurs. They were going to attack. The man on the camel threw a bucket over the young dinosaur. The dinosaurs attacked and the Vikings came and killed one dinosaur. Then the commander in the chair threw a bomb on the dinosaurs and all of them died.

The men (seven) who were living took the statue and the egg, made themselves an airplane and managed to go home.

Discussion

Ari Tray 7

There appears to be a regression in Ari's work, as he returns to complex conflict and death. His story even tells us that the first protagonist is killed. There is terrific aggression and great carnage. This is the first time that we have seen such hurt inflicted on the human beings in the story. Although seven men escape with their lives and the treasure, there was a huge price to pay. The therapist suspects that something difficult and painful has occurred at home, but is not aware of a specific event. She recalls that he was more withdrawn than he had been in prior sessions and seemed to have returned to his own private world.

It is painful to see this regression, particularly after he has made such progress in his work. However it is imperative that we not look at this in isolation, but consider it in the context of his overall sandplay process. Significantly, he still has the beautiful egg in the nest and the Statue of Liberty alongside the scene of the battle. Even in the middle of this carnage he has access to the newly found resources that anchor him in the Self. The Statue of Liberty was the last figure he put in the tray. This was directly preceded by the skull. Symbolically Ari acknowledges the losses in his life, yet still has a touchstone in his inner truth. He balances these resources with the pair of Vikings on the left side of the tray that were protagonists in Tray 4.

The soldiers he chose to use in this tray are very small. In prior trays he has used the larger ones. The warriors have decreased in size and there is no hero here. He has an equal number of soldiers and dinosaurs. However Ari's expression of anger is much more open and obvious than in the past. It appears that after Ari integrates psychic material, as he does in Trays 4 and 6 he freed up to openly express his anger. (Trays 5 and 7) His psyche is strengthened and he is better able to tolerate the forces of his disappointment and fury. But like his soldiers, he would like to make an airplane and get away from his painful home life.

Ari Tray 8

Ari Tray 8a

Ari Tray 8b

Ari's Story
Tray 8

The Four Keys

Once there was a man who had a shop where he sold animals. Once when he came to his shop all the animals had left. The animals took his gold. He saw footsteps that headed to the desert where nobody dared go to. When he arrived at the desert he saw his gold and still more treasure. He also saw his animals and more bad animals (insects, monsters and crocodiles).

On one of the stones he saw a double-sided sword. When he took the sword the bad animals were going to attack him and he saw a green monster that was their chief. He saw also his dog and it ran to attack him because the monster had hypnotized it. The man stunned the dog. The monster ordered the other animals to attack. The man saw that the red dinosaur was good and it helped him.

A strange man who was a statue in a box appeared. He brought a spider, the foot of a living bird and a scorpion, which were supposed to attack the man. But then the dinosaur jumped on the wasp and ate it and gave the man one of the keys.

At that point one of the frogs fell from the pile of frogs while the dinosaur got another key. The man and the dinosaur ran to the chest where the mice were and put the two keys in the chest. The crocodiles came with another key and the dinosaur ran to them and ate them. The dinosaur put this key in the chest.

Then all the bad animals ran to the last key that was beside the spider and all the good animals (snail, frogs and dog) came and attacked them. The man grabbed the key and was able to open the chest and he found loads of gold. He took all the gold and went home with his animals.

Discussion

Ari Tray 8

In Tray 8 Ari temporarily leaves the battlefield and moves toward a more civilized world, where there is a shop. Although the shopkeeper must go into the desert and recover the stolen treasure, Tray 8 is much less savage than the last and prior trays. When we see movements from primitive, dark places to scenes of ordinary life over the course of a sandplay process, it generally indicates that the new psychic capacities that have been tapped in the depths of the unconscious are being integrated into consciousness. Although threats, such as the crocodiles and the wasp, do remain, Tray 8 is much more organized than many of Ari's prior trays. Ari's story tells us that the protagonist owns a shop, clearly a more conscious domain than the warring primitive creatures that precede it. In addition, this new region is populated with several non-threatening, and in some cases, helpful creatures. The shopkeeper has a black and white dog that is helpful in recouping the lost gold, although he was temporarily hypnotized into doing bad deeds. It is interesting that the dog had been hypnotized. Perhaps Ari begins to "wake up" to the realities of his outer life and is accessing resources that will allow him to maintain his personal integrity and continue to grow in the midst of the family pain.

Continuing the transformational symbolism, there is a large brown snail sitting next to a baby snail, which is perched on top of the black stone. This is what Dora Kalff (2003), referred to as the *mother-child unity*. Kalff observed that the pairs of mothers and children frequently appear in sandplay work when new psychic qualities are just beginning to develop. This impending development is mirrored by the green frogs, which symbolically carry transformative energies, and by the tiny turtle hatching from the egg, directly in front of the protagonist. Both snails and turtles carry their homes on their backs. Being 'at home' wherever they go, they symbolize a vital working relationship between the conscious personality and the Self (De Vries, 1984).

Continued growth and development is also present in the small heart-shaped box of seeds Ari places to the left of the pedestal. This image of seeds safely contained within a heart is powerful and deeply moving, as it symbolically embraces a potential for Ari's continued growth in a loving and compassionate manner. Doing his sandplay series has allowed this young boy to access psychic qualities of compassion and wisdom which will develop and come to realization as he continues to grow. The four mice on top of the treasure chest affirm Ari's ability to break through the confines of his current helpless position in the family. In nature, mice are able to pierce through the most foreboding impediments. They can chew through just about anything and can squeeze through the tiniest of holes. Symbolically they carry a resolute and penetrating energy that finds its way through the most difficult circumstances (Waldau, 2006).

It is interesting that the red dinosaur that is usually found on the enemy team is now a helper figure. It appears that there is further integration of some shadow material here. What was once perceived as a threat is now an asset in service of the Self.

The Chinese mask in the brocade box in the far right corner functions as a shaman. He uses a scorpion, a spider and the foot of a water bird to do his medicine. Curiously, Ari tells us that this "strange man" from the far off place was supposed to attack the man, but does not follow through with it. Because China is so distant from Ari's native Iceland and an unknown culture it may be that he is accessing psychic qualities that are very remote from his conscious position to find his own medicine and healing.

Ari positions four crocodiles in an unusually tidy row near the base of the shaman. In addition, there is another small one in the central lake. The crocodile can be highly dangerous in nature. Mythology is filled with tales about the power of these creatures. In early Ethiopian and Hebrew lore, the crocodile is a demonic creature that lives underground or under water and perpetrates evil deeds (Langton, 1949). Psychologically these are the dark, unseen operations of the shadow. In Jungian personality theory the shadow consists of psychic qualities and issues that have been conscious but were intolerable to the ego, the conscious position. Thus they are forced back into the shadows of the unconscious, but continue to apply pressure to become conscious and see the light of day (Jung, 1981). Because they rumble around below the surface of consciousness, they are perceived as very threatening and frightening. As the youngest child in a family where the parents have divorced, there is bound to be conflict that Ari has not been privy to. Divorce can be a frightening mystery. As the row of crocodiles is placed at the foot of the medicine man, it appears that Ari's psyche begins to acknowledge and address the issue of the family shadow. It is interesting that the smallest crocodile is not a part of this group but is in the pond by himself. Ari is the youngest of three brothers. Perhaps he separates himself from the family to attain some perspective on the situation. It may be that this is the observing aspect of the psyche that has achieved sufficient distance to obtain some perspective on the darker side of the family story. In Indian mythology, the holy river Ganges is said to ride on the back of a crocodile which carries the dangers of death, as well as the abundance of life (Darian, 1978). Regarding the crocodiles from this perspective it appears that acknowledging the family shadow entails Ari's acceptance of his many losses and in doing so his life becomes fuller.

Ari Tray 9

Ari Tray 9a

Ari Tray 9b

Ari's Story
Tray 9

The Viking

Once there was a man who was called Lalli. He was taking a walk at the zoo. A black panther attacked him and let all the animals in the zoo go free. A monster arrived and changed itself into a vampire. Then stars fell and one of the stars landed on the man. A Viking came and helped him stand up. The vampire came and ate the man. The Viking killed the vampire with his sword and it vomited up gold and magic books. It also threw up crocodiles, elephants, bears, rhinoceros, hippopotamus and the man. The man was dead. The Viking attacked the vampire and killed it. The crocodiles ate all the fish that were in the zoo.

A pig with a beer came and hit everyone with his beer except the Viking and the good animals.

Gold came up from the earth and the Viking took all the gold. He was about to leave when the guards arrested him because he hadn't paid to get into the zoo. Then the guards discovered the man was dead and thought that the Viking had killed him. So the Viking was put into prison. A man in the prison came with a rope. He and the Viking wanted to try to flee. A helicopter arrived and the man fled. The Viking went to the ship and fired cannon balls at the helicopter then sailed home with the gold.

Discussion

Ari Tray 9

Ari's story takes an unexpected turn when the panther opens the cages and releases all of the animals in the zoo. Symbolically it appears that the instincts are now freed, and as might be expected, they are a little unruly to begin with. The animals in this tray are more highly developed than the dinosaurs and insects of prior trays. There are many mammals here, including bears, hippos and elephants. The crocodiles go about their business and eat the fish. The little pig has a beer. Perhaps this is the part of Ari that would have liked to be numb to the troubles in his family. In his story however, the pig uses the beer as a weapon to hit the bad guys. In some way Ari is more accepting of his circumstances and acknowledges the cycle of birth and death, of gain and loss, as the natural course of things.

Curiously the release of the animals is repeated when the vampire regurgitates them along with jewels and books. What was formerly sucking the life blood from his psyche now gives birth to a wealth of instinctual energy, the inner world riches of jewels and the wisdom of books. The jewels from the prior tray have multiplied and are disbursed throughout the tray. There are many of them and they are readily available.

Transformation by being swallowed is a mythic theme of profound change, such as we see with the Biblical story of Jonah and the Whale (Eliade, 1996). Another mythic account of transformation by consumption is found in the Nordic tale of the *Yggdrasil*, the World Tree (Sturluson, 1984). In this version a huge serpent named Nidhogg lives at the root of the World Tree, the mythic account of all aspects of life and death. Nidhogg's domain is in the underworld, the darkness, where he viciously gnaws at the roots of Yggdrasil and devours corpses. As a depiction of transformation, encounters with Nidhogg concern radical change through psychic death and loss. In Ari's story the dead man, his lost innocence, is vomited up at his feet so he can be clearly seen. However, transformation has occurred and he arrives with the treasures and wisdom of the jewels and books. Although frightening and painful,

Ari's journey into the darkness provides him with the naked truths of his experience of the family dissolution. Ari is more accepting of his circumstances, and has the necessary tools to acknowledge the cycle of birth and death, of gain and loss, as part of his path and of what makes him who he is. Even after the battle the story tells us that the Viking protagonist was imprisoned twice: once for the minor violation of failing to pay the zoo's entrance fee; and secondly for being falsely accused of a murder. As Ari's psyche provides him with the capacity to see the facts of his losses it also prepares him for the understanding of its lack of justification. Ari has undergone substantial psychic development through his sandplay work, but the sadness and the inequitable nature of his experience of loss must still be grieved consciously.

Five stars fall from the sky. One hits the man temporarily knocking him down. The star is a beautiful symbolic image of Ari's wholeness as a human being. Moreover the symbolism of the number five is repeated in that there are five five-pointed stars. In the story the stars fall to the earth. As a symbol of completeness, these stars are connected to the heavens above and are grounded on the earth below. When we consider this symbolism along with the release of the animal instincts, it appears that the fullness that emerges in Ari is rich instinctual energy that will allow him to take care of himself, to honor his feelings and experience and to find his way through the world. As this development takes place a small bird sits on a pearl that Ari tenderly placed underneath as an egg. As a symbol of the Self, this pearl is also an egg, and holds the promise of something new to come.

Ari Tray 10

Ari Tray 10

Ari's Story
Tray 10

The Good Soldiers and the Bad Ones

Once there was a warrior who was a commander and he was going to take a vacation with all the soldiers. They went to Egypt. They walked around the country and examined it. They saw a cave full of dinosaurs. They heard a warning bell then bunches of dinosaurs and soldiers attacked them.

Way back in the cave were the chief dinosaurs. They were the only ones that had wings. All of the soldiers attacked the dinosaurs. The bad soldiers came and a war broke out. Then some Indians came along with more bad soldiers. A bad one shot at the leader so the good ones got angry and threw bombs at the bad ones. Then some good soldiers sneaked up and killed the bad chief of the dinosaurs.

Then more men came out of the earth. They were skeletons. They killed all the good ones except five and the monsters killed three of them. Then one of the soldiers threw a timed atom bomb and ran to the airplane. His buddy ran to another airplane. They flew away and the desert exploded.

Discussion

Ari Tray 10

Ari was not feeling very well when he came to sandplay this day. Here good soldiers are fighting with bad soldiers, dinosaur monsters, skeletons and Indians. The chief of the good soldiers is the man in the far right corner. He lies prostrate on his back. In front of him but in a vertical position are two Vikings, a muscle man and a little man in black with a pistol. The chief has higher status than these men but he is not in a strong position.

In Tray 10 Ari grieves the loss of power to change what has happened in his life. Looking back through the early phases of Ari's sandplay process there appears to be an alternating pattern of confrontation-battle-discovery of assets-escape themes followed by themes of sadness-hopelessness and/or loss. In Tray 1 we see struggle and the discovery of assets. There is a battle between men and dinosaurs. A magician discovers magic books and a soldier discovers treasure. This is followed by themes of loss, grief and hopelessness in Tray 2.

Following the battle a single soldier and one monster engage in what is a nearly futile struggle for the soldier. In Tray 3 the theme of the discovery of assets returns. This is followed by themes of loss in Tray 4 where a man is killed by bears and is buried in a box. A Viking is also killed. Tray 5 returns to themes of struggle and the discovery of assets. There is a battle between dinosaurs and men and the protagonists recover the gold. Tray 6 repeats the theme of struggle and asset discovery when a single man confronts several adversaries before discovering the jewels. In Trays 7 through 10 the themes of loss and grief become more pronounced. In Tray 7 a man crashes his boat on an island filled with dangers and threats. Dreadful battles ensue with terrible losses of life. Tray 8 repeats the themes of loss and struggle with a pet store owner who is robbed of his gold. Following a great struggle he recovers the gold and returns home.

Ari's discovery of new possibilities and inner strengths in Tray 9 is followed here in Tray 10 by a raging battle. In Tray 10 Ari again works with hopelessness, futility and loss. In this story a vampire eats a man then vomits up his corpse for observation and the Viking protagonist is falsely imprisoned. The two protagonists barely escape with their lives. The animals are primitive, terrifying insects and crocodiles with soldiers in their mouths. The soldier in his story intended to take a vacation, but ended up in the middle of a huge fight. He is even attacked by skeletons of things from the past.

The meaningless nature of the fight conveys the sadness of the divorce and Ari's inner struggle to accept it. Clearly he cannot control or change his experience and he recognizes that such experiences come unannounced. The dramatic changes in his family life have wounded him deeply. Yet his growing capacity to "voice" his anger in the sand tray is admirable, and a necessary step in his healing and development.

In the near center is a striking pair of black and white panda bears. These were the second items Ari placed in his tray, immediately after the big piece of dead wood in the near right corner. While one of the most savage battles he has encountered rages in this tray, this pair of black and white pandas, like the Chinese symbol of the yin yang, carry the opposites that prefigure the birth of new psychic qualities. This is the pair of opposites, the archetypal duality that arises when the undivided wholeness separates into the original duality, which underlies material manifestation (Kalff, 2003). Perhaps the strengths that the immobilized chief carries will rise to prominence in what follows.

As means of transportation Ari uses five airplanes. In his stories Ari has often mentioned airplanes but here he actually puts them in the tray. There were no real planes in the collection at that time so Ari cleverly used the vertebrae of a sheep. Two airplanes leave Egypt with the two good soldiers that overcome the slaughter. As they leave the desert there is a huge explosion from an atom *bomb* one of them threw when flying away. Perhaps Ari is developing the inner abilities that will allow him to leave the battle behind.

Ari has three green trees and one large dead tree in his tray, indicating that although there has been loss and death there is the promise of new growth and development. This is also reflected in the numerous large rocks from which Ari built a cave and places around the tray. While he is powerless to change his circumstances he is developing a sound, solid base on which to stand.

Ari Tray 11

Ari Tray 11a

Ari Tray 11b

Ari's Story
Tray 11

The Man with the Dinosaur

Once there was a man who had a dinosaur and he went everywhere. One time he went to a cave and lots of soldiers and animals came out of the earth and attacked the soldiers. Then the man had his dinosaur attack the soldiers.

The commander came and told the little soldiers to go to the cave and see what they could find. They found a golden egg. The dinosaurs came to be guards to protect the egg. The officers came and told the soldiers that the dinosaurs were only puppets. Then one of the soldiers pushed the puppets and took the egg and he exploded. The soldiers saw that there were landmines around the egg.

The soldiers arrived with guns and shot at the crocodiles that were trying to eat their friends. Men came and threw bombs at the animals. They circled around the man with the dinosaur and shot him. They exploded all the mines and took the egg and went home.

Discussion

Tray 11

In Tray 11 Ari encounters another brutal battle however there is less chaos and more order than much of the combat he has come across before. The king is the first figure Ari placed in his tray. Someone is in charge and oversees the events. The king is different than the exaggerated muscle man, who was the hero in Ari's prior trays. Here the chief wears the robes of authority, and carries a royal staff. He does not outwardly carry the brute strength of the muscle man, but bears an inner strength that speaks of true empowerment.

Diagonally across from the king is a man riding the large red dinosaur. In Tray 11 the red dinosaur that has frequently been the most powerful of the primitive enemy creatures now comes under the control of a man. It is also encircled by soldiers. What was once dangerous and out of control is now tamed and in the service of the men. The threats to Ari's psyche are subsiding and he harnesses new strengths, as his development continues. This theme is mirrored in the story when we learn that the dinosaurs that stand guard over the egg become harmless puppets. What once seemed very threatening to him no longer poses any danger.

When a soldier prematurely attempts to take the prized egg, he steps on a land mine and is destroyed. We are reminded of the mythical theme of the dragon protecting the precious pearl of the Self. It is not easy to obtain and can be approached only with the wisdom of having undergone the difficult work of transformation. Not just anyone can succeed at this (Eliade, 1991). This is a heroic journey where great sacrifice and loss precede growth and maturity.

The battlefield is strewn with the corpses of many dead soldiers and animals. Ari has had a huge price to pay for the transformation demanded by the changes in his family. Essentially he has had to surrender to the loss of himself as a young boy under the protective care of the parental archetype. He has had to undergo radical intrapsychic changes that allow him to experience himself as an individual boy with a separate mother and father. In the free and protected space of the sandplay he has been able to accomplish this very difficult task. Given his original level of withdrawal it is difficult to imagine what other avenue would have facilitated this substantial task in such a brief period of time.

Ari Tray 12

Ari Tray 12a

Ari Tray 12b

Ari Tray 12c

Ari's Story
Tray 12

The Baby Turtle

Once there were two turtles in the sea. One day one of them laid a turtle egg. After some months a baby turtle came out. Other animals from the sea came to protect the little one because there were monsters that were going to kill the turtle.

Tiny soldiers came and wanted to save the turtle. When they came they sank into the sand. Then a big soldier came with three other soldiers. They couldn't sink because they were so big. They started to shoot at the dinosaurs. Then the commander of the dinosaurs arrived with two of his friends and the soldiers killed them. A big dinosaur arrived with another one on his back and a crocodile attacked it.

All the dinosaurs were dead except one that was hiding in the sand. The scorpion saw it and was going to sting it, but the dinosaur went down deeper in the sand and came up beside the lake. Then it flew and got the egg but the little one sprang out. The dinosaur could not carry the egg and a shark came and ate the dinosaur.

Discussion

Ari Tray 12

Ari has come a long way in his sandplay journey. In his final sandplay Ari's focus comes to the center around the large water opening. Directly in the middle of the lake is the little family of turtles, which were the first figures Ari placed in the tray. The baby sits between the mother and father turtle. Significantly the parents are now separated and the newly hatching baby is positioned to have a relationship with both the mother and the father. Symbolically Ari is reborn. He has undergone the intrapsychic transformation required to adjust and survive in his newly-configured family.

There are still threats to safety, but it is interesting that he harnesses the powers of the crocodiles, the scorpion, and the shark for protection. While they are able to save the fragile little creature there is still a great deal of anger present that needs to be addressed and properly channeled.

A three-headed green monster sits above in the rocking chair, appearing to have an overview of the three green turtles in the pond below. Perhaps this three-headed monster is the family shadow. It may be that the anger surrounding the new birth below is the anger remaining in the family from the divorce. While Ari's newly developing sense of self is born and remains safe, it is a fact that he must deal with the anger and resentment that color the family atmosphere.

Ari completed his sandplay series without the traditional process pattern of descent, centering, and ascent that we see in some of the cases. Ideally, we would like to see Ari be able to continue with sandplay however the school year had ended and we were not able to continue. Even so, it is clear that he did a lot of good work and made substantial development. We recall that Ari had virtually shut down following his parents' divorce. He stopped making progress in school, and fell behind his peers in his physical growth. Sandplay provided this child the opportunity to work through some profoundly painful and confusing issues, and allowed him a safe outlet for his anger. Although we would like to see him be able to continue with sandplay, he ended the school year a much better adjusted boy, able to function in his family and social situations and he was back on track with his school work.

The Sandplay Work of Alda:
Girl 4th Grade – Age 9

Alda's Sandplay Work – Overview

Alda was a gentle girl who had problems with her schoolwork and labored away at it very slowly. Alda was diagnosed with dyslexia. She hesitated a lot and was always erasing what she had just written. Alda was terribly shy but when she participated in class performances she seemed to take on another character that sang and danced with ease. She dressed like a girl much older in these performances and her dances were daring. At the same time Alda was socially isolated in class. Her teacher recollected that once when the class was discussing the dangers of smoking she broke down and became inconsolable. Alda told the teacher that both her parents smoked. Her teacher surmised that Alda was probably worried about several issues concerning her parents.

Alda's eyes easily filled with tears. She had a very insecure self image and was never satisfied with anything she did. She was two full years behind in both reading and mathematics. Her countenance was quite different when she came to her sandplay sessions. She was quietly confident and satisfied with her sandplays.

Her family history was stressful, with an alcoholic father and an older sibling who was drug addicted. There was a suspicion that Alda had been sexually abused. At the time of the suspicion the child welfare board got involved because of the father's alcoholism but nothing was proven and the investigation was dropped. The girl was often anxious and worried and suffered from somatic complaints such as headaches. Both parents, especially the father, were reluctant about Alda participating in the study, but they finally gave their consent.

In the year Alda participated in the study she made considerable progress in reading, although she remained far behind her classmates. She also made progress in spelling and written expression. She had very little confidence in mathematics and her performance continued to be poor.

On WISC III Alda scored low average (81/92). She made significant progress in Freedom from Distraction (17 points) considerable progress in Perceptual Organization (12 points) but Processing Speed went down a little (–3 points).

According to her self assessment at the end of the school year on the Beck Inventories her anger and confusing behavior had increased considerably. The study of Alda's work and the knowledge of her hard life help us better understand her anger and low self evaluation. We can only hope that the psychic strengths Alda accessed in her sandplay work will serve her later in her life.

According to Alda's teachers she had clinical symptoms of ADD at the beginning of the school year but the symptoms had decreased by the end of the year. On the Achenbach Scale the teachers' assessment of Physical Complaint and Social Isolation was striking. Complaints were up to clinical limits at the beginning of the year, but symptoms had diminished significantly by the end. Similarly Alda's teachers' pretest on her Depression and Anxiety scores were up to clinical limits, but had lessened by the end of the school year. According to her parents however, symptoms of Depression and Anxiety had increased at the end of the school year. Perhaps what the parents saw as depression and anxiety was their misinterpretation of Alda's growing emotional awareness of the abuses and losses she has suffered.

Alda was highly enthusiastic about sandplay and participated wholeheartedly. Unlike her slow pace with her schoolwork she worked fast in sandplay and actively moved figures around. It was striking how often she hid things by digging them in the sand or otherwise. Alda never used water in her trays however openings to the blue bottom appeared in nine. Often she used the same or similar objects from one tray to the next. None of these objects appeared more frequently than the black spider, which was found in nine trays. Alda's trays contained a lot of conflict themes. Magic appeared in all of the trays. Oppositions, treasure and terror appeared in nine trays; poison and caves in six; and a place for growth and change in five. Alda tended to make long stories that were often confused and dreamlike.

Alda Tray 1

Alda Tray 1

Alda's Story

Tray 1

The Power

> *This one is evil – the Devil* (vampire in near right corner) *and he wants to rule the whole world because the globe is in front of him. This lady* (far left corner) *wants to find out what is going on and the monkey is very surprised. The evil one has collected things. He stole them and hid them. He uses power and magic to get things.*

> *The bones are there to mark the place where he buried the treasure. He also hid things under the bridge. The key to the chest is hidden, too. There is poison in the brown bottle* (behind vampire in near right corner)*.*

> *The spider is poisonous, a tarantula, and it is the pet of the Devil.*

After making the tray, she made several comments.

There is something missing (she added a man with a gun pointing at the woman).
He is working for the Devil.
Dinosaurs are hunting.
The ladybug is a harmless little bug.
The shell is a trap.
The Devil succeeds in changing the world and makes it evil.
A grey rat works for the Devil.
The girl (woman) *did get the treasure box however.*

Discussion

Alda Tray 1

Alda's first tray shows a clear opposition between what is evil on one side and what is innocent on the other. On the evil side of the tray there is a vampire, a tarantula, a man with the gun, a grey rat, poison and a crocodile. On the innocent side is a dark woman Alda refers to as a "girl," a monkey, a ladybug and a white mouse. Alda tells us that the evil vampire rules over the entire world. He uses magic to steal things then secrets them away. He hides what he steals under the bridge and buries them in a pink heart-shaped box marked by the crossbones. Alda also attempted to bury the larger treasure chest but was not successful. The evil one's helper is a man with a pistol who aims a gun at the black woman in red in the far left corner. His pet is the tarantula, which Alda calls a poisonous spider. There is also some poison in a bottle behind the vampire. The dangerous and oppositional theme is underscored in the central lake area by the crocodile and its prey, the white mouse.

The symbols Alda chooses for her first tray are fascinating. The vampire, although commonly thought of as masculine was originally a feminine form of the devil in fifteenth century Germany and Czechoslovakia (Russell, 1977). These female devils were thought to steal children and roast them for dinner. Clearly Alda draws from the collective unconscious when she tells us in her story that this vampire is *...the evil one, a devil.* Jung referred to the repository of all human knowing as the *collective* (Jung, 1981). Very likely carried in the DNA, the collective unconscious contains the archetypal underpinnings, or templates, of human meaning-making. An example of what Jung meant by the collective is the appearance of parallel themes in the religions and mythologies across cultures. The underlying essence of these themes is similar and assumes the appearance and characteristics of the particular culture. Alda certainly had no knowledge of the vampire as an evil feminine energy that destroys childhood, yet her unconscious found the perfect symbol she needed to begin her work in sandplay.

Similar feminine child-destroying symbolism is carried by the crocodile, the large spider and the ladybug. While untrue in nature, there is a common belief that the mother crocodile devours some of her hatchlings as she carries them in her mouth to the water. In the Egyptian *Book of Going Forth By Day* a crocodile monster devours those who do evil deeds (Budge, 1904). In addition, the large black spider is associated with its capacity to weave a beautiful web on its lighter side, and with trapping and devouring prey on the darker side. The ladybug, which Alda is clear to describe as such a harmless little bug is trapped in the large shell. This little bit of innocence is held captive. It is important to be aware that the issues that arise from Alda's history are mirrored in her inner world by wounding to an archetypal feminine, mothering, and masculine, fathering energies. Given the repitition of this devouring theme in the symbolic content of Tray 1, it appears that the issues Alda will address in the sandplay work ahead concern the destruction of her innocence and a lack of protection.

Alda's story tells us that the lady wants to find out what is going on. However this is a dangerous undertaking and a man with a gun aims directly at the young woman. In the tray he is the tiny dark figure to the immediate left of the woman, directly in front of the rose petals. Alda is under threat by the masculine and she is not protected by the feminine. She is surrounded by dangerous and devouring figures. The treasure, the truth and goodness of the Self, has to go underground in the heart-shaped box and is marked by the cross she makes out of bones. The rose petals in the two upper corners look like tears.

The wild cats are positive symbols. They are powerful and ably take care of themselves (Sunquist & Sunquist, 2002). Symbolically wild cats are associated with the Self in that they move in concert with what is required at the time. In ancient Egypt cats were thought to be feminine in nature (Malek, 1997). They bore wisdom in a non-verbal way. They were considered superhuman by virtue of their certainty and the consistency of their behavior in the wild.

It is significant that Alda, being fair skinned, chooses a dark female figure to play such a prominent role in her sandplay. Perhaps the dark skinned figure carries shadow qualities of the natural strength of her feminine nature that had to be repressed into the unconscious as a means of coping in her dysfunctional environment. Over the course of her work we would hope to see these qualities reemerge and become available to her for her self-protection.

The whale in the central lake is also symbolically significant. In nature the whale must dive deeply for food and then resurface for air. As symbols and in mythic themes, the whale is associated with what is called the *night sea journey*. The gravity of this form of psychological change becomes visible in Jung's description:

> *...a descent into Hades and a journey to the land of ghosts somewhere beyond this world, beyond consciousness, hence an immersion in the unconscious* (Jung, 1985, par. 455).

This is a descent into the unconscious, beyond the boundaries of what is known. This is where the individual undergoes radical transformation. As with the Biblical story of Jonah and the whale, mythic tales frequently involve being swallowed by a dragon or sea monster (Jung, 1985). It appears that Alda's sandplay work will entail some very demanding passages.

In addition to this impending descent into the unconscious, Alda places a small monkey and two pairs of feathers behind the woman along the far wall of the tray. The feathers, coming from birds that fly, imply that ascent is possible and that the spirit is accessible. The agile monkey also carries similar qualities, in that it is so adept at climbing. Dora Kalff referred to the monkey as, *"...the initial impulse to the spirit"* (1988, Conference Notes). The feathers and the monkey provide a sense of hope among the many horrors, and carry the psychic assets that Alda has available to her to undergo the difficult work ahead. The large red lobster in the lake is also a psychic asset, in that lobsters feed off of the waste at the bottom of the water. Symbolically speaking they clean up what is old and what is not in service of the Self. The two dinosaurs on either side of the lake may indicate that the issues Alda contends with are very old. The appearance of dinosaurs may signify painful conditions that have a long family history, perhaps going back generations.

The primary issue appears to concern awakening the feminine energy that will serve her growth and development. Alda's aim is to find the intrapsychic feminine energy that can hold and love her. She needs to develop a feminine nature that can be fierce when necessary, one that can drive away danger and protect her. At the same time she needs to access the inner masculine energy, the *animus* that can lead the way. Alda has to reconcile the wounding she has suffered from her outer world parenting with the intrapsychic archetypal mother and father.

The first figure Alda put in the tray was a bridge however she returned it to the shelves. Later in the construction of the tray, after pairing off the positive and negative elements, she replaced the bridge over the lake. In doing so, Alda forms a means of connecting the opposing sides of the issues, creating the hopeful possibility that she will be able to reconcile the opposing forces in her psyche. As she concludes her story Alda tells us that the woman got the treasure box at the last minute. This is not a believable ending, as the devil appears to still rule the world and it is too early in her process for such a resolution. Clearly Alda wants to regain her own heart, her own spirit and the Self. This part of her story, along with the bridge added late in the making of the tray give hope that she may be able to do so through her sandplay work.

Alda Tray 2

Alda Tray 2a

Alda Tray 2b

Alda's Story

Tray 2

The Dark Cave

This is a magician (the tall figure wearing a hat in near right corner). There is poison in the bottle and poisonous apples and berries in the brown cup. This girl is looking for jewelry and she has watchdogs. The pistol man is trying to stop her. She lifts her hands when the man aims at her.

There are a lot of animals, sharks and other dangerous ones. The purple snake is a python and it can spit poison. The giant ant can give an electric shock. There is one little innocent ladybug.

The magician tells the man to take the woman to prison.

There is a small boy playing outside and he went into a cave and the crocodile came and ate him for lunch.

The man put the woman into the prison. The monkey somehow gets the key to unlock the treasure chest and the prison. Then they got away.

The dog bit the man in the foot. The man was so hungry that he ate a poisonous berry. He did not die but changed into a mouse.

The women managed to get one necklace from the chest but the magician continues to rule the world.

Discussion

Alda Tray 2

In Alda's second tray many figures and themes return from Tray 1, but with some significant changes. The dark woman from Tray 1 reappears. She returns to the far left corner, but is now accompanied by two sturdy guard dogs and the tiny monkey. In nature dogs are loyal and instinctive. Symbolically they carry these same qualities. There are two dogs protecting the woman. The number two symbolically indicates that something new is emerging from the unconscious. Drawing from the symbolism of numbers, we recall that psychic development progresses from an undivided whole or "one," which then divides into a duality. This duality or "two," is a pair that begins to be able to see or reflect itself. These are new psychic qualities that are just being born and will need to be nurtured (Kalff, 2003). As this is a pair of dogs it appears that there is new development emerging in her instinctual abilities. The monkey now sits on the edge of the tray on the left side of the woman. The inclination to the spirit is now *at hand* and is also protected by the pair of dogs.

The evil vampire from Tray 1 is now a magician who has a muscular body guard by his side. He still has a globe of the world in front of him and keeps a tarantula as a pet. The wild cats, the whale and the dinosaurs reappear from Tray 1, suggesting that these powerful symbolic energies continue to work in Alda's psyche. She continues her descent into the depths of the unconscious to confront her obstacles and to access the qualities she needs to overcome her issues. The final figure Alda places in the tray is the little ladybug from Tray 1. It sits in a large shell on the right side of the tray near the evil adversary. The danger and threat remains. Apart from the shelter of the shell, the ladybug is defenseless. While the dark woman now has the protection and guidance of the dogs, the ladybug remains exposed and on her own.

Alda completes her landscape with a number of green trees. Trees are rich symbols. Among other possibilities they symbolize the feminine principle, the nourishing, sheltering, protecting aspect of the Great Mother (Neumann, 1972). Trees also speak of growth and development. These are positive, nurturing qualities that begin to counterbalance the darker part of the feminine principle that appears in the devouring crocodile. While Alda continues to work with the feminine and masculine energies, the green trees bring a more protective and nurturing aspect of the feminine. At the same time however, the devouring side remains present.

In the middle of her narrative, Alda injects a horror story about a defenseless little boy who enters a cave. Inside the cave he is surrounded by terrifying animals, including a python, a giant ant and a crocodile. As we see in the tray, the crocodile devours the boy. Alda's exact words were, …(*he*) *ate him for lunch.* Just as soon as she says this she returns to the story of the woman and her adventures. In Tray 1 the crocodile was stalking the white mouse. In Tray 2 it devours a little boy. Alda introduces the positive, innocent animus of the little boy but he is in a very weak position and is devoured. The therapist was very concerned by this tray and contacted the school psychologist. Together they decided to watch over the girl and to follow closely what happens next.

Things are not as covert as they were in the first tray where objects were stolen by magic and hidden away. Here the conflict is more directly visible. Toxic berries and a bottle of poison are out in the open. It is likely that this refers to Dad's alcoholism and the resultant effects on the family. In Alda's story the man ate one of the berries and changed into a mouse. He became an animal and was no longer governed by human qualities. Poison is a prominent metaphor in Alda's sandplay, perhaps carrying the pain and loss of the damage her father's "poison" has done to her.

Alda tells us that the man puts the woman in prison. However the monkey is able to free her and open the treasure chest. Symbolically the inclination toward the spirit liberates her and adorns her with a necklace from the treasure chest. Even though the magician continues to rule the world, the feminine nature now has a connection to the spirit that can set her free.

The necklace is an interesting symbol in that it is circular and made of jewels. It carries the qualities of the crown, the mark of the earthly royal rulers, as well as the heavenly ruler, or the Self. In addition it is associated with fertility and sexuality (De Vries, 1984). Given Alda's history with allegations of sexual violation, the necklace becomes a complex symbol in her process. While it carries the potential for wholeness and re-ordering to the Self, its associations with sexuality carry a heavy shadow. In her story the woman is given the necklace immediately after being released from her imprisonment by the evil man. The proximity of being put in prison by the man and the sexual connotations of the necklace are seriously disconcerting. In addition to its positive qualities it may be that the necklace is also the burden Alda bears for being her father's prisoner.

Alda Tray 3

Alda Tray 3a

Alda Tray 3b

Alda' Story
Tray 3

The Power of Women

These two, a sister and a brother, were searching for their dog. The dogs went into a cave and barked and barked. The kids went into the cave. It opened and they went in.

Here is a globe which was ruled by a man in Australia who is now dead. There is a book and in it there is a spell. If you recite it you can have power over the world. The magician is trying to get to the globe to control the world.

The old woman was going to feed the ducks with some bread but she got lost and went into the cave.

The magician owned the cave but had not been there for a long time. The Australian kept the book in the cave and hid the key in the candlestick (far right corner). The magician had a daughter who was angry with him because he betrayed her a lot. Now he wanted to rule the world as a way to do something for her.

The bears are the guards of the magician and the tarantula, too. The frogs are poisonous and the Australian owns them.

The daughter of the Australian was going to visit him but her trip took such a long time that he was dead when she arrived. The Australian was also a little bit bad. The magician and the Australian had at first been good friends. The Australian was so silly that he had told the magician about the book and the globe and then the magician had sent the tarantula and the python to kill him.

The kids were in a treasure hunt and they found their dogs.

The egg was magic. If it opens all wishes come true. A princess had owned it but the magician stole it. Only a woman can make a wish. Elves come out of the egg.

The magician did not manage to control the world. The kids felt sorry for the seal which was whining and the girl managed to get the (magic) book and started to read and then a light beam appeared and she could rule the world and the egg opened. The boy ran at the egg but then it closed. It was only the girl who could make a wish. Then the magician suddenly became an ordinary man.

The Buddha has a camera in his eyes and takes photos of the Australian for the kids. The magician's owl is so smart. It has a power that sends a beam out on the book but now the girl knows the spell by heart and could continue to rule the world.

Alda Tray 3

Discussion

Alda appeared to struggle as she constructed Tray 3. She took many figures from the shelves only to return them soon after. The woman from Trays 1 and 2 was in this group. She changed things around a lot as she made the tray. She seemed a little insecure and looked at the therapist several times during her play. Her ambivalence and insecurity may indicate that the aspects of her ego structure that are impeding her continued growth and development are beginning to deconstruct as she moves into a new region of the psyche.

This is reflected in Alda's story which is wandering and dreamlike. A magician and an Australian somehow fuse into one another and become two sides of the same person as do their two daughters. The magician is evil, the Australian a little less. The daughter of the magician is angry with her father and there is a lot of secrecy associated with him. The daughter of the Australian takes a long journey to visit her father but he is dead when she arrives.

The story begins with a brother and sister, a paired balance of masculine and feminine energies. They embark on a journey to find their dog that has gone into a dark cave. Once in the cave the male and female counterparts each assume two roles, dividing into their light and dark qualities. It appears that with the male protagonists Alda manages to differentiate two sides of the masculine archetype experiencing it as ambivalent and betraying, and at the same time desirable but unattainable. The feminine archetype is characterized as a girl that is on the one hand, very angry at her father and at the same time ready to undertake a long journey to see him.

Tray 3 was made October 24th which is Women's Day in Iceland. There were many news items about women's rights as well as class discussions. This no doubt influenced Alda's choice of subject when she entitled her story *The Power of Women*. In her sandplay and storytelling, Alda's work centers on the power of the feminine. Notably only the girl can open the beautiful green egg in the near left corner. The story tells us that when the boy ran to the egg it closed, denying him access. The egg is a symbol of fertility and the germ of all creation. When the girl obtains control of the magic book she rules the world, the egg opens and she makes a wish. Then many transformations occur. The magician loses his supernatural ability and becomes an ordinary man. He no longer has the mysterious power over her that he once did. As the magician loses his influence, the brother of the girl becomes a positive animus figure. The little defenseless boy in the last tray that was devoured by the crocodile is changed. He becomes an ally, although he is still very young.

Another positive quality appears in the near right of the tray with the mother bear and cubs, a *mother-child unity*, a symbolic precursor to new psychic development (Kalff, 2003). Just as with the birth of a new child into the world, new psychic qualities symbolically make their initial appearance as mothers and children. In nature the bear is a fierce and protective mother. The hatching hen that sits just beside the large green egg in near left corner is another positive feminine figure. It is interesting that Alda placed the bear and her cubs very close to the magician, the evil masculine figure in the near right corner. Perhaps the newly emerging psychic qualities concern a mother bear-like fierceness that will allow

Alda to protect herself from the negative influences of males in her outer world and their intrapsychic counter parts. It is hopeful to see some development of inner strength in the feminine. At the same time many dangers continue in the darker side of the feminine. The devouring crocodile remains in a central position and the spider sits near the magician. As we saw in Tray 1, both carry dark feminine qualities.

The two butterflies in the near left corner underscore the transformation that takes place. In nature the butterfly begins life as a caterpillar and transforms into a magnificent flying creature. Symbolically they carry qualities of rebirth and resurrection. This renewal symbolism is reflected in the red starfish, which is also known for its regenerative abilities. The starfish sits at the feet of a statue of the god Krishna which indicates transformation of spirit. Alda also placed a large figure of the Buddha in the far left corner and put the tiny monkey from Trays 1 and 2 on top of his head. This Buddha's hands are raised above his head holding balls of rice, indicating nourishment and wealth. This growing presence of spirit is mirrored in the birds and feathers that appear in all corners with the exception of the near right where the magician stands. Symbolically it appears that in spite of the many remaining dangers Alda has the intrapsychic nourishment she needs to follow her inclination to the spirit, the Self.

Alda Tray 4

Alda Tray 4

Alda's Story

Tray 4

Mischievousness

The girl often went down to the sea because her father had been a fisherman but his ship had sunk. Nobody knew about the shark in the sea. These three kids are scamps and the spider is their pet. They are teasing the girl. The leader of the kids (one with blue cap) *pushed the girl into the water with a stick and her sister* (woman in red in far right corner) *comes on the black horse and saves her. The kids took the horse but the sisters found it again.*

The leopard understood the girl well because when he had been little he had been teased and put into the water. He teases the kids and frightens them. He is dangerous and not dangerous.

The girl always had some food with her and ate on her way to the sea. She does not have many friends, only her sister and the cat. She did have a best friend and that was her dad but he died when the ship sank.

(Makes a little hill and puts the hippopotamus on top of it).

The wild animals are not dangerous except for the rhinoceros (near left corner) *and the big hippopotamus. The girl was mostly in the lighthouse* (her home). *Her room was where the upper window is. The three kids lived where the lower window is. They were always breaking windows. They climbed to the top of the lighthouse and broke the light bulb.*

The girl's mother was a stewardess and the airplane had crash-landed and so she did not have parents anymore. Her sister took care of her.

The girl knew where the ship was but her mother and her sister would not believe her. But they found the ship.

(She raises the sailing ship in the far left corner).

Her father was under the ship and very wounded, but they managed to save him.

Discussion

Alda Tray 4

In this tray the main character is a little orphan girl whose mother and father have both died in tragic accidents. Neither parent is present in the tray. Alda's story tells us that the mother had been a stewardess and died in an airplane crash. Equally catastrophic, the father died when his fishing boat sunk. Alda continues to work with the feminine and the masculine, mother and father, here facing the loss of their inability to properly care for her. In her play Alda grapples with this terribly sad fact. Perhaps she begins a phase of grief, of surrendering her hopes that everything will be all right, and that Mom and Dad will change and be available to her in the ways she needs. Recognition and grief for her losses is a necessary step before she will be able to access the parental archetype in her own psyche.

Several elements return from Tray 3. There are three mother-child unities - the giraffes, the elephants and the hippopotamuses. A bird and a butterfly are placed on top of a green tree lending hope that spirit is present and that transformation is taking place. Directly across the water from the little girl there is a turtle emerging from the sea.

Symbolically turtles carry energies of wholeness. The shape of the turtle's shell combines the archetypal forms of the square and the circle. The underside of the turtle's carapace is square in shape and the top side is round. Archetypally the square and the circle combine the earth, the square, with the heavens, the circle, indicating wholeness (Kalff, 2003). In addition, turtles, like snails, carry their homes along with them, symbolically indicating the wholeness in the fundamental home of the Self. Perhaps the combined presence of the turtle and the butterfly accentuates the quality of this transition as a possible union of opposites in her inner world (Bradway & McCoard, 1997).

The dark woman in red reappears. In Tray 1 she set out to discover, "...*what is going on*" and in Tray 2 she was, "...*looking for jewelry and she has watchdogs*." In both cases she was threatened by a man. In this tray this dark female figure rides in on a dark horse to rescue the little girl. She is the little girl's sister and caretaker. While dangers do remain, this positive feminine figure brings nurturing qualities out of the shadows and into the light. Interestingly the sisters live on the top floor of a lighthouse, the structure that guides the ships in the darkness. It appears that in Tray 4 Alda accesses sufficient inner resources for self nurture and care. With this in place she may be able to find her way through the psychic and emotional darkness she experiences. Although new inner resources are emerging, the question remains whether or not she will be able to manifest them in her outer world, given the realities of her family setting.

The fact that the two sisters live high in a lighthouse may indicate that they are not quite grounded. Living at the top of a tower might also provide a better overview of the situation. The lighthouse where the sisters live is not completely safe as the three mischievous kids reside on the floor directly below them. Alda tells us that among other things they break windows and destroy the light bulb in the lighthouse.

The little girl has allies. She has two friends in her sister and her cat. There is a bright red ladybug in front of the cat. Generally considered a sign of good fortune, the ladybug is helpful to farmers, as it destroys the aphids that can harm the crops. We recall from previous discussions that its bright red color is associated with passion and fire. In folklore it is considered very lucky if a ladybug lands on you, however it must be allowed to fly away on its own (De Vries, 1984).

Alda has an additional resource in the leopard, which is a strong wild cat. The leopard is sympathetic to the little girl's situation and understands how it feels to be teased and bullied. Alda comments that he is both, ...*dangerous and not dangerous.* While very kind to the little girl, the leopard makes a point of frightening the scamps. In nature leopards are strong and swift. They prowl at night and see keenly in the dark. This attribute lends them the symbolic quality of vigilance (de Gubernatis, 1978). The helpful animus that emerged in the previous tray as the little girl's brother now assumes a more aggressive role in the leopard.

The figure Alda used for the brother in Tray 3 is now one of the teasing boys. In her story Alda tells us that one of the brothers pushed the little girl into the sea with a stick. Like the stick, the rhinoceros in the near left corner is an aggressive phallic symbol. As she taps the more protective inner strengths of the leopard Alda is able to begin to address the abuse that she has experienced. While sexual abuse remains unknown as a fact, the aggressive symbolism in her work might indicate a violation of sexual boundaries. In any case, we can confidently say that Alda's developing inner resources will give her the capacity to be vigilant and to address inappropriate intrusions to body, mind and spirit that she has experienced.

It is interesting that one of the menacing boys had a pet spider. Symbolically, the spider carries the positive qualities of industry for its ability to weave a beautiful, mandala-like web. It concerns creativity and finding coherence in life by the thread that connects the past, present and future. The negative qualities have to do with being trapped in the web and devoured. Much like the alligator the spider is associated with dangerous and devouring mothering (Neumann, 1972). In her story Alda tells us that the spider is the naughty boy's pet. Symbolically the negative mothering is kept by, or in service to the negative masculine influence. Perhaps this pairing of the boy and his spider reflects the unhealthy relationship between Alda's mother and father as the codependent partner and the alcoholic.

According to Alda the father had been the little girl's best friend and she knew where her father's ship had sunk. Alda shares a piece of insight and wisdom here about the love she has for her father and the sense of betrayal and loss that she now feels. Alda changed the story at the end by raising the sailing ship from underneath the sand in the far left corner and restoring the father to life. Perhaps Alda felt vulnerable, exposed or guilty having killed the father in the story, so made attempts to have everything appear all right toward the end.

In spite of her efforts to mask the more painful aspects of her work a centering begins to take place in Tray 4. The little girl in the central area of the tray is courageous. She has a lot of potential as well as a lot of troubles. She provides for herself by taking provisions when she goes to sea. As a final gesture, Alda thoughtfully placed the tiny pink flower at the feet of the little girl. This and the red starfish may be precursors of the Self.

Alda Tray 5

Alda Tray 5a

Alda Tray 5b

Alda's Story
Tray 5

The Magic Flower

This is the leader of the lions (far left corner) *and this is the leader of the frogs* (right near corner). *The girl and the boy were friends and after school they always went into the woods to fish in the lake. The boy went inside the red circle* (circle of red beans around the magician near center) *and the magician stopped time.*

The girl's parents, her favorite horse and her friends are there (man with glasses, girl with ponytail, boy with green cap and boy with blue cap and blue trousers). *The queen and her sister came into the land from China because the magician made them.*

If anyone drinks from the brown bottle and eats the green and the red berries (far left) they take all the power from the magician. The bad animals guard them (lion, frogs and big spider). The crocodile is chasing the girl. The owl on the magician's shoulder is watching. The ladybug is kind. All the animals can talk. Some of the bad animals, like the snake, the seal, the rhinoceros and the little spider were against the magician. The black leopard is helping the girl. The magician can change the weather.

The girl's flower gives her power. The magician is trying to negotiate with her and wants to get the flower. He promises to trade it for his power but he doesn't do it. When he gets the flower a big storm comes. Time starts all over again and everything gets better. Only the magician and the girl can move. Everything else is frozen.

Discussion

Alda Tray 5

Alda was particularly enthusiastic about her sandplay this day. The little girl returns from Tray 4 and stands in the center of the tray on a small bridge of sand that spans two lakes. Directly in front of her is an evil magician and behind her is an aggressive crocodile. Alda's protagonist now stands between the negative feminine force of the crocodile and the negative masculine energy of the evil magician. In this tray it appears that Alda directly addresses the psychological impact of the issues surrounding her inadequate and perhaps dangerous parents, particularly the father. This is emphasized by the central location of this activity and by her statement that, "*Only the magician and the girl can move. Everything else is frozen.*"

The magician is flanked by the queen of China on the left and by Mulan on the right. Symbolically the queen is a powerful ruler who wields great authority. Alda tells us that this queen has come from very far away. Mulan is the fictional character who dressed as a man to fight in the war. While the negative mother figure of the crocodile remains directly behind the little girl these two figures carry the positive feminine strength Alda needs to confront the issues with her father.

As her final gesture Alda pairs the woman in red with the Native American king, placing them behind the little girl and the crocodile. This couple is a balance of masculine and feminine energies with regal qualities. Standing beside the king, the woman in red assumes the appearance of a black Madonna. In Catholicism the dark-skinned black Madonna contrasts sharply with her tall white counterpart in the Virgin Mary. While it is likely that the origin of the black Madonna stems from the incorporation of local deities into the early church, she has come to represent the darker archetypal qualities of the feminine that are not otherwise expressed in Catholicism. The black Madonna symbolically carries the earth goddess as giver and taker of life. She is the feminine embodiment of the divine. She simultaneously carries qualities of female sexuality and of what is divine, which are not present in the holy Virgin (Preston, 2010).

The frequency of Alda's use of the dark woman throughout her process attests to the significance of the symbolism the figure carries for her. In this tray she pairs this earth goddess energy with the Native American king who is also a man of the earth. The strengths carried by the dark feminine have matured and have joined with an equally grounded, safe masculine figure. Synchronous with confronting the evil father, Alda accesses archetypal parental energy, forming an inner world model of healthy safe parents that she can draw upon to help guide and direct her through her life.

Like the Madonna, the little girl's protector leopard is also black. In Tray 4 the leopard helped the girl by sympathizing and understanding her pain. Perhaps the capacity to understand her own pain and losses is emerging from the darkness of the shadows to assist her in her journey.

In Alda's Tray 5 the girl has a magical flower that gives her power. The magician wants this flower and steals it from her through trickery and lies. As soon as he has the flower in his possession a terrible storm breaks out. If Alda was sexually violated this tiny flower appears to carry the innocence and virginity that were stolen from her. While the facts of this part of her history remain unknown it is clear that in her work in the sand tray she faces the reality of the harm done to her by a malevolent masculine force. Having done so, Alda moves abruptly to obscure the harsh reality by adding a positive ending to the story, *"Time starts all over again and everything gets better."*

There is a magic circle of bright red beans around the magician. Perhaps this is Alda's attempt to control this unsafe male energy by marking him off as separate and further identifying him as dangerous. Perhaps they are drops of blood that attest to her wounding. Throughout the landscape there are many treacherous animals. Even with her new psychic strengths there is still a great deal of danger. Irrespective of her own growth and development the fact remains that Alda's family life is painful and unstable. As a child she has no option but to return to this home.

Alda Tray 6

Alda Tray 6

Alda's Story
Tray 6

The Yellow Statue

There were bad men and good men and bad animals and good animals. Some of the good animals like a pig, a dog, a hen and a horse went over to the bad world.

The bad men catch fish in the lake (an invisible streak in the sand). *The bad animals did not believe in the Statue of liberty but believed in the yellow statue. The gods in the corners* (left corners) *did something for the animals. It was possible to go into the big owl* (right of yellow statue) *and see what was happening in the world of the good animals. You had to recite a spell to let the gods and the owl do their work.*

In the good world there were small elves. A man was feeding his animals. The sheep was giving birth to two lambs. The good animals had been calm but when they saw the bad animals they became excited and they were also very hungry. The man had gone camping to search for a treasure and had left four bowls of food for the animals, but they had finished that long time ago.

The man's wife had left the treasure on a mountain. A soldier had taken the woman when she was digging and put her in a prison and took the treasure for himself. The man went searching for the treasure and got the idea to go into the world where the yellow statue rules. He found the treasure and fought with the soldiers and won. Then he went searching for his wife and managed to get her out of the prison and they went home and took care of the animals and everything became good.

Discussion

Alda Tray 6

On this day Alda arrived for her sandplay session looking tired and unhappy. The teacher had previously let me know that there were more difficulties at home concerning Alda's older sibling's drug addiction. The instability in her home life shows in her work in Tray 6. The level of organization and symbolic coherence of Tray 5 is absent and the tray becomes somewhat chaotic and crowded. Alda's story was equally meandering and confused. A regression has taken place. The clarity and strengths that Alda was developing have been overshadowed by outer world pain and disorder.

While she attempts to fashion a thematic conflict in her story it soon becomes ambiguous and the boundaries that divide the good animals from the bad are blurred. Looking at the tray there is a profusion of wild and domestic animals mixed together, positioned with no discernable direction or purpose. Alda tells us in her story that some of the animals from the good side go over to the bad side.

The animals are hungry and the man who cares for them left them without adequate food. In addition his wife is absent. The animals have essentially been ignored, if not abandoned. Their needs are not being met. However there are two images of positive mothering in the sheep that has just given birth to two lambs and the bear with her cubs. The abundance of animals might indicate a sudden activation of Alda's instincts and emotions resulting from the turbulence at home. As we have seen before, a child that is not taken proper care of and whose natural emotional needs have not been met may turn inwardly to seek support from what is at his or her disposal intrapsychically. Even in the midst of the turmoil and unclarity Alda does have access to these two archetypal mothers to help sustain her. This is a very positive development.

An additional resource is available in the two divinities. Alda tells us that they are able to help the animals if the proper spell is used. The two birds in the far right of the tray reinforce this connection to spirit. Throughout her work we have seen that Alda has an inherent relationship with spiritual energies greater than herself. In Tray 1 she used the feathers and the tiny monkey. In Tray 2 the monkey returned as a helper to the dark woman. In Tray 3 she placed a starfish at the feet of Krishna, and in Tray 4 the spirit was present in the bird and the butterfly. Given her few outer world resources it is encouraging that Alda is able to sustain a relationship to the divine.

Finally, in her accustomed attempt to end on a happy note, Alda tells us that the husband liberated his wife and together they went home with the treasure and took care of their animals. Sadly this happy ending does not feel plausible.

Alda Tray 7

Alda Tray 7a – *View from left side of the tray*

Alda Tray 7b – Detail

Alda's Story
Tray 7

The Bear and the Woman Journalist

There was once a powerful man who was watching the earth. A woman was spying on him and tried to find some information for the newspaper because she was a journalist. She wrote about the powerful man and his spiders. The shell had powers and was the home of the spiders. The servant of the powerful man captured the journalist for spying. He asked his master what he should do with the woman. The master said, "Put her with the fox and the black leopard."

A fortuneteller owned the treasure chest and said that the powerful man would become evil and that he would have a lot of animals but that he would not be kind to them. When the animals were crying or naughty the powerful man took revenge and changed them into statues. He changed the seals, the dinosaur, the goat, the gorilla, the hippopotamus and the turtles.

The bear and the journalist managed to run away from the powerful man because the prison wardens were afraid of the bear. The bear became the pet of the journalist woman. The man had made a deal with the bear that if it ever managed to get free he would take away a lot of power from the man. After that the statues became living animals again. They were nicer than before and all lived safe and sound.

Discussion
Alda Tray 7

On this day Alda was focused and appeared more secure. Her story concerns an unkind man who had influence over the people and animals. The dark woman appears here as a journalist who is gathering information about him to report in the newspaper. Now there is a part of Alda's feminine nature that seeks to know the truth about her circumstances. She is ready and willing to look directly at her suffering and the hurt caused by her family life. However the woman is captured by the muscular servant of the all powerful ruler and is held in a menacing scene on the left side of the tray. As much as she would like to reveal the truth Alda recognizes that she is captive and helpless to do anything about it. This sense of powerlessness is repeated when Alda tells us that when the many animals the magician owns do not obey he punishes them and changes them into statues. They have no choice in the matter. They dare not question his judgment as he will literally take their lives away.

The woman and her captor face the evil man directly across the tray in the center right. He stands between two stone pillars on top of which are his pet spiders. Again the spider is the pet of a negative and dangerous masculine force as it was in Tray 4. In Tray 7 Alda tells us that the spiders live in the large shell. Directly in front of the shell she partially buries a small box that she filled with little treasures: a leaf and a colored stone. These precious things are in the clutches of the spiders that live there. Alda repeats the theme from Tray 4 that she cannot rely on the protection of a mother figure that takes instructions from a dangerous man. She needs a mother who is a powerful feminine force that will protect her offspring like the fierce mother bear. Toward the end of her story Alda symbolically joins the woman with the bear forming an alliance of archetypal mothering. Underscoring this inner source of positive mothering energy are two mother-child pairs. There is a turtle and a baby hatching from an egg in the near center and a mother giraffe with her little one close to the magician and his terrible pets along the far right of the tray. The proximity of the giraffes to the evil man seems to emphasize that the only good parenting Alda will have comes not from her outer world parents but from an inner source in the unconscious.

As she constructed the tray Alda originally placed the scorpion, the octopus and the rhinoceros in the central lake. She later moved these dangerous animals to a smaller lake in the far right corner and outlined the larger lake with a beautiful pattern of red beans and stones. Perhaps she is trying to clear the way, to make a pathway or direction for the dark woman to follow. Perhaps she is marking the lake as a sacred space that is available to the woman. Even so at the very end of the play when she looked up and said, "That's it" she hastily added a crocodile and a dinosaur as if to emphasize the fact that she remains burdened with a negative mother image and that it is an old story.

Alda Tray 8

Alda Tray 8a

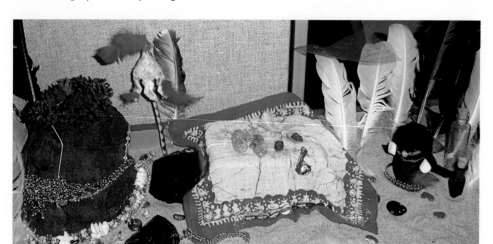

Alda Tray 8b

Alda's Story
Tray 8

The Wishes

There was a man who was not really a leader but he was chief in the country. There were a lot of foreign people who came to this country. This was not really a land but an island. The foreigners came to look around.

If you found a magical egg you could get five wishes fulfilled. The person who owned the egg was a man who had an accident. There was also a leaf owned by a spider man. It was not really magical. It was evil. You could stop the world with this leaf. There was a mask in a locked box hidden under the flower (Alda was not able to find a mask so said there was "a make-believe mask" in the box). *When you put on the mask you became really strong and also a little bit funny.*

There was a little girl who was trying to get the leaf, the egg and the mask but she did not manage. The man who owned the egg was also the owner of the mask and he was a good friend of the chief. When they had been younger they had been business partners but then he had an accident. The chief got everything but when he took the egg, the face of the wounded man (his friend) appeared and said that there were other people in the world and he should not make wishes just for himself. The chief thought about that. He had made four wishes: 1. That he would be rich; 2. That everybody would listen to him; 3. That he could do everything he wanted; and 4. That he would have a good wife. Then the spirit came and the chief took back all the wishes except the one about the good wife. After that the country became better and water and animals arrived.

After she finished telling her story she added:

Elves are living in the big stone. There is poison in the bottles – not really poison but just for animals and foreigners. The blue stone in front of the flower can tell about the weather. You look into it and a picture of the weather appears. The foreigners look at the gloves and the shoes (on platform in far center).

Discussion

Alda Tray 8

Although Alda's story tends to wander and be confusing, she does some very important work in Tray 8. In this tray Alda marks all four corners with tall feathers. As we have discussed elsewhere the feathers carry the spirit. They are from birds that fly through the air to higher places. When similar vertical or sacred objects are placed in all four corners of the tray we know that the client's psyche makes a special point of demarcating what is held in the tray as of great significance. The attention to the four corners acts much as would putting a frame around what is contained in the tray. In some cases the four corners function to provide additional containment for the material that arises in the tray. Also the corners can define a sacred space. Alda's use of the tall feathers adds the dimension of verticality, indicating a connection of what is below to what is above. This is the axis between the underworld and the heavens that archetypally carries the spiritual dimension of life (Eliade, 1974). Because the number four and the four-cornered square represent the archetype of the earth and material reality, marking all four corners with feathers grounds the psychic qualities they frame in material reality.

In the far left corner Alda carefully and lovingly adorns a large stone with jewels and pine cones further anchoring her work in that which is solid and treasured, or the Self. She places three beautiful pieces of obsidian around this sacred sanctuary.

In the far center of the tray Alda creates an alter-bed-like structure, covering it with a red and white handkerchief that looks as if it is splattered with blood. On top of the red and white covering she carefully places the vestiges of a little girl - a tiny pair of mittens, a tiny pair of red shoes, a small red brooch and a tiny white down feather. Perhaps this is a sacrificial altar upon which Alda has lost the precious qualities of her childhood: her capacity to handle things - the mittens; a solid footing - the empty shoes; her beauty -the colorful jeweled broach; and her innocence -the down feather.

Alda buries a large heart-shaped box directly at the base of the altar. Perhaps this is a representation of the place of sexual violation and what necessitated her loving heart to go underground, to be submerged and remain unseen. It is interesting that the bed-like structure is placed between the sacred rock to the left and the selfish vampire chief to the right. With the support of what is sacred Alda is able to look at the abusive perpetrator, her sacrifice and the losses she has sustained.

Alda describes the man as the chief, but emphasizes that he is not really a leader. He is responsible for the world but is incompetent at caring for and guiding his people. He has two bottles of poison beside him as if to underscore the danger of his presence. The two additional male figures Alda introduces in her story further describe the masculine deficiencies. One man is a spider who can stop the world and the other is wounded. This one has a magic egg and a mask that makes him act strong and funny. All of these male figures appear to describe aspects of her father's alcoholism: he has bottles of poison; he sometimes acts strong and funny; he is ineffectual as a father; and is as poisonous and engulfing as a spider.

On the left side of the tray Alda creates a small altar out of shells and jewels. She puts the black spider on the altar and marks the space with a small chain. Outside the altar space directly to the right she buries a small heart-shaped box and places a flower on top. Directly in front of the altar is the blue stone that reveals the weather report. With stones and red beans Alda shapes a pathway from the chief in the far right corner to the small altar. With the solidity and strength of the Self configuration in the large decorated stone in the far left corner Alda is able to confront her abuse and her losses. She then creates a link with a colorful pathway between her abuser and the sacred altar space. Confronting her wounding, Alda sacrifices her innocence and acknowledges her painful experience as a part of her passage. Psychologically the engulfing spider no longer holds her in his grasp, but is placed in the hands of the power of the divine Self. To emphasize this new freedom and her developing capacity for oversight Alda places the Statue of Liberty in the near left corner and a lighthouse in the near right.

With a final elegant gesture Alda places the blue stone directly in front of the little altar space clarifying that this is where you can go to see the weather, what is in the atmosphere and how things are in truth. While Alda's father remains a threat in her outer life she now has the psychic structures in place to clearly distinguish his ill deeds from the truth of who she is. We can only hope that she is somehow able to sustain and nurture this budding awareness sufficiently to allow it to fully develop and strengthen, and that the dysfunction of her family does not inflict further damage that interferes with her growth.

Alda Tray 9

Alda Tray 9a

Alda Tray 9b

Alda Tray 9c

Alda Tray 9d

Alda' Story
Tray 9

Rich or Poor

This is one world and then there is a second world.

On one side is a rich woman who has a lot of food and fancy things and on the other side there is a couple and they are poor and do not have much to eat.

The rich woman wants a full plate of food and then she is going to have dessert. The couple was also having some food but the only thing they had was a shell with some fish in it. They had to eat that same thing over and over. The woman went down to the shore to fetch more food. Then she came across a box that contained a magic stone, gold and six wishes. She went to the man and told him about this. He said it was a gift from God.

Some weeks passed and there was a report about the magic wishing stone in the newspaper. The rich woman was selfish so she took her dogs to search for it. She found the box with the stone. After she had used five wishes a spirit came out of the box and told her that there were people other than her in the world. The spirit said that there were many people that did not have much to eat. Then the spirit left and the woman wished that she could take back her five wishes. She wished that the world would be better and that people would have more to eat and that they could live in better houses.

When the couple returned home their bowl was filled with meat. A helicopter was waiting for them and they went to visit their family. They lived well as it should be and had enough to eat. There were dangerous animals where the couple was living and they were in danger. The rich woman was not really happy.

Discussion
Alda Tray 9

In her last tray Alda confronted the painful abuse she has experienced, acknowledged it as a reality and surrendered her pain and loss to the divine. Here in Tray 9 she begins the process of integrating her newly developing understanding of her experiences into a more mature awareness of who she is. She divides her tray into two worlds contrasting an affluent land with an impoverished and unsafe one. In her story Alda characterizes the imbalance between the two worlds, telling us that one is prosperous but self-centered, and the other is harsh and dangerous.

After a visit by a wise spirit, the wealthy woman becomes aware of people other than herself. Although she uses her final magic wish to create a better world where people have better houses and plenty to eat, many dangers remain and the poor couple is left in jeopardy. Alda said that the moral of this story is not to be selfish and that being rich is not equal to being happy.

Alda joins her two worlds with a bridge to establish a connection between these very different psychic qualities. While Alda attempts to balance or integrate her new resources into the deprived parts of the personality many threats remain. Perhaps she has suffered too much wounding for her to bring about this level of integration at this stage of her life. In spite of these continued challenges we see evidence of new psychic qualities emerging in the many pairings in the tray. There are two dolphins, two seahorses, two pairs of dogs and a pair of turtles with a baby hatching out of an egg. In number symbolism we recall that a pair of objects carries newly emerging psychic qualities. We can think of it as two beings born from the undivided wholeness of number one. These qualities will develop into three, which indicates that the new energies are on the move (Eastwood, 2002). They are dynamic and growing.

The dolphins carry playful, intelligent energy. In addition, the dolphins are known to act as midwives when the whales deliver their calves (Waldau, 2006). Symbolically they help facilitate new developments.

The symbolism of the seahorse is particularly significant in Alda's work. As we have discussed previously, in nature the male seahorse carries the eggs while the embryos develop (Indiviglio, 2001). They are good, caring, protective fathers. Perhaps this pair of seahorses indicates that Alda is intrapsychically tapping the archetype of the father. Having access to this good fathering energy in her inner world will allow her to develop the qualities that a girl with a healthy outer world relationship with her father might possess. These qualities would include a balance between discipline and love that supports and guides her continued development into womanhood. This potential for wholeness is reiterated in the five pointed starfish, which represents the *anthropos*, as seen in Da Vinci's well-known drawing of *Vitruvian* Man, or whole person: two arms, two legs and the head. As this symbol appears so frequently, let's explore it more in depth.

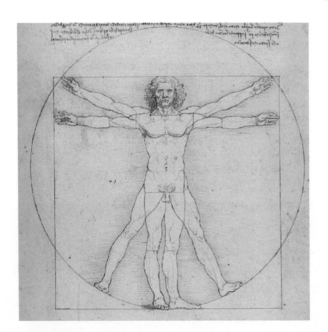

Leonardo da Vinci's – *Vitruvian Man*

For a little more background on this figure, Marcus Vitruvius was a Roman architect in the first century bce who wrote *De Architectura,* a well-known piece on structure in architecture. Describing the appropriate structural balance for a temple he said:

> *Similarly, in the members of a temple there ought to be the greatest harmony in the symmetrical relations of the different parts to the general magnitude of the whole. Then again, in the human body the central point is naturally the navel. For if a man can be placed flat on his back, with his hands and feet extended, and a pair of compasses centered at his navel, the fingers and toes of his two hands and feet will touch the circumference of a circle described therefrom. And just as the human body yields a circular outline, so too a square figure may be found from it. For if we measure the distance from the soles of the feet to the top of the head, and then apply that measure to the outstretched arms, the breadth will be found to be the same as the height, as in the case of plane surfaces which are completely square* (Vitruvius, 2008, p. 3).

Leonardo da Vinci had access to Vitruvius's notebooks and drafted the diagram that is so well known today. The figure is of great symbolic significance as it combines the five-pointed figure of the whole person along with the combination of the circle and the square.

Although Alda has awakened many highly positive psychic possibilities through her sand-play it remains to be seen how much she will be able to fully realize in her current stressful family environment. The equivocation in her story's ending appears to indicate that the hoped for outcome of her earnest efforts is uncertain. Alda tells us that the rich woman was not happy and the poor couple lived well with enough to eat, yet had to contend with dangerous animals. If not realizable in her childhood, we can hope that she will be able to cultivate these powerful potentials in her adulthood.

Alda Tray 10

Alda Tray 10a

Alda Tray 10b

Alda Tray 10c

Alda Tray 10d

Alda's Story
Tray 10

Sisters in Danger

Once there were two sisters. They went searching for their mother and father because they had not seen them for a long time. They went to a foreign country. The girl was trying to get some food when a cheetah arrived and jumped on her. The black leopard frightened off the cheetah. The cheetah ran away and her sister managed to save her.

A mean man hid their father and mother and turned them into big snakes. There was a bear that was just a little bit good. He jumped on the man. At that moment the man fired a gun at the big sister but missed her.

The bird was very nice and helped the big sister rescue the little sister. They decided never to come back to this country. The best thing was that they found their mother and father, but they had become snakes because the spider had changed them. The mother and father became human again and took the girls to Canary.

Discussion

Alda Tray 10

During this session Alda constructs her tray slowly, having just recovered from a bad cold and the flu. She creates a large jungle filled with serpents and wild cats. Her final gesture was to place a spider in the feather house located in the far left corner of the tray. She tells a story of two sisters whose parents are missing and have been turned into serpents. The two sisters join forces to recover them and must undergo many dangerous trials. In the language of the symbols it is clear that Alda is aware that the parenting she needs has been absent, and is in fact dangerous. In this tray we see that the good fathering energies tapped in the pair of sea horses in Tray 9 evolves into the more conscious quest to recover her archetypal parents here in Tray 10. In spite of the perils, the girls are assisted by powerful animal energies that shield them from danger. The leopard chases the cheetah away and the bear attacks the man who threatens them with a gun. Because wild animals behave instinctually in nature they also carry this energy as symbols. In this tray Alda activates the assistance of her instincts to protect her.

Once again Alda's Tray 10 includes a conflicting admixture of hazards and positive elements. As we have discussed, given its mandala-like web, the spider can carry the positive energies of the weaver of the thread of life. On the other hand it can be negative and devouring feminine energy. Alda's story tells us that this is an evil spider. Here it is perilously close to the precious little pink flower in the feather house in the far left corner. At the same time the central presence of the starfish, the three turtles and the abundant green vegetation is a positive clustering of healing and transformative energy.

After encountering many dangers, the sisters find their parents who have been changed into snakes by the evil spider. At the end of the story the parents become human again and take the girls to Canary, a popular Icelandic resort location. This happy ending with the family going on a holiday trip is fanciful, and contradicts the dangerous content of the tray and the story. Although the wild animals appear at home and are comfortable in their natural environment and some of them are helpful, it is interesting to note that Alda left the cheetah at the throat of the little girl at the foot of the mountain in the far right corner. Alda titled her sandplay *Sisters in Danger* and it appears that they remain in danger in spite of the many helpers and assets she has developed.

Alda Tray 11

Alda Tray 11a

Alda Tray 11b

Alda's Story

Tray 11

The Niece

There was a family who invited Indians, Vikings, elves and princes to a feast. It was very merry. This is the house and the garage (far left corner) and there is food and fire in the garden. The uncle sits in the chair in front of the fire and tells stories. The woman (in red and lying in center) is the sister of this man. She is not really dangerous but she is under a spell. Her mother is the woman with the black hair (far left) and her father is a Viking. Her footprints appeared behind the house and the bears asked for a security guard and for other animals to help. The woman had taken a key which could open a storage room where a jewel was kept that could rule the world. The security guard lost his power when the jewel disappeared.

They looked everywhere for the jewel and found it at last and the bear family got it again. It gave off a sound when the woman left the house. The woman went to prison but she kept a little piece of the jewel and had it on an earring. She continued to rule the world a little bit. When she got out of the prison everybody became friends again.

Some years later the family of elves gave a party and invited the bears, Indians and Vikings. A fire got out of control but they managed to put it out.

Discussion

Alda Tray 11

A merry party takes place in this tray however a tragic story unfolds at its center. Alda tells us that the niece is under a spell and she has stolen a jewel that gives her power over the world. When she is found out she is locked away in prison. However she manages to keep a little piece of the jewel and "...*continued to rule the world a little bit.*" She is imprisoned for her daring and manages to keep a tiny bit of the jewel. Following her release everyone reconciles but the situation is flammable. How could it be otherwise when the young feminine energy must resort to thievery to obtain the jewel that gives her power over her life? She is punished for claiming the self autonomy to which she is naturally entitled. And in the end the niece manages to retain only a vestige of her power.

As she approaches the end of her sandplay work Alda repeats the theme of growth and loss that we have witnessed in many prior trays. Here in Tray 11 in the guise of a happy party the theme assumes the sad tone of a loss of hope. Alda becomes aware that in spite of all of her earnest efforts, she is only able to hold onto a crumb of her Self. Her life simply does not provide the safety and support she needs to explore and cultivate the development of her true personality. While she consciously continues to try to make things positive and acceptable, her unconscious reveals the hopelessness of her fate. The anxiety underlying this awareness is reflected in the crowded, agitated quality of the construction of the tray, where the niece does not stand on her own two feet, but lies prone in the tray. While Vikings, elves and princes are guests at the party, the blood sucking Dracula lies in bed in a prominent central location. In addition the cheetah, which was at the throat of the little girl in Tray 10, now assumes a central position in the scene. The two heart-shaped boxes, which in former trays were filled with treasures and buried, are here exposed and empty. No longer does she have hope of treasures to discover.

Alda is aware that she has one more sandplay session. Although she has confronted some formidable issues and has accessed many psychic strengths during her process, we do not see the closure and resolution that we would hope to see at this stage of the work. Alda appears to have arrived at a level of understanding that her home environment cannot support her development and the best she can do is to hold onto that tiny bit of jewel and to survive.

Alda Tray 12

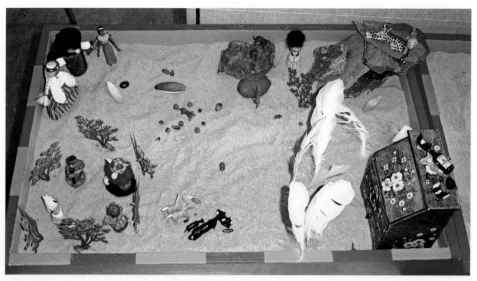

Alda Tray 12a

Alda Tray 12b

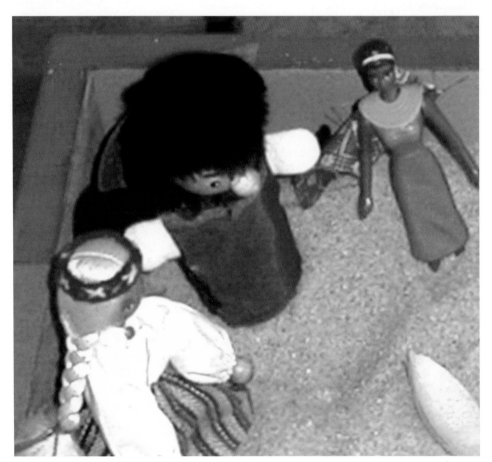

Alda Tray 12c

Alda's Story

Tray 12

The Magic Book

They were having a meeting about changing the world (Indians, dwarfs and Vikings). *The woman* (black hair, far right) *had a birthday. She was the queen of the lions and the leopards. She got a lion cub for her birthday. She did not want that. She wanted a magic book that was in the cave. With it she could rule the world. Nobody knew about the magic book except her husband and the maids, who once had been rich girls. The key to the chest was in the lion cave but nobody knew that. The man who owned it disappeared and changed into a stone which looked like a man. The girls had had many horses but the king had them now because he had taken them from the girls.*

One day the queen was tidying up in the lion cave and found the key. She was glad but did not know which lock the key would open. She went to the jewel cave and tried the key but it did not work. She tried again and heard music. The stone man was singing. The queen opened the lock and managed to get the book and the crown. This was the next to the last day the crown would work. She wished she could rule the world and would get her children (the two girls) *back. She wished her husband* (the king) *would not decide what she should do.*

The Indians, the elves and the Vikings (near left) *were talking about how they could help the queen get rid of the king. They teased the king by putting a fly in his soup. At last the king gave up and went to Egypt to rule there. Soon he left and went to Iceland and there he ruled some time but learned how to give orders and not be too pushy.*

He went back to his own country. At first nobody would talk to him but then they saw that they could trust him. He became a king again and married the queen again. She had become much more interesting and funny. The girls became freer and got their horses back.

Discussion

Alda Tray 12

As Alda brings her sandplay work to a close she engages in a story that sums up her family circumstances. A father, the bad king, has taken the horses away from the two daughters.

The horses are their vehicles and their personal power. His wife, although a strong woman who lives with the wild cats, is greatly under his influence and does what he says. Wishfully Alda engages in a story to remove the father from the family. And in her characteristic way of attempting to make everything all right she arrives at the unbelievable conclusion that the father returns as a kind and trustworthy man.

However the elements of her tray belie this happy ending. As her final gesture Alda places the reclining pig holding a liquor bottle on the blue dresser between an old man and woman, and sprinkles the red beans and berries in the center. In former trays these berries have been poisonous. The poison berries and the indolent pig with the liquor undeniably refer directly to the toxic effects of the father's alcoholism, which is protected by both parents.

Alda has done a tremendous and courageous work in her 12 trays. She has accessed many resources and has done her best to free them and integrate them with the aim of leading a healthy psychological life. But Alda does not control her life situation and dangers are still lurking. We can only hope that the strengths she has accessed in her sandplay will serve her healing and development, once she is able to leave the painful influences of her family.

The Sandplay Work of Filip:
Boy 3rd Grade – Age 8

Filip's Sandplay Work – Overview

Filip was a sweet and delicate boy. He was quiet and often in his own world. The teacher and his parents reported having concerns about his "peculiar ideas and behavior." The teacher said that Filip did not hear the instructions she gave to the whole class but needed them told to him personally. Furthermore to understand the directions, he needed to be looked directly in the eyes. She emphasized that Filip's tendency to daydream was so extreme that he could not sit by the window or he would, "…instantly go outside in his mind." He would often lapse into his own fantasy world and it would be difficult to drag him back to reality. He played a lot fantasy games, especially with one classmate, often with his fingers under the table or outside during recess. He was very easily disturbed by his environment and commonly overreacted to sound, smell or sight. Filip was also terribly absentminded during class performances and sometimes regressed to the behavior of a much younger child. To this day he is quite timid. Filip had good support from his parents and grandparents and was apparently spoken to and read to regularly. His vocabulary was rich.

The teacher reported that Filip held low opinions of himself, could be hard on himself and that was typically self-reproaching. When criticized it was not uncommon for him to break down, cry and become sure that he was at fault. Filip's teacher said that even his classmates realized how profoundly kind Filip was and often tried to convince him that he was good enough. He once became inconsolable when he accidentally stepped on a piece of wood that caused a blow to the cheek of a classmate, causing it to bleed. The little girl that had been hit went to Filip and tried her best to comfort him, but to no avail.

On the WISC he scored low average, Full Scale IQ (71/80). He made good progress in Verbal Comprehension (82/102) with an improvement of 20 points. According to his parents Filip showed more signs of anxiety, depression, self-effacement, malaise and lack of focus than peers at the beginning of the school year. In fact symptoms were up to a clinical limit on the Achenbach Scale. By the end of the school year these symptoms had diminished, as well as had his strange thoughts and behavior. The parents also stated that the anxiety had reduced greatly. In contrast to the parents' significant pre-test assessment, the teacher's assessment of Filip on the Achenbach Scale was considerably under clinical limits at the beginning of the year. The teacher's posttest assessment agreed with the parents' that anxiety and depression had diminished at the end of the school year.

According to the parents Filip had symptoms of ADD up to clinical limit in the beginning of the school. This lowered considerably by the end of the school year. The teacher reported some symptoms of ADD at the beginning of the year but by the end of the year they had diminished almost 50%. Symptoms of hyperactivity were reported by the parents but they had lowered dramatically at the end of the year. No symptoms of hyperactivity were reported by the teacher. Filip's self assessment was above average. Filip made progress in reading and was above average in his class at the end of the school year. His progress in mathematics was rather poor and he made little progress.

Filip was extremely interested in doing sandplay and was both focused and meticulous in his work. Filip talked a lot about what he was doing while playing in the sand. He seemed pleased with his work and often asked the therapist whether or not she found it "awesome." Filip's trays have a lot of grace and a personal tone. Once he placed the figures he did not move them about much, but sometimes adjusted things a little bit to be certain they were in the exact place he wanted them. He did not work much with the sand. He never used much water and when he did it was mainly for making quicksand. Similar objects can be seen repeatedly in his trays: colored stones (treasure) in all his trays, men, soldiers and trees in ten trays. He used statues, houses, vases and a chest in eight trays. The humans are masculine in ten trays. Females appear only twice. In one tray an extraterrestrial of an unknown gender appears.

The themes are many and appear repeatedly. Opposition, struggle and treasure appear in 11 trays. A rescuer appears eight times, danger seven times, a journey six times and magic five times. Filip told stories with ease and his imagination was rich. His stories are filled with treasure hunting, wars and battles. Even with all of this activity and fighting he maintained a kind voice that reflected his sensitivity. The titles of his stories carried an adventurous tone. For example: *The Beautiful Jungle and The Dangerous Statue; The Secret of the Pirate Funfair; and The Dragon Warrior and Tai Long.* Filip's stories were picturesque and sometimes influenced by films he had seen. All his stories ended on a positive note. Filip generally used the full forty minutes he had for his play and storytelling.

Filip Tray 1

Filip Tray 1a

Filip Tray 1b

Filip's Tray 1 – Divisions

Filip's Story
Tray 1

The Treasure in the Jungle

Once upon a time in Africa there were many dangers. People needed cowboys to protect the territory. There were also Indians.

It was said that there was a huge treasure in the forest and that the soldiers owned the treasure.

One day a man who was a detective came. He sneaked past the Indians and the dinosaurs. Then he told the soldiers that cowboys would attack them if they did not give him a little bit of the treasure. The cowboys had owned the treasure before the soldiers, because they busted into the territory and took it. The soldiers gave the detective a little bit of the treasure and he left and gave some to the people.

Notes During Construction:

Filip first placed the houses, later pouring water in the basin, and said, *For the gods.*

When he positioned the turtles, he commented, (they) *can be handy.*
Filip identified the man with the brief case as a detective.
Cowboys and Indians are good, and the soldiers are bad, he said.

Discussion

Filip Tray 1

Filip divided his first tray into four distinct areas, with no connections between them. On the diagonals we see the village or ordinary life in the far right corner, counterbalanced by a rich but chaotic wealth of treasures in the near left. Crossing this is a second diagonal that has dangerous, almost chaotic energies at both ends. The near right corner feels particularly threatening, with the water areas unclearly defined, the boat out of water, deadly "quicksand" and the small ponds crowded with huge sea animals. Filip has an abundance of inner treasures, however the lifeless village on the opposite end of the diagonal indicates that these resources do not connect to ordinary life. As a first tray it appears that the issues Filip will address in his sandplay process involve the integration of these psychic assets into ordinary life. In order to accomplish this he will need to address the ominous dark energies carried by the ends of the opposite diagonal.

Filip's clever story and carefully constructed sandplay demonstrate his verbal and spatial strengths. However it appears that there are significant gaps that prevent the use of his gifts in a meaningful and productive way in his school work. He must find ways to bridge these isolated areas of functioning and develop the means to integrate them into a working whole.

The story tells us that it is the detective who was able to cross into the area of the stolen treasure and to return some of it to its rightful owners. The detective crosses the limits, the boundaries dividing the separate sections, and serves as an initial bridge between two different areas. A detective is a person that explores and inquires to solve a mystery. This detective is a strong and hopeful indication of an inner resource Filip can draw upon to reveal the answers to his dilemma. It is interesting that the detective carries a blue case, as blue is frequently associated with the divine. In Hinduism, the gods related to Vishnu are depicted with blue-colored skin (Reyna, 1993). In Catholicism, blue is associated with the Virgin Mary (Glazier & Hellwing, 2004), and in Judaism blue is connected with the glory of god and is ritually used in sacred garments (Goodenough, 1992).

In the area just beyond the center Filip places a tower, a church and a dinosaur. Perhaps this is a summary statement of the work he faces ahead in his sandplay process. Being phallic-shaped, it may be that the tower has to do with something in the masculine, some-thing up high –perhaps something neurological. The dinosaur tells us that this issue is very old. The church mirrors the spiritual inclination carried by the blue valise. Filip's journey may address some difficulties he has with his thought processes. They may have their roots in early neurological developmental problems. In order to overcome these obstacles he will need to draw upon the spiritual, the inner truth, or Self, in Jungian psy-chology. Filip further demonstrates his sensitivity to the spiritual dimension when he adds water to the candle holder basin, and asks the therapist if she knows what that means. He answers that, *"…it is for the gods."* There is also a pair of turtles standing by the detective. When Filip placed the two turtles he commented *(They) can be handy!* They can indeed. Symbolically they carry qualities of integration and wholeness. As we have seen, turtles have a round-shaped carapace and a square-shaped belly, thus integrating the archetypal shapes of the circle, the masculine energy, with the square, the feminine. Their proximity to the detective with the blue case adds further strength to the healing potential of Filip's sandplay work.

Filip's sectioning of his first tray is significant in light of the contemporary thinking on ADHD, which holds that the principle problems of this disorder have to do with the dys-functions in what is called the "executive function" of the prefrontal cortex (Biederman, Monuteaux, Doyle, Seidman, Wilens, Ferrero, Morgan & Faraone, 2004). This is the area of the brain that synthesizes, evaluates and makes action plans out of often conflicting sensory input. It has to do with sorting out what is right or wrong, what the consequences of different choices are and making choices based on inner goals. The trend in the field now is to view ADHD not as a static neurological, psychological or biological deficit, but as an underlying developmental function. Taking this approach to ADHD inherently means that the deficit can be addressed by working with these underlying developmental processes.

The processes involved in executive functioning are complex and varied. They include tak-ing in and processing sensory information, then making choices based on these percep-tions. This is a very involved and intricate mental procedure, particularly because each child processes sensory information in different ways. If the child has hyper or hypo sensory sensitivities in one or more sensory input channel, he or she begins the decision making process with faulty information (Greenspan & Wieder, 2009). Uncomfortable or skewed input from the senses then moves through the limbic system where an emotion or feeling tone is assigned to the information. This further distorts the incoming neu-ral signals. Thus the signals moving toward the prefrontal cortex, if they even reach this level of brain function, are inherently faulty. This form of faulty information processing can result in the characteristic hyper or hypo focused attention styles of the ADHD child. ADHD thus has to do with the neurological *vertical integration* of input from lower brain structures into higher, specifically in this case, sensory input through the limbic system to the prefrontal cortex. ADHD can be thought of as non-existent or faulty connections between these regions of the brain. We know that Filip suffers a number of sensory input issues, exhibiting high auditory, olfactory and visual sensitivity. While diagnosis and treatment of sensory deficits is a task for the psychotherapeutic clinical setting, it is likely that Filip addresses such isolated brain functions and the need to make connections in the spatial construction of the four separate areas in his first tray. If so, what we would hope to see as his process continues is the meaningful and useful bridging and integration of these disconnected elements.

Filip Tray 2

Filip Tray 2a

Filip Tray 2b

Filip Tray 2 – Divisions

Filip's Story
Tray 2

The Beautiful Jungle and the Dangerous Statue

Once upon a time there were people who lived on an island and they were very happy. Some men went to find a pyramid and the pyramid was big and it was in the jungle. Then it happened that they found a statue. When they took the statue home with them they wiped the dust of it and then the statue's mouth opened and a smoke came out along with plenty of enemies who took all their gold. Then a bottle with poison came out and the ghost knight appeared.

Then the men fled into the jungle and they sent cowboys to fetch the gold again. It was very beautiful in the jungle. They saw a little fort and an Indian with an axe. The cowboys continued and found the tower with the statue and the ghost knight. They tripped on a rope and the cork popped out of the bottle of poison. Then lots of enemy watchmen came.

A bunch of cowboys came and circled the enemies. They caught them and put them in the prison tower and locked them up. The statue and the ghost knight argued about whose fault it was. Then the men gathered the gold and went home.

Discussion
Filip Tray 2

Here ordinary life is integrated with the archetypal world. The happy islanders go into the jungle to find a pyramid, the apex of which, according to traditional symbolism, is the highest spiritual and initiatory attainment (De Vries, 1984). In the jungle they also find a statue that they take home with them. The statue is horrific. It becomes animated when dust is wiped of it and smoke ensues from its mouth, followed by a number of enemies, who take the people's gold. The cowboys are sent to fetch the gold again and they manage to do that and come home with it. In the end the enemies are captured and put in jail.

The themes of divisions and attempts to connect returns from the last tray but many things have changed. Here the tray is divided into two sections, not four. Furthermore sections have changed sides from the last tray with the village on the left and archetypal world with the jungle that contains the stolen treasure, on the right. This tray is more organized than the previous tray. The treasure is more spread out, and its contents are more clearly visible. The water area is much clearer now and it is filled with sea life. Here the boat is ready to go to sea. Also, there is no quicksand.

On their way to fetch the gold the cowboys see an Indian in a little fortress. The Indian's fort is centrally located. This appears to be the beginning of a way to bridge the two areas of the tray and is the first indication of a center.

In Tray 2 the number of positive animal energies multiplies. There are two owls, which are the first figures Filip put in his tray. He places them in the center, one in front of the tree and the second directly behind. Owls carry symbolism of wisdom from their characteristics in nature. They have keen eyes that can see in the dark, and they are able to turn their heads so far as to appear to see all around them (Waldau, 2006). Three elephants, one black, one grey and a small white one move toward the central area. Elephants are symbols of strength and fidelity (De Vries, 1984). In nature they are able to clear a path through the densest jungle (Waldau, 2006). Symbolically elephants bear these qualities that can clear the path, find the way and remove obstacles (de Gubernatis, 1978). There are also three mice surrounding the fort. In nature mice burrow and make entrances. As we have previously seen, mouse symbolism concerns action and thought that is penetrating and tenacious (de Gubernatis, 1978). A powerful lion stands in the far center and the two turtles from the last tray return. Some scary animals also return from the previous tray, including the scorpion and a number of dinosaurs, reminding us that the issues Filip addresses have a long history and that addressing them directly can be frightening.

There are three statues of divine figures in the tray, representing Filip's potential for a spiritual inclination. Filip places a wooden statue of Buddha in the village, a Hindu deity in the village in front of the cowboys, and he elevates a second Hindu god on the candlestick-altar in the jungle. In Filip's story the statue moves from the jungle to the village. This movement of the spirit from the archetypal world into the ordinary world is mirrored in his placement of the Hindu deities in both worlds. Thus Filip forms a bridge that links the inner world of the spirit to the outer world of daily life.

It is interesting that the story tells us that the statues are dangerous and contain enemies. In addition Filip says that the four bottles and a vase, all symbols of the feminine receptive principle, contain bad spirits and poison. Like the scary dinosaurs and the scorpion, these elements may be experienced by his conscious mind as frightening or dangerous. Because these are new qualities that are emerging from the unconscious, they are still unknown to the conscious mind and are first perceived as threats. In spite of the potential threats the treasure is recovered and all enemies are safely locked away. As his work progresses we will hope to see Filip strengthen his capacity to openly embrace his spiritual dimension. With his characteristic humor, Filip moves from the sublime to the silly by bringing his story to a close with an argument between the ghost knight and the statue over who was to blame for their getting thrown into jail.

Filip Tray 3

Filip Tray 3a

Filip Tray 3b

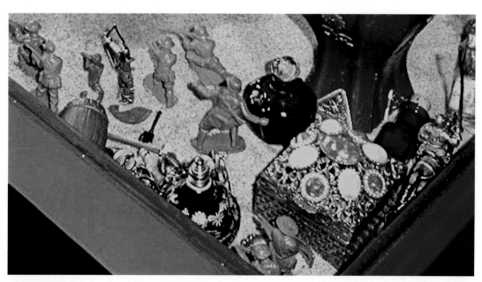

Filip Tray 3c

Filip Tray 3 – Divisions

Filip's Story

Tray 3

The Treasure Symbols

Once upon a time there was a very beautiful country but there were many dangers. There was quicksand and Indians and soldiers. Then it happened that soldiers came to the country with a big treasure and they had heard that there were diamonds owned by Indians and cowboys in the land.

The chief of the soldiers ordered the army to attack and it was a long, long battle. But they didn't notice that one Indian and one cowboy sneaked to the soldiers' treasure and took it. Then the big tower opened and they found the statue and they took it as well.

The officer became furious and wanted to drink whiskey. He became very confused and he demanded another bottle so the soldiers gave him another one. But they forgot to read on it and there was poison in the bottle and all of them tasted it and they all died.

Filip tells the therapist that the treasure signifies many different things:

> *Gold is the mountains*
> *Pearls are the sea*
> *Diamonds are volcanoes*
> *And the necklace is the jungle*

Filip added that the wood statue could give the Indian and the cowboy good advice and "*…then it turned around.*"

Discussion

Filip Tray 3

In Tray 3, the central fortress housing the Indian in the last tray is replaced by a large open space. To the left of center is a large lake that has several canoes sitting on its bank. In addition, the blue boat from the far right corner in Tray 2 crosses the tray and now sits inverted in the near left corner. Beneath it are several jewels. It appears that there are ample resources available to navigate these waters.

The central, protected space that appeared in Tray 2 has here grown into a sizeable and rich area where something new or different can emerge. This possibility is underscored by the lake, which opens to the waters and the unknowns of the unconscious. Perhaps we can anticipate that new psychic qualities will emerge out of these depths and will have ample room to develop.

However there are threats. Filip tells us that the soldiers are actually a troop of bandits that carry other stolen treasures with them. As a line of defense, Filip creates a stream of wet sand, which he calls "*quick sand*," between the lake and the enemies. The soldiers invade this beautiful and peaceful land and carry out an attack. They want to acquire even more wealth and plan to steal diamonds from the cowboys and Indians. As Filip's psyche opens to new possibilities, threats and insecurities continue to appear. Will the newly emerging capacities be safe enough to develop and grow into consciousness? What aspects of Filip's psychic functioning have robbed him of his full functioning? One wonders if, in terms of Filip's learning difficulties, he has inner treasures that are very valuable, but not necessarily recognized in the ordinary learning environment of the school room. Or possibly that he has inner treasures that he has not yet been able to neurologically integrate in an operational way.

Filip's story tells us that the greedy invaders don't succeed, and that a courageous Indian and a cowboy team up and manage to seize the treasure. In addition they find a magical statue that turns around on its own volition and dispenses sage advice. By stealth and cunning the brave heroes are able to sneak by the guards. They cross into the enemy camp and recoup the stolen goods. In addition they access ways of sound decision making with the statue.

Filip employs an odd pair of champions in his choice of the cowboy and the Indian. Traditional lore regards these as oppositional enemies. However, working together symbolically, this pair of opposites is able to penetrate into a foreign camp where they are richly rewarded. In spite of the threats, he is able to access new riches within himself. These are riches that can help direct him and guide him.

The brave heroes do not destroy the invaders. Interestingly, the enemies destroy themselves with their reckless consumption of poison. They are out of control, and are not capable of taking care of these treasures. Although they bring treasures, they lose them for lack of vigilance. They do not know the enormous value of what they have, and are incapable of making use of these riches. In his allegory, Filip tells us that some assets have been unmanageable and wasted, but are now in far more capable hands. Perhaps he is beginning to form the neurological pathways that lead to a greater level of vertical integration that will properly connect his lower brain functions with higher thinking capacities.

It is interesting that Filip clarifies that the treasures are actually elements from nature: mountains, sea, volcanoes, and jungle. He calls his story *The Treasure Symbols*, acknowledging that there is great significance to their meanings. These treasures are not simply pretty things or trinkets that can be destroyed. Rather they are rich aspects of the earth that support life. In the joint effort of a pair of opposite energies and their penetration into a foreign place, Filip's psyche has pierced into new regions of mental possibility, accessing new qualities and potentials. In addition, these are qualities that endure. They must be honored and cared for.

Filip Tray 4

Filip Tray 4

Filip Tray 4 – Divisions

Filip's Story
Tray 4

The Fortress in the Jungle

There once was a jungle. In it was a little fort. In the fort was a good team. The army was clever, but one day bad guys arrived. The army thought about what it could do. The soldiers got an idea and whispered one to another. Then the war started. The bad guys came to get the treasure. When they were in the jungle they heard, "Stick it up" and the soldiers circled around the bad guys.

The chief of the bad guys got angry and yelled at his men. They wondered how the soldiers were able to find them. The soldiers said that they decided to wait until they came into the jungle and then they would circle around them. The bad guys decided to flee and the soldiers became happy every day.

Discussion
Filip Tray 4

In Filip's prior trays we have seen movement of figures from one side to the other creating a bridge between the two worlds. However the ordinary world and the archetypal world have otherwise remained separated. In Tray 4 the beginnings of an integration of these two elements takes place in the left portion of the tray. A fortress protects this new-found combination of treasures, gods and ordinary life. The new psychic capacity, the archetypal content, that has emerged is young and vulnerable. It is tender and must be protected and allowed to develop. The story indicates that the enemy is now outside of the fortress. And once again the pair of owls in the far left corner returns to anchor this work in wisdom.

Coincident with the new psychic content emerging in Filip's Tray 4 we see an abundance of square and circular forms. These are feminine and masculine energies, respectively. At this point in his process these energies remain archetypal and are not yet integrated or united. The figures are scattered about but there is not yet a figure that combines the two shapes, creating a new level of psychic integration. The square shapes of the fortress and the things inside it, such as the chest, a house, and the table saw, emphasize the need for an archetypal union of the square and the circle.

In sandplay it is common to see opposing energies prior to the emergence of new psychic qualities (Kalff, 2003). As the psyche prepares to give birth to new mental capabilities, the pressure of the opposition grows. This frequently culminates as equally balanced opposite forces that face each other in a powerful dynamic tension. Subsequently, new mental capacities begin to emerge. The new qualities must be nurtured as they begin to move into consciousness. Importantly, the new psychic qualities must also be brought to the center. By centering, the psyche acknowledges that the new abilities arise out of, and are part of the totality of the Self, the center of the personality.

While it is important to be aware of the patterns of psychic healing and transformation as they appear in sandplay, we must also be aware that the psyche has its own trajectory and follows no rules or templates in its change and development (Turner, 2005). As we see in Filip's Tray 4 new qualities are being integrated at the same time other new capacities are beginning the initial stages of development. This example of simultaneous developmental processes occurring in the same tray, or series of trays, is not unusual and underscores the necessity for proper training to practice sandplay. The healing and development processes that occur in sandplay can be highly complex and difficult to understand.

Four dinosaurs are situated nearby the quicksand. In the last tray there was a great deal of poison. Now we have the protection of an antitoxin that works against the effects of poison. The dinosaurs circle the quicksand and the antitoxin perhaps indicating there are now ways to deal with the very old issues. However the relatively large bottle stands on the right side of the tray where the darker forces are located and it is in the quicksand. Is it in danger of being swallowed up, or is it emerging from the depths?

It is interesting how the characters assume different roles from tray to tray. Soldiers are now on the good team and the Indians and cowboys are the enemies. The enemies have also changed sides in the tray when compared to the last tray. Perhaps Filip is unclear about which elements of his psyche are destructive to his functioning, and which are positive. Or perhaps this change in roles and sides is more about his attempt to make neurological connections.

Filip Tray 5

Filip Tray 5a

Filip Tray 5b

Filip Tray 5 – Divisions

Filip's Story

Tray 5

The Tyrant

There was once a land where there was a little town. But it was not much fun to live there because in the land was a tyrant. The tyrant wanted only to gain money and more money. He went searching for people who had money and took their money. The people said this was unfair and wanted to kill him.

The tyrant got news that men with guns and arrows were coming to attack him and he became mad with anger. He ordered his watchmen to plant some dynamite but they said, "But if we plant dynamite and you will be too quick to explode it then you will blow us up, too." He then told his men to go and fight with their weapons.

When the good team saw all the soldiers their chief said, "This could be hard and they might beat us. I got a better idea. We send a letter and in it will be written that we surrender. Then I will dress like a waiter and I go with poisoned water and give it to the tyrant."

They sent the letter and the tyrant became very glad and decided to give a party. He asked for a drink and then the good chief came disguised as a waiter and gave him the poisoned water. When the tyrant tasted the water he crashed on the floor and started to strangle himself. Then he died.

The soldiers fled in their canoes and wrote a letter and said that they would never come back. Then the good team came and took all the gold.

Discussion

Filip Tray 5

Filip was very happy to come to the sandplay session and talked a lot during his play. He began his work with two figures from the film about Mulan, while talking about the film. Then he returned the figures to the shelves. This was uncharacteristic for this child, who always selected his figures with certainty. Perhaps he was beginning to reach beyond his accustomed expectations and was more willing to experiment with new ways of being.

As in Tray 4, the village and the treasure are on the left side of the tray. In Tray 5 the bad team led by the nasty tyrant surrounds this village. Like Tray 4, the good team appears as cowboys and Indians and is positioned on the right part of the tray across from the big water opening. The fort is less rigidly walled than it was in the prior tray. Here he has an indication of walls around the fort and has placed some of the treasures outside in the near left area. The large water opening indicates that he has ready access to material from the unconscious.

Spiritual elements return in this tray in the center right above the cowboys and Indians. Here Filip clusters the three statues from his last tray: Vishnu, the four-armed Hindu deity considered the Sustainer of life; beside him a dancing baby Krishna holding a *laddu*, a special sweet made for festivals; and the wooden bust of Buddha. Next to the three deities Filip fashions an altar with a red ruby offering. While telling the therapist that the good team believes in the gods he marks this sacred area with two tall black feathers and carefully makes quicksand around it to protect it from harm. He also makes a quicksand trap to protect the good team from incursions from enemies in the near right corner.

This is the first appearance of feathers in Filip's work. As we have seen, the feather is a powerful symbol of the spirit and birds. According to ancient cultures feathers were used to communicate with the gods. In ancient Egypt the funerary judgment rites included weighing the deceased's heart against a feather as a measure of divine order and earthly transgressions (Wasserman, 2008). Filip mirrors the feather qualities with the tiny glass bird that he places on the top of the palm in the near right corner.

In this tray, Filip repeats the themes from Tray 4. These include a greedy tyrant and his evil team, and a good team that is smarter, using treasure, poison, and cleverness. The tyrant is without sympathy or good qualities and is a devouring menace. Once again, Filip uses his cleverness and humor to deal with these negative forces. In this tray, he has the good side send a false letter of surrender, and disguises the captain in the costume of a waiter, who serves the tyrant poison. His humor is delightful and rather well developed for a child of his age. The greedy tyrant is outwitted by this small, but shrewd group of men with guns and arrows. The tyrant's watchmen flee and the tyrant is poisoned. Filip told the therapist that the tyrant wanted only to be rich and that he had no pity for the poor. "*He takes everything from them. He is greedy,*" he said.

While Filip again divides the areas of the enemies from those of the protagonists, there is a great deal of interchange and movement between them. First we learn that guns and arrows are coming to attack. The good team delivers a letter proposing a scheme, and this is responded to in turn. The pseudo waiter once again travels across to the enemy team to deliver the poison.

Bones are strewn around the tray, indicating that some things have died. Some psychic qualities that have not been serving him are no longer needed. Death has taken place which gives room for birth or resurrection.

It is interesting how frequently Filip uses the bright red table saw in his trays, and frequently as a part of what he calls the treasure. Is this the treasured fantasy of a little boy who would like to someday have his own table saw? Perhaps its presence has more to do with the bright red color, which is the color of deep feeling, passion and anger. He needs this energy to continue with this difficult psychic reordering.

Filip Tray 6

Filip Tray 6

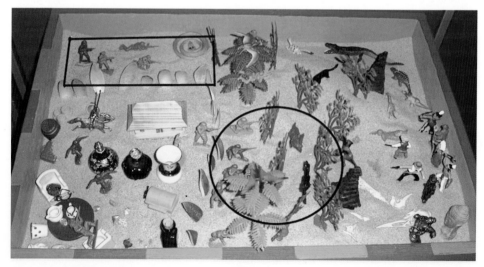

Filip Tray 6 – Divisions

Filip's Story
Tray 6

The War Against the Nazis

There was once a beautiful country and the people believed in the gods. But one day the Nazis came and they wanted to walk away with all the gold the people had. The people said, "Don't take it all from us." But then the officer laughed. He said, "Next time I will take still more" because he was so greedy.

One day the people said, "We should do something about this." Then one of the soldiers said, "We could call the English and the Americans." The soldiers sent a letter to England and the United States and asked for help. They got help and fought well and chased off all the Nazis.

Discussion
Filip Tray 6
Filip was happy to come to sandplay, and constructed his tray with the story of the Second World War in the background. Once again, he was very pleased with his construction, and asked the therapist if she didn't find it an excellent picture.

In this tray a forest has grown in the central area where the big water opening was located in Tray 5. While there is still an opening to the blue in the far right corner, it is smaller. It appears that the qualities that Filip accessed through his large opening to the unconscious in the prior tray are now growing in the green trees of the forest. In this tray Filip continues with his characteristic themes of greed, theft, battle and restoration of treasure to the rightful owners, but for the first time the problem is solved by asking for help. Perhaps this is a positive transference statement about the benefits of the work he is doing with his therapist in sandplay (Jung, 1985).

The table and tea set, located in the near left corner, were the first items Filip placed in the tray. The Indian with the bow and arrow sitting at the table was the last figure. When something new surfaces from the unconscious we frequently see feeding and nourishing themes. Just as with a newborn child, what is new in the psyche must also be fed for it to develop properly. In Tray 6 a forest grows and develops in the former lake area, and the psyche now has a place to feed and take sustenance at the tea table. Significantly, a member of each team sits at the table. It appears that the disconnected parts of the psyche have come together to take nourishment. With this balanced union of opposites there is abundant possibility for new growth.

Containers and vases have appeared in each tray of Filip's process. The container or vessel is frequently considered the wholeness of the feminine, the Great Mother, or source of all being (Neumann, 1972). Containers are also the alchemical vas, where qualitative transformation occurs (Jung, 1968). In this tray Filip outlines the tea table area with two rows of containers. Inside of this square area he scatters jewels. The joining of the opposites at the tea table is contained within the boundaries of the four vessels and the treasure chest, and the sacred quality of this new union is marked with the bountiful jewels.

Patterns of opposite but balanced energies are present throughout Tray 6. On the diagonals there is an interesting juxtaposition of the healing, nurturing qualities in the near left corner and the primitive, devouring animal forces in the far right corner. On the opposite diagonal, the bad team gathers in the far left, and the good team with the gods is in the near right. Mirroring this opposition are the representatives of the two opposing teams, who come together to take tea in the near left. With elegant simplicity Filip brings together all of the struggles between the primitive, destructive forces in his psyche and the battles he has fought with them, and unites them in a healing ritual of tea.

Filip Tray 7

Filip Tray 7

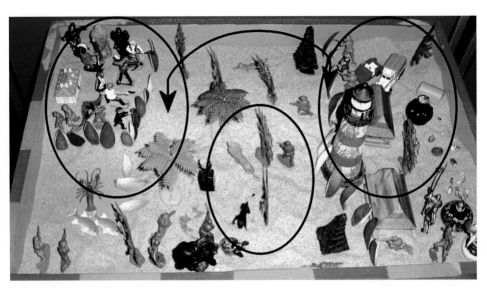

Filip Tray 7 – Divisions

Filip's Story
Tray 7

Indiana Jones and the
Lost Wicked Robbers from the Wild West

Once in New York, Indiana Jones was talking to some other men. He said that he was going to find the treasure chest but then one of the men showed him photos of the wicked men that were also going to hunt for the chest. Indiana Jones was shocked when he saw the photo because it was the bad man who had asked for the statue and had deceived him.

Indiana Jones traveled to a woman he knew and asked her to give him the necklace her father had given her because on it was a drawing showing where the treasure chest was to be found. She told him to come the next day.

Then he met the bad men and they wanted to get the necklace, too. The chief of the enemy team got the necklace and burned himself. Then he went to get the treasure chest. Indiana Jones and his friends followed him in a jeep with a machine gun. Indiana Jones went on the truck where the treasure chest was

*hidden and he took the truck from the Nazis and pushed the chief out of the car
and he drove to Cairo and sailed to New York with the treasure chest.*

Discussion

Filip Tray 7

The first thing Filip put in the tray was a red ruby. He commented that this was a magic stone and that he wanted to make a treasure. While placing pearls, pieces of gold and colored stones around the ruby he said that the bad guys, the Nazis, had stolen the treasure. Once again he pairs two teams against each other. The good team seems now to be placed in upper left corner with the three god statues while the bad team is dispersed around the tray. While the theme of conflicting forces continues there is greater balance and symmetry in the overall construction of this tray. The enemy fort occupies the right portion of the tray, and is distinguished by an orderly row of fencing made from the oval-shaped wood chips. Behind the fence the lighthouse tower stands in a central position, and is flanked by a pair of wooden buildings. The area of the good team is also marked off with fencing in the far left corner, leaving a large central open area with trees, wild animals and enemy soldiers.

It is interesting to look at the groups of twos and threes in this tray. Symbolically the number two indicates the emergence of something new. Pairs appear in the tray as fish, trucks and two powerful beasts: a lion and a black panther. The two fish symbolize energies related to temporal and spiritual power. The pair of sturdy trucks may carry energies related to the physical body, as they are a means of conveyance and are driven by people. Taken together, this symbolically carries the body and spirit, constituting the essence of a whole human being. Additionally, the two powerful wild cats symbolically carry the powers of the instincts. The lion is known as the king of the animals, the courageous and powerful ruler of the jungle. In early Christian lore the panther was said to save people from the Evil One or the devil (Waldau, 2006). Like the lion and other large wild cats, the panther is known for its fierce stealth and power (de Gubernatis, 1978). Its dark coat is often thought to carry the dark feminine forces, although some cultures also associate it with the sun and the masculine (De Vries, 1984). The strength of the two cats is underscored by the three elephants that stand in the near central area of the tray, in the vicinity of the panther. In addition to their devoted familial caring, elephants are also symbols of strength and power. They represent perseverance, are very hard working and are known for their memory, wisdom and dignity (Waldau, 2006). Filip uses three different elephants: a large black one; a smaller one that is adorned for a ceremony; and a tiny white one that stands just along the inner edge of the near side of the tray. The white elephant is often related to compassion and kindness.

It appears that the qualities of these five wild animals, the two big cats and the three elephants, are coming together in the central area of the tray to form the beginnings of a whole, strong and capable person.

In numerical symbolism groups of three carry dynamic energies of growth and creative power (Eastwood, 2002). In Filip's Tray 7 there are three elephants, three statues of deities and three red objects. The red objects, the lobster, ruby and truck, are of particular interest. Red is a color of strength and passion as well as the active, masculine principle (Gage, 2000). The fiery red truck is a sturdy vehicle and seems to indicate that Filip's strengths and passions are developing and are on the move. The large red lobster in the pond with the two fish is another indicator of positive development, in that the lobster cleans away the waste at the bottom of the pond, clearing the waters and symbolically making the unconscious more accessible. Paired here with the two fish we might infer that a purification of the spirit is taking place. The third red object is the ruby, a treasure of magical quality, likely to be a precursor of the Self.

It is deeply touching how Filip uses the three deities in tray after tray, and makes reference to the good team having, "...*belief in the gods*." In spite of his many difficult struggles with learning and his painful sense of being somehow different, or flawed, Filip's work to clarify, reorder and connect aspects of his psychic functioning is always anchored to central principles that are greater than himself. In Tray 1, we recall that he adds water to the ritual basin, "...*for the gods*," and uses divine images in each of his following trays. Although he has no conscious idea about the meaning of the three deities he uses, they are clearly significant to his work and form a core point around which his work revolves.

Filip Tray 8

Filip Tray 8

Filip's Story

Tray 8

The War Between the Big Fortress and the Little Fortress

Once in South America there were three fortresses. The big fortress was owned by colonel Welduko. The middle fortress was from an ancient time. The one who owned that was an Indian chief. In the tiny fortress were guards of the jungle.

Once colonel Welduko stole some diamonds from the Indian chief. They started to argue. Then a war started. The massacre was horrible. The guards of the jungle had enough of this noise, disturbance and stupidity and they built a wall between the two enemies to make them stop. Then the enemy teams tried to break their way through. The guards of the jungle asked them why the enemy teams were fighting and they did not remember the reason. Colonel Welduko suddenly remembered and said: "Sorry I stole the diamonds." The Indian chief said: "You can just keep them." And the story has come to an end.

Discussion

Filip Tray 8

The first figures Filip placed in Tray 8 were the two trucks from last tray. Here they are lined up and are ready to leave the battle field. The treasures - the red ruby, diamonds and pearls - are collected and safely stored in the big chest. The three deity figures appear again but are now dispersed and more integrated with what is going on around them. The single tower from Tray 7 now becomes two, indicating further development of Filip's strength and capacity for oversight, or understanding.

While he creates two opposing forts in the sand, his story progresses and the battle that has taken place in all of Filip's trays eases down and finally comes to an end. In Trays 1 through 7 the conflicts always concerned a desirable treasure that had been stolen by greedy and cruel enemies. In Tray 8 peacemakers appear as jungle guards and they build a wall between the two camps in an effort to stop the fighting. Filip's story about this tray demonstrates his characteristically witty humor and his deep understanding of human nature. Filip says that the enemies are still determined to continue fighting, but have in fact forgotten the purpose of their battle. They make peace when the enemies understand the absurdity of their situation. During sandplay Filip asked the therapist which side she wanted to be aligned with, and then informed her that the good ones are on the right side. He mentioned that the jungle guards are ...*sort of wild.*

Given the richness of his imagination, it is probably no surprise that his peacemakers are colorful characters. Symbolically they function as archetypal wise men that are able to bridge the conflicts and resolve the tensions. By definition the energies that perform this function must be outside of the norm of what is expected. These are new qualities that emerge out of the pressures of the disparities of the struggle. In Jungian personality theory the "somewhat wild" peacemakers are the product of the transcendent function that occurs when the polarities of the ego's position are no longer tenable (Jung, 1981). When the conscious position, the ego, encounters a circumstance that it is not capable of dealing with, the ego engages in an intense effort to address the issue by using the skills or psychic qualities that it currently has. However these abilities are not adequate to deal with the new challenges. The unconscious then produces an equally powerful and likewise inadequate psychic product to try to create stability in the current unbalanced situation. An example of this might be a person who feels that he is not worthy in a particular situation. Because this attitude is terribly off balance with the psyche's central organizing principle of the Self, the unconscious produces another attitude to counter balance it. In our example, this person might feel superior. So the psyche oscillates back and forth between inadequacy and superiority until it comes to a standstill by the equal force of the polar opposites. The pressures of the equally powerful poles of the opposition force the psyche down into the unconscious to access new psychic material, which then resolves the conflict. In his Tray 8 Filip's psyche develops qualitatively and accesses new qualities and abilities, leaving the old conflicts behind. In fact he tells us that they cannot even remember what the fight was about.

With the exception of Colonel Welduko's horse, it is noteworthy that there are no longer any animals in the tray. As Filip resolves the conflict he enters a world where there are only human beings and gods. He moves away from an archetypal battle of primitive forces into a more human and civilized sphere.

Filip Tray 9

Filip Tray 9a

Filip Tray 9b

Filip's Story
Tray 9

The Dragon Warrior and Tai Long

Once in Egypt there was a place that was so special that you can't imagine it. It was a temple. And if you go into the temple you drift to China as it was in ancient times.

There was a kid that had a stupid dad. The dad sold noodles and he had a restaurant. The kid dreamed of becoming a dragon warrior rather than serving noodles but his father would not hear of that.

One day when the boy was serving guests noodles in the restaurant, three men from the temple of the warriors came and they posted a letter. In the letter it was written that Ungvey the master of the temple was going to choose a dragon warrior.

Now we shall go to the temple of the warriors. There Ungvey was speaking to his apprentice. He said that Tai Long (a bad one) would return.

Now we shall take a trip to the prison where Tai Long is. The messenger went with the master of the prison and showed them where Tai Long sat. Then Tai Long broke the chains he was in and managed to get loose. Ungvey had chosen the boy as a dragon warrior and he trained him. In the evening Tai Long went to the temple and the dragon warrior fought with him. The boy made the Mutsi finger grip and Tai Long exploded.

After that, all lived happily in the temple of warriors in China.

Discussion

Filip Tray 9

Filip began his work saying he wanted to make a magic pyramid and later identified it as an Egyptian temple. He said that when one enters this temple, he or she is transported to a place beyond ordinary time and space, specifically, "*…one drifts to China as it was in ancient times.*" Notably different than his prior trays, this scene radiates a mystical numinosity. This is the *temenos*, the sacred space. It is serenely quiet and aesthetically pure. Filip's Tray 9 is what is known as the *manifestation of the Self* (Kalff, 2003; Turner, 2005). In this sand tray Filip touches the deepest part of the psyche. He anchors his newly developed psychic capacities in the central archetype of the personality. In Jungian personality theory the Self is considered the source of all manifestation as well as the goal to which it returns (Jung, 1980). In the Western Bible this might be likened to the description of man (being) made in the image of God. Specifically, we read in Genesis 1:26-7 (Revised Standard Version):

> God said, 'Let Us make man in Our image, according to Our likeness… And God created man in His own image, in the image of God He created him.

When the sandplay client has sufficiently addressed his or her conflicts and is able to access new psychic qualities that will allow him or her to live in the world with newly developed mental abilities and capacities, the process returns to the center. Prior to the new qualities moving into consciousness the psyche must first acknowledge their source in the Self and their alignment with the central archetype. In this way the new abilities move into consciousness with the ego's recognition of their accord with the Self. In so doing the ego becomes more aligned with the Self and acknowledges the superior authority of this central archetype.

The wholeness of the Self is inherent in the underlying construction of his temple where Filip used cork disks aligned in three rows of three to fashion a square built of round forms. In so doing he archetypally unites the spirit of the heavens, the circle, with the manifest body of the earth, the square. Atop the temple, he places the wise owl that has appeared in many of his prior sandplays. He marks the sacred space with two wooden pillars, which he topped with jewels. The ruby which has figured prominently in his struggles for the treasure in prior trays now sits on the temple in all of its glory. The holiest place, or *sanctum sanctorum*, at the center right of the tray is set apart by a delicate fence of wooden disks and the statues of Krishna and Vishnu, behind which the bust of Buddha is elevated on the altar.

On the left portion of the tray a solitary turtle swims in the stream. Echoing the rewards of the steadfast pace of Filip's own journey in his sandplay work, the little turtle carries its home on its back. It is whole, persevering and at home with itself. In addition, the turtle sits by a butterfly-like construction Filip fashioned out of a twig and two wooden disks. The butterfly symbolizes the transformation process, as it evolves from the lowly caterpillar to a magnificent winged creature. Perhaps this serves as a bridge to cross the water and enter the sacred temple area where one is transformed in the Self.

Filip's story of the hero, the son of a poor noodle seller, who becomes a dragon warrior and conquers the evil Tai Long, mirrors the transformative themes carried in the symbols in his sand tray. In his story, which Filip tells the therapist is based on a film he saw, the hero develops special powers and tools which he uses to overcome difficult tasks. Although Filip draws from the themes and characters of a popular film, it is his own myth, the story of his unconscious that unfolds in the sandplay. The battles are over. The newly developed psychic qualities acknowledge their source in the Self, and are now positioned to become conscious.

Filip Tray 10

Filip Tray 10a

Filip Tray 10b

Filip's Story
Tray 10

Wonder Star

Once there was a star and it was named the Wonder Star. It was not an ordinary star because an extraterrestrial lived on it and it was amazing. The wonder being was happy and felt good.

One day it woke up and went for a walk. It decided to go through the garden. Then it came to a cave and got shut inside it. Its protection weapon was a very weak electric current which could become great if it became angry. It was so sad and hurt that much electricity came and it exploded the stones from the cave. When the light shone into the cave the wonder being saw lots of diamonds. It took some diamonds and left the cave. It found the day enjoyable.

Discussion

Filip Tray 10

The impact of the centering of the Self that occurred in Filip's last tray is evident in Tray 10. On one hand we are introduced to the peaceful and comfortable home of the extraterrestrial, an alien being that is newly arrived from outer space. This home might denote the ego that begins the process of integrating the newly developed qualities into the conscious mind. Certainly these new psychic qualities would seem rather "alien" to the ego (Jung, 1970). The little green extraterrestrial, at home in his curiously furnished house, is a perfectly suited symbol of Filip's transformed psyche. This outer, more conscious world is balanced by the cave, the inner world, which Filip tells us is filled with precious jewels.

When Filip made this tray he and his classmates were working on a unit on outer space, stars, extraterrestrials and spaceships, and he draws from this theme in his sandplay. Filip was very creative in finding things that he could use. The extraterrestrial is the small prickly green rubber ball sitting on a white chair at the table and his space ship is a golden lamp part in the near right corner. In addition he uses other objects in inventive ways to represent furnishings in the extraterrestrial's house. He used bird bones for lamps and a sea urchin for a sofa. A heart-shaped plastic box is a pond in the extraterrestrial's garden. Filip made a big cave out of stones. He decorated the largest rock with jewels, which required a lot of concentration on his part, as they repeatedly slid off and had to be repositioned. Filip was extremely happy with his tray and asked his therapist six times whether she did not find it splendid. Concern and loving-kindness is felt throughout the tray. A baby crib in the near left is ready for his newborn Self to rest in. Filip put water in the heart-shaped pond and reverently anointed the big stone, bestowing protection and honoring the sacred nature of the treasured home of his inner world.

Filip now has access to his inner world and has a way to discover his own resources. Filip's story tells us that the extraterrestrial becomes locked in the cave and is able to free himself with the help of his electric current weapon that is activated in correspondence with the measure of his feelings. Because he was so sad and hurt, a great current is generated, which detonates and reveals a wealth of diamonds. The choice of a mild electric current as a protection device is fascinating. Perhaps this current in the cave can be understood as a metaphor for well functioning neurological connections between the conscious and the unconscious mind, as well as the vertical integration of input from lower brain functions and the limbic system with the prefrontal cortex. It is highly interesting that it is only when the alien demonstrates the courage to acknowledge and respond to his feelings that the treasure is discovered. It appears that through his sandplay work, the impediments in the neural functioning underlying the ADD are now being bridged with a healthy, vital neural integration. It is also fascinating that the extraterrestrial did not feel the need to take all of the diamonds from the cave. The story infers that he is able to return. This pathway remains open to him and there is an active connection between these areas of his mental functioning.

Filip Tray 11

Filip Tray 11

Filip's Story

Tray 11

The Queen and the Chief

Once there was a beautiful country but something was the matter. The island was divided into two parts. A queen of half the country had a huge treasure. On the other half was a chief. He had no treasure.

Then the war started because both wanted the whole country. Many people fled, but the queen won and then the queen and the chief decided to negotiate and have peace and they lived happily ever after and built a bridge between the two parts of the country.

Discussion

Filip Tray 11

Filip was very happy to come to his sandplay session this day, and began his work by placing trees and creating a long water course in the center of the tray. Soldiers figure in the scene again. At the time he did this tray, Filip was eight years old. Soldiers are a common and normal figure used by boys of this age, who are beginning to deal with issues about their role as males (Turner, 2005). Although this tray reminds of us of his prior battles, it is qualitatively different, for here he directly addresses the central value of the feminine.

This is the first tray in which the female plays the major role. In Tray 7 a female is mentioned in the story but is not to be found in the tray. In this tray Filip crowns the queen by placing a small golden ring on her head, and entitles the story *The Queen and the Chief.*

There is a lot of treasure on the left part of the tray where the queen reigns. In contrast, the chief has no treasure in his land on the right. Filip tells us that they go to war and the queen is the victor. However, instead of taking over the chief's lands, the queen and the chief enter into a cooperative agreement. They establish peace and build a bridge between them.

In this tray, the feminine is elevated to a highly respected position, a respect that is appropriate for the male psyche. In Jungian psychology the queen might be regarded as a prefiguration of the anima, which Filip will develop more fully during his adolescence (Jung, 1981). Although Filip is too young for the anima to emerge, his psyche acknowledges and recognizes the essential value of the feminine. The story tells us that the masculine has no treasure without the feminine. In this tray, the masculine aspect of Filip's psyche recognizes its origins in the feminine. The conscious, rational aspects of the psyche acknowledge the value and necessity of the unconscious, feminine. In the female psyche, the animus, or masculine energy is required to bring order and definition to the undefined darkness of the feminine. Conversely the male psyche, which is predominantly rational, must accept the presence and importance of the feminine in order to find balance and wholeness in the Self. The allegory of Filip's story tells us of the precious value of the treasures of the feminine and how they are needed for the full development of masculine personality.

If we consider Tray 11 in the context of his overall sandplay process, we can see how the new psychic qualities that Filip has tapped are becoming conscious. The conscious position may be seen in the chief's masculine team on the right side of the tray. This region begins with no treasures, however they need treasure. In contrast, the new psychic capacities Filip has developed over the course of his sandplay work can be seen as the rich treasure trove under the command of the queen, on the left side of the tray. The queen's land is the feminine, or the unconscious that Filip has accessed throughout his process. The treasures are abundant here, but they are not yet conscious.

We recall that after confronting many conflicts in Trays 1 through 5, Filip began to find resolution in the reconciliatory tea party of Tray 6. Having done this, new psychic qualities emerged and continued their development in Trays 7 and 8 as the battle finally came to an end. In Tray 9 Filip's psyche, now transformed, returned to the center of the Self. The psyche acknowledged the Self as the source of the new abilities. After this the process of setting the new qualities in place to become conscious occurred. In Tray 10 Filip discovered a completely novel and rich world for his "alien" newly-developing self. Finally, this is followed by a dramatic enactment of the archetypal procedure the newly forming qualities follow to enter the domain of consciousness. Filip plays this out in the discrepancies, imbalance and eventual cooperation between the masculine and the feminine energies in Tray 11. And with this archetypal collaboration, Filip tells us that, …*they all lived happily ever after.*

Filip's work in sandplay is a remarkable demonstration of the depth and resilience of the human psyche when given the opportunity and circumstances necessary to facilitate healing and development. Filip has clearly undergone tremendous transformation. The *"free and protected space"* that Kalff described as the two primary components necessary to facilitate this order of change have allowed Filip the safety and possibility to address his conflicts; to access new psychic abilities; to anchor the work in the center of the Self; and to integrate these new abilities and perceptions into the conscious personality (2002).

Filip Tray 12

Filip Tray 12

Filip's Story
Tray 12

The Secret of the Pirate Funfair

Once a long time ago there was an old pirate amusement park. It was divided between the pirates. The captain of the pirates owned the Ferris wheel, the steersman owned the ghost cave, the cook owned the carousel and the pirate who tasted the food owned the roller coaster. All the other pirates owned the target together.

In a closed house was a treasure chest and in the chest there were loads of diamonds, emeralds, rubies, yellow diamonds, violet diamonds, pearls and gold nuggets.

Many visited the funfair. One day the island where the fair was sank to the bottom of the sea. The treasure disappeared with it, but it was said that the pirates lived in the water and the funfair continued to work in the ocean. And now the story has come to its end.

Filip Tray 12
Discussion

In the beginning Filip made a circular water hole, which he enlarged and changed into a great river that traveled from the left to the right sides of the tray. He then covered it with sand and announced that he knew what he wanted to do and that he would call his story, "*The Secret of the Pirate Funfair.*" It was only at the very end of his story that he revealed the secret that the funfair had sunk and continued to operate in the underworld. After he disclosed the secret, he succinctly concluded, *And now the story has come to its end.* So Filip's sandplay work reached its conclusion.

The tray is quite different from former trays. Here the soldiers are the visitors to the carnival. Filip was creative in finding things he wanted to use in his amusement park and was patient as he constructed the rides and amusements. This funfair took great persistence to create, as structures repeatedly fell, requiring him to build them again and again. He made a Ferris wheel and a roller coaster car out of cheese boxes; a carousel out of a wooden bobbin, cork disks, some sticks and horses; a haunted house out of rocks; a shooting gallery target out of a tiny basket; and a roller coaster out of chopsticks that he carefully balanced on top of rocks.

Along the far part of the tray Filip has his signature spirituality as a backdrop to his funfair. In place of the three deities he now has three white feathers. The Indian chief sits atop the altar overseeing the carnival, and the jeweled treasure box sits beside the altar. He created a carnival that a child would enjoy, and in his own delightfully loving way, Filip tells the therapist how much he has gained from his sandplay work, and that it continues to work in his inner world. The resources he has discovered in himself through his sandplay process function in his depths and he now takes them away as his own.

Throughout his work Filip demonstrated a touching warmth and intelligence, combined with a delightful sense of humor and an eagerness to explore and grow through his imaginative play. Through the sand, the symbols and his stories Filip has developed a sense of confidence and capability. Of course he will continue to have struggles with his school work, but now he believes in himself. Moreover he has activated a powerful spiritual connection that will continue to nourish his growth and development. It is always a gift to work with a child like Filip, for in the end we feel we are the recipients of a great blessing that sustains hope in human possibility. Filip closes his work saying, "*...and now the story has come to its end.*" So it has and we say, "*...thank you Filip.*"

Concluding Remarks

In the sandplay processes of the four children presented we have been able to track the progress that was measured by the test scores through the changes in the symbolic content of the trays and the stories. Due to the fundamental paradigmatic differences between the qualitative symbolic work in the tray and the quantitative measures of the test instruments it is not possible to directly correlate to skills such as improved Verbal Comprehension scores or overall IQ measures with the right hemispheric sandplay and story making process. Yet the case analyses clearly show that the children addressed their inner conflicts or deficits and that they were able to progress through many of their intrapsychic challenges toward more integrated in-tact mental functioning. Even Alda's work demonstrated an impressive capacity to address her issues and to develop new strengths through her sandplay and story making. Sadly however, her family environment did not support her continued development. The imaginative work in the sand tray gave the children access to skills and abilities that were previously unavailable to them and the storytelling activated their language centers while continuing their right hemispheric symbolic process. The test results affirm in several cases that the children's skills showed significant improvement following their play experience in the sand.

The research on this topic is rather new and more studies will need to be undertaken to further develop the thesis. However as an initial foray into the area of the effects of imaginative play through sandplay and storytelling on learning and development, this study most certainly supports the observations of many prominent child development specialists who have long averred that children's learning occurs in play and in relationship.

We realize that funding for education is limited and that additional resources for schools are scarce. We also understand, along with many other caring professionals, that many of our children are not getting the education they need to carry them through life as productive citizens. Too many schools have given unwarranted focus to test taking. This is not learning. With their focus on testing teachers are unable to help children learn to think and process information in creative ways. Many excellent teachers are terribly frustrated that they are unable to practice their craft. We firmly believe that education must return to considerations of children's developmental needs. Curriculum designers and superintendants must heed and put into practice the thousands of solid research studies that clearly conclude that children have different ways of learning, and that all learning and creative thinking is facilitated by play. We are firmly convinced after many years of sandplay practice and by the results of this study that the freedom and the safety of the symbolic play of sandplay and imaginative storytelling can be of tremendous benefit in the educational setting. While we keep the sandplay within the tray, or box, our thinking as children's advocates must extend outside the box of current educational delivery. We need to provide the children the means by which we know they learn, and we need to return the right to teach to our many wonderful and dedicated educators.

The need to learn and develop is inherent to the human experience. This is true for adults as well as children. As a final word, it is our hope that we can design our learning environments to offer creative opportunities that nurture our children and allow them to blossom. This is a process that has no end. Jung (1981a) reminded us of the life-long need to care for these aspects of ourselves.

> For in every adult there lurks a child - an eternal child, something that is always becoming, is never completed, and calls for unceasing care, attention, and education. That is the part of the human personality which wants to develop and become whole (pp. 169–170).

We hope that in some way our work here makes a contribution to this effort.

Resources

For information on training requirements to practice sandplay therapy, workshops & how to locate a Certified Sandplay Therapist – CST, or Certified Sandplay Therapist Teacher – CST-T in your region:

International Society for Sandplay Therapy
www.isst-society.com
Martastrasse 140
8003 Zürich
Switzerland

E-mail: isst.bamert@gmail.com
Phone: 0041 (0) 44 558 97 96

Sandplay Therapists of America
www.sandplay.org
PO Box 4847
Walnut Creek, CA 94596
USA

E-mail: sta@sandplay.org
Phone: (925) 478-8103

For mental health professionals interested in training to become sandplay therapists:
Barbara Turner, PhD
Certified Sandplay Therapist – Teacher
Registered Play Therapist – Supervisor
PO Box 305
Cloverdale, CA 95425 USA
www.barbaraturner.org

E-mail: drbarb@barbaraturner.org

For online courses in foundations and theory of sandplay therapy:
www.temenospress.com/learning

For books written and edited by Dr. Turner:
www.temenospress.com

Glossary of Jungian Terms

Anima and Animus

The contra-sexual qualities in the male and female psyches respectively. For a balanced personality the masculine psyche needs to be in a cooperatively working relationship to the anima, the inner feminine and the feminine psyche must have a healthy relationship with the animus. It is the anima and the animus that show the way to the central archetype of the Self.

Anthropos

The whole, balanced human being.

Archetypes

The core or essential templates of human psychic life. The inherited aspects of the psyche that structure human psychological experience. The unconscious is made up of archetypes.

Collective Unconscious

Composed of instincts and archetypes. Contains all of human kind's potentials and histories. The collective unconscious reaches across all time and cultures. Images and symbols are the language of the unconscious. Myth and fairy tale are its stories. In the brain, the collective unconscious is a right hemispheric function.

Compensation, Compensatory Product

The quality produced by the unconscious to restore psychic balance when the ego is not aligned with the Self. The compensatory product is as out of balance as is the ego's misaligned thought, idea, self perception. However the psychic tension created between the two opposing misaligned products stimulates the production of the symbol from the unconscious that will resolve the ego's dilemma, restore balance to the psyche and bring the ego into proper alignment with the Self.

Consciousness

The psychic material that is available to awareness. The domain of the psyche characterized by what Jung called the *four functions,* or means whereby we receive information from the inner and the outer world.

Directed Thinking
The mode of thinking characterized by rationality and reason. This is based in logic and is a left hemispheric process.

Ego
The central feature or organ of consciousness. The ego tends to hold tenaciously to what it knows. The goal of individuation is to bring the ego in greater alignment with the central archetype of the Self, such that the conscious awareness acknowledges its source and goal in the Self.

Fantasy or Undirected Thinking
The mode of thinking characterized by unconscious processes. This is an image and feeling-based right hemispheric process.

Feminine
The female psyche is primarily feminine in nature, characterized by receptivity, generativity and collective cooperation on the light side. The dark side of feminine energy can be fiercely engulfing and destructive.

Four Functions
Four modes of perception through which the individual receives information from the inner and outer world. *Thinking, Feeling, Sensation and Intuition.* Each individual is characterized by varying combinations of these qualities. An objective of the individuation process is to be able to distinguish or *differentiate* what information we are receiving through which mode of functioning.

Individuation
The process of aligning the ego to the Self. This occurs through the assimilation of the shadow, diminishing the layer of the personal unconscious that separates the conscious personality from the unconscious.

Masculine
The male psyche is primarily *masculine* in nature, characterized by rationality, logic, protectiveness and assertion on the positive side. On the negative side, the masculine can be rigid, controlling and violent.

Personal Unconscious
The area of the unconscious that is closest to conscious awareness. Contains the shadow.

Polar Opposition

Occurs when the ego is misaligned to the Self and the psyche is out of balance. The compensatory product is produced in an attempt to restore order. However the compensatory product carries energies that are exactly opposite those carried by the misaligned product. This creates a condition of polarized energies that bring the psyche to a standstill. The polarized energy builds into a great pressure that dives down into the unconscious to access new psychic material that carries the qualities necessary to resolve the ego's issue.

Self

The central archetype of the unconscious which gives order, form and meaning to human existence. The Self is the source of all being and the goal to which is returns.

Shadow

Awareness of personal characteristics that have been held in consciousness, but were too difficult for the ego to bear. The qualities are repressed back into the unconscious and are carried just below the level of awareness. These qualities can be either negative or positive traits. For example, being very stingy is a negative quality that an individual may find hard to accept. Thus, this is forced back into the shadow. If an individual has always been treated as though they were not smart, his or her real intelligence, a positive quality, may be contained in the shadow.

Symbol

The image and feeling-based psychic product produced by the unconscious to facilitate ego development and greater alignment with the Self. The symbol arises when the conscious position lacks the skills necessary to resolve a current crisis. The symbol compels the unconscious and the conscious mind to bring about psychic growth and development.

Transcendent Function

The process of transcending, or *climbing across,* the gap in the polar opposition that occurs in the ego during an intrapsychic or adaptive crisis. The transcendent function occurs when the ego is forced to hold both poles of the opposition in consciousness at the same time. This results in the untenable position of the simultaneous conscious obligation to both the certainty of the fact of one pole and its antithesis at the other. This stalemate causes a buildup of psychic pressure that has nowhere to move. It is thus forced down into the unconscious where it accesses new psychic material that will resolve the ego's crisis, and align the ego more to the Self.

Unconscious

The part of human mental functioning that lies beneath ordinary awareness. New psychic products emerge out of the unconscious. The unconscious precedes what is conscious. This is a right brain quality and is characterized by images.

Undirected or Fantasy Thinking

The mode of thinking characterized by unconscious processes. This is an image and feeling-based right hemispheric process.

References

Achenbach, T.M. (1991). *Manual for the Child Behaviour Checklist/4-18 and 1991 profile.* Burlington: University of Vermont, Department of Psychiatry.

Adam, J.M. (1985). *Le texte narrative. Traité d'analyse textuelle des récits.* Paris: Nathan.

Adler, A. (1970). *The education of children.* Salt Lake City, UT: Gutenberg Publishers.

Arbib, M. (2002). The mirror system, imitation, and the evolution of language. In C. Nehaniv, & K. Dautenhahn (Eds.), *Imitation in animals and artifacts* (pp. 229–280). Cambridge, MA: MIT Press.

Armstrong, T. (1999). *7 Kinds of Smart: Identifying and developing your multiple intelligences.* New York, NY: New American Library.

Arnold, E. (1970). *The song celestial the Bhagavad Gita.* London: Routledge & Kegan Paul Ltd.

Badenoch, B. (2008). *Being a brain-wise therapist: A practical guide to interpersonal neurobiology.* New York, NY: W.W. Norton & Company, Inc.

Barkley, R. A. (1990). *Attention-Deficit Hyperactivity Disorder: A Handbook for diagnosis and treatment.* London: Guilford Press.

Barkley, R. A., Murphy, K.R., and Bush, T. (2001). Time perception and reproduction in young adults with attention deficit hyperactivity disorder. *Neuropsychology 15,* 351–360.

Beck, J.S., Beck, A.T., Jolly, J.B. and Steer, R.A. (2006). *Beck Youth Inventories of Emotional and Social Impairment.* 2. Ed. San Antonio, TX: Psychological Corporation.

Bergström, M. (1998). *Neuropædagogik: en skole for hele hjernen.* København: Hans Reitzel.

Biederman, J., Monuteaux, M.C., Doyle, A.E., Seidman, L.J., Wilens, T.E., Ferrero, F., & Faraone, S.V. (2004). Impact of executive function deficits and attention-deficit/hyperactivity disorder (ADHD) on academic outcomes in children. *Journal of Consulting and Clinical Psychology, 72*(5), 757–766.

Birnbaum, R. (1979). *The healing Buddha.* Boston, MA: Shambala Publications.

Birren, F. (1961). *Color psychology and color therapy: A factual study of the influence of color on human life.* Whitefish, MT: Kessinger Publishing, LLC.

Blakeslee, S. & Blakeslee, M. (2008). *The body has a mind of its own: How maps in your brain help you do (almost) everything better.* Kindle edition. New York, NY: Random House Digital Inc.

Boleyn-Fitzgerald, M. (2010). *Pictures of the mind: What the new neuroscience tells us about who we are.* Upper Saddle River, NJ: FT Press.

Bradway, K. & McCoard, B. (1997). *Sandplay – Silent workshop of the psyche.* New York, NY: Routledge.

Brown, S. & Vaughan, C. (2009). *Play: How it shapes the brain, opens the imagination, and invigorates the soul.* New York, NY: Avery.

Budge, E.A.W. (1904). *The gods of the Egyptians: Studies in Egyptian mythology.* Chicago, IL: Open Court Publishing.

Cajete, G. (1999). *Native science: Natural laws of interdependence.* Santa Fe. NM: Clear Light Books.

Campbell, J. (2008). *The hero with a thousand faces.* Novato, CA: New World Library.

Cattanach, A. (1994). *Play Therapy. Where the Sky Meets the Underworld.* London: Jessica Kingsley Publishers.

Chodorow, J. (Ed.) (1997). *Jung on active imagination: Key readings selected and introduced by Joan Chodorow.* London: Routledge.

Coe, Michael D. (1972). "Olmec jaguars and Olmec kings". In E.P. Benson (Ed.), *The cult of the feline.* (pp. 1–12). Washington, DC: Dumbarton Oaks.

Cooper, J.C. (2004). *An illustrated encyclopaedia of traditional symbols.* London: Thames & Hudson.

Damasio, A. (2010). *Self comes to mind: Constructing the conscious brain.* New York, NY: Pantheon Books.

Darian, S.G. (1978). *The Ganges in myth and history: A study of mythology, symbolism, sculpture, and history of the Ganges river.* Honolulu, HI: University Press of Hawaii.

de Gubernatis, A. (1978). *Zoological mythology or the legends of animals.* New York, NY: Arno Press. (Original work published 1872).

De Vries, A. (1984). *Dictionary of symbols and imagery.* Amsterdam: Elsevier Science Publishers B.V.

Doidge, N. (2007). *The brain that changes itself: Stories of personal triumph from the frontiers of brain science.* New York, NY: Penguin.

Dong, L. (2010). *Mulan's legend and legacy in China and the United States.* Philadelphia, PA: Temple University Press.

Dreikurs, R. & Dinkmeyer, D. (2000). *Encouraging children to learn.* London: Routledge.

Eastwood, P. S. (2002). *Nine windows to wholeness. Exploring numbers in sandplay therapy.* Honolulu, HI: Sanity Press.

Eliade, M. (1974). *Shaminism: Archaic techniques of ecstacy.* Princeton, NJ: Princeton University Press.

Eliade, M. (1991). *Images and symbols: Studies in religious symbolism.* Princeton, NJ: Princeton University Press.

Eliade, M. (1996). *Patterns in comparative religions*. Lincoln, NE: University of Nebraska Press.

Elkind, D. (2007). *The power of play: Learning what comes naturally*. New York, NY: Da Capo Press.

Ferguson, G.W. (1966). *Signs and symbols in Christian art*. Oxford: Oxford University Press.

Finke, R. A. (1986, March). Mental imagery and the visual system: What is the relation between mental imagery and visual perception? Recent work suggests the two share many of the same neural processes in the human visual system. *Scientific American, 254* (3), 88–95.

Fox, C. (1993). *At the very edge of the forest: The influence of literature on storytelling by children*. London: Cassell.

Frazier, S. H. (Ed.). (1975). *A psychiatric glossary: The meaning of terms frequently used in psychiatry*. New York, NY: American Psychiatric Association.

Friedrich, P. (2006). Revolutionary politics and communal ritual. In Swartz, M.J.; Turner, V. & Tuden, A. (Eds.), *Political anthropology*. Chicago: Transaction Publishers.

Gage, J. (2000). *Color and meaning: Art, science, and symbolism*. Berkeley, CA: University of California Press.

Gallese, V. & Lakoff, G. (2005). The Brain's Concepts: The Role of the Sensory-Motor System in Conceptual Knowledge. *Cognitive Neuropsychology 22*, 455–79.

Gallese, V. (2007, April). Before and below 'theory of mind': Embodied simulation and the neural correlates of social cognition. *Philosophical Transactions of the Royal Society: Biological Sciences, 362* (1480), 659–669.

Gazzaniga, M.S. (1998). *The mind's past*. (Kindle Edition) Los Angeles, CA: University of California Press.

Gimbutas, M. (1982). *The gods and goddesses of old Europe: Myths and cult images*. Berkeley, CA: University of California Press.

Glasser, W. (1975). *Schools without failure*. New York, NY: Harper and Row.

Glazier, M. & Hellwing, M.K. (Eds.). (2004). *The modern Catholic encyclopedia*. Collegeville, MN: The Order of St. Benedict.

Golinkoff, R.M., Hirsh-Pasek, K. & Singer, D.G. (2006). Why play = learning: A challenge for parents and educators. In Singer, D.G., Golinkoff, R.M. & Hirsh-Pasek, K. (Eds.), *Play = learning: How play motivates and enhances children's cognitive and social-emotional growth* (pp. 3–14). Kindle Edition. New York, NY: Oxford University Press.

Goodenough, E.R. (1992). *Jewish symbols in the Greco-Roman period*. Princeton, NJ: Princeton University Press.

Greenspan, S. I. & Wieder, S. (2009). *Engaging autism: Using the floortime approach to help children relate, communicate, and think*. Cambridge, MA: Da Capo Lifelong Books.

Guðmundsson, E., Skúlason, S. & Salvarsdóttir, K. S. (2006). *WISC-IV IS. Mælifræði og túlkun*. Reykjavik: The Psychological Corporation.

Haber, R.N. (1983). The impending demise of the icon: A critique of the concept of iconic storage in visual information processing. *Behavioral and Brain Sciences, 6*, 1–11.

Hausman, G. & Hausman, L. (2000). *The mythology of cats: Feline legend and lore through the ages*. New York, NY: Berkley Trade.

Hellige, J.B., Laeng, B. & Michimata, C. (2010). Processing asymmetries in the visual system. In Hugdahl, K. & Westerhausen, R. (Eds.) The two halves of the brain: Information processing in the cerebral hemispheres, (pp.367–415). Cambridge, MA: MIT Press.

Henderson, J. L. (1990). Ancient myths and modern man. In C.G Jung (Ed.), *Man and his Symbols*. (pp. 104–157). London: Penguin Arkana.

Homer's *Odyssey*. (2000). Lombardo, S. (Trans.). Indianappolis, IN: Hackett Publishing Company.

Howard, J.H., Howard, D.V., Japikse, K.C. & Eden, G.F. (2006). Dyslexics are impaired on implicit highter-order sequence learning, but not on implicit spatial context learning. *Neuropsycholgica, 44*, 1131–1144.

Huizinga, J. (1955). *Homo ludens: A study of the play-element in culture*. Boston, MA: Beacon Press.

Iacoboni, M. (2008). *Mirroring people: The new science of how we connect with others*. New York, NY: Farrar, Straus and Giroux.

Indiviglio, F. (2001). *Seahorses: Everything about history, care, nutrition, handling, and behavior*. Hauppauge, NY: Barron's Educational Series.

Jung, C.G. (1968). *Psychology and alchemy*. Princeton, NJ: Princeton University Press.

Jung, C.G. (1970). *Civilization in transition*. Princeton, NJ: Princeton University Press.

Jung, C.G. (1976). *Symbols of transformation: An analysis of the prelude to a case of schizophrenia*. Princeton, NJ: Princeton University Press.

Jung, C.G. (1977). *Psychological types*. Princeton, NJ: Princeton University Press.

Jung, C.G. (1979). *Freud and psychoanalysis*. Princeton, NJ: Princeton University Press.

Jung, C.G. (1980). *The archetypes and the collective unconscious*. Princeton, NJ: Princeton University Press.

Jung, C.G. (1981a). *The development of personality*. Princeton, NJ: Princeton University Press.

Jung, C.G. (1981b). *The structure and dynamics of the psyche*. Princeton, NJ: Princeton University Press.

Jung, C.G. (1985). *The practice of psychotherapy: Essays on the psychology of the transference and other subjects*. Princeton, NJ: Princeton University Press.

Kalff, D.M. (1988). *Sandplay in Switzerland*. (Seminar notes). Zurich: University of California at Santa Cruz.

Kalff, D. M. (2003). *Sandplay: A psychotherapeutic approach to the psyche*. Cloverdale, CA: Temenos Press.

Konorski J. (1948). *Conditioned reflexes and neuron organization*. Boston, MA: Cambridge University Press.

Kris, E. (1988). *Psychoanalytic explorations in art*. New York, NY: International Universities Press.

Langton, E. (1949). *Essentials of demonology: A study of Jewish and Christian doctrines, its origin and development*. London: AMS Press Inc.

Lakoff, G. (1987). *Women, fire, and dangerous things: What categories reveal about the mind*. Chicago, IL: University of Chicago Press.

Lewin, K. (1935). *A dynamic theory of personality*. New York, NY: McGraw-Hill.

Luria, A.R. (1932). *The nature of human conflicts*. New York, NY: Liveright.

Lüthi, M. (1986). *The European Folktale: form and nature*. Bloomington: Indiana University Press.

Malek, J. (1997). *The cat in ancient Egypt*. Philadelphia, PA: University of Pennsylvania Press.

Martin, T. (2005). *The world of whales, dolphins, & porpoises: Natural history & conservation*. Minneapolis, MN: Voyageur Press.

Martindale, C. (1989). Personality, situation, and creativity. In J. A. Glover, R. T. Ronning, & C. R. Reynolds (Eds.). *Handbook of creativity*. (pp. 211–232). New York, NY: Plenum Press.

Mayes, C. (2005). *Jung and education: Elements of an archetypal pedagogy*. Lanham, MD: R & L Education.

Neill, A.S. (1984). *Summerhill: A radical approach to child rearing*. New York, NY: Pocket Books.

Neumann, E. (1972). *The great mother: An analysis of the archetype*. Princeton, NJ: Princeton University Press.

Noyes, M. (1981). Sandplay imagery: An aid to teaching reading. *Academic Therapy, 17* (2), 231–237.

Opie, I. & Opie, P. (Eds.). (1972). *The classic fairy tales*. London: Addey and Company. (Original version by Grimm, J. & Grimm, W. published 1853).

Opie, I. & Opie, P. (Eds.). (1997) *The Oxford dictionary of nursery rhymes*. London: Oxford University Press.

Ouvinen, P. and Stam, B. (1999). *Jag tycker jag är* (I think I am). Psyckologiförlaget AB.

Oztop, E., Kawato, M. and Arbib, M. (2006, April). Mirror neurons and imitation: A computationally guided review. *Neural Networks, 19* (3), 254–271.

Paley, V.G. (2005). *A child's work: The importance of fantasy play*. Chicago, IL: University of Chicago Press.

Penfield, W. (1977). *No man alone: A neurosurgeon's life.* New York, NY: Little, Brown and Company.

Piaget, J. (1962a). *The language and thought of the child.* London: Routledge & Kegan Paul.

Piaget, J. (1962b). *Play, dreams, and imitation in childhood.* New York, NY: Norton.

Pinker, S. (2007, January). The mystery of human consciousness. *Time, 29.*

Ramachandran, V.S. (2000, May). Mirror neurons and imitation learning as the driving force behind "the great leap forward" in human evolution. Paper for Edge.org.

Reyna, R. (1993). *Dictionary of Oriental philosophy.* New Delhi: Munshiram Manoharlal Publishers.

Rizzolatti, G.; Fadiga, L.; Gallese, V. & Fogassi, L. (1996a). Premotor cortex and the recognition of motor actions. *Cognitive Brain Research 3,* 131–141.

Rizzolatti, G.; Gallese, V.; Fadiga, L.;& Fogassi, L. (1996b). Action recognition in the premotor cortex. *Brain 119* (2), 593–609.

Rogers, C. R. (1977). *On Becoming a person. A therapist's view of psychotherapy.* London: Constable.

Russell, J. B. (1977). *The devil: Perceptions of evil from antiquity to primitive Christianity.* Ithaca, NY: Cornell University Press.

Sacks, O. (1990, November). Neurology and the Soul. *New York Review of Books, November 22.*

Salman, S. (1997). The creative psyche: Jung's major contributions. In Eisendrath, P.Y. & Dawson, T. (Eds.), *The Cambridge companion to Jung.* (pp. 52–70). Cambridge, MA: Cambridge University Press.

Samuels, A., Shorter, B. & Plaut, F. (1997). *A critical dictionary of Jungian analysis.* London: Routledge & Kegan Paul.

Sherab, K.P. & Tsewang, K. (2010). *The Buddhist path: A practical guide from the Nyingma tradition of Tibetan Buddhism.* Ithaca, NY: Snow Lion Publications.

Singer, J. (1995). *Boundaries of the soul: The practice of Jung's psychology.* Dorset, U.K.: Prism Press.

Singer, J.L. (1999). Imagination. In Runco, M.A. and Pritzker, S.R. (Eds.), *Encyclopedia of Creativity, II,* (pp. 13–25). London: Academic Press.

Singer, J.L. (2006). Learning to Play and Learning Through Play. In Singer, D.G., Golinkoff, R.M. & Hirsh-Pasek, K. (Eds.), *Play = learning: How play motivates and enhances children's cognitive and social-emotional growth,* (pp. 251–260). Kindle Edition. New York, NY: Oxford University Press.

Singh, V. (1994). *The river goddess.* London: Moonlight Publishing.

Sperry, R.W. (1976). Hemispheric specialiation of mental faculties in the brain of man. In T.X. Barber (Ed.), *Advances in altered states of consciousness & human potentialities, Volume I.* (pp. 53–63). New York, NY: Psychological Dimensions, Inc.

Stewart, L.H. (1992). *Changemakers: A Jungian perspective on sibling position and the family atmosphere.* London: Routledge.

Storr, A. (1989). Individuation and the Creative Process. In P. Abbs (ed.), *The symbolic order: A contemporary reader on the arts debate.* (pp. 183–197). London: The Falmer Press.

Sturluson, S. (1984). *The prose edda: Tales from Norse mythology.* Berkeley, CA: University of California Press.

Suler, J. R. (1980). Primary Process Thinking and Creativity. *Psychological Bulletin, 88,* 144–165.

Sunquist, M. & Sunquist, F. (2002). *Wild cats of the world.* Chicago: University of Chicago Press.

Tatar, M. (1987). *The Hard Facts of the Grimms' Fairy Tales.* Princeton, New Jersey: Princeton University Press.

Turner, B.A. (2005). *The handbook of sandplay therapy.* Cloverdale, CA: Temenos Press.

Turner, B.A. (Ed.). (2004). *H.G. Wells' floor games: A father's account of play and its legacy of healing.* Cloverdale, CA: Temenos Press.

Turner, V. (1990). Are there universals of performance in myth, ritual and drama? In R. Schechner and W. Appel (Eds), *By Means of performance. Intercultural studies of theatre and ritual,* (pp. 8–18). Cambridge: Cambridge University Press.

Unnsteinsdottir, K. (2002). Fairy tales in tradition and in the classroom: Traditional and self-generated fairy tales as catalysts in children's educational and emotional development. (Unpublished doctoral dissertation). University of East Anglia, Norwich.

Vedfelt, O. (1992). *Drømmenes dimensioner. Drømmenes væsen, funktion og fortolkning.* København: Gyldendal.

Vitruvius, M.P. (2008). *De architectura, libri.* Charleston, SC: BiblioBazaar. (Original work published in first century bce).

von Buchholtz, J. (2007). *Snow White – She was quite a ninny, wasn't she?!* Atlanta, GA: C.G. Jung Society of Atlanta.

von Franz, M. L. (1989). *Eventyrfortolkning. En introduktion.* København: Gyldendal.

von Franz, M. L. (1990). *Individuation in Fairy Tales.* London: Shambhala.

Vygotsky, L. S. (1978). *Mind in Society. The development of higher psychological processes.* M. Cole, V. John-Steiner, S. Scribner & E. Souberman (Eds.), London: Harvard University Press.

Waldau, P. (Ed.) (2006). *A Communion of subjects: Animals in religion, science, and ethics.* New York, NY: Columbia University Press.

Wasserman, J. (Ed.). (2008). *The Egyptian book of the dead: The book of going forth by day.* Chicago, IL: KWS Publishers.

Wechsler, D. (1992). *Wechsler Intelligence Scale for Children. 3th ed. UK. Manual.* London: The Psychological Corporation.

Weinrib, E.L. (2004). *Images of the self: The sandplay therapy process.* Cloverdale, CA: Temenos Press.

Wickes, F. (1988). *The inner world of childhood.* Boston, MA: Sigo Press.

Wilson, F.R. (1999). *The hand: How its use shapes the brain, language, and human culture.* New York, NY: Vintage Books.

Yang, C.K. (1961). *Religion in Chinese society: A study of contemporary social functions of religion and some of their historical factors.* Berkeley, CA: University of California Press.

Zelan, K. & Bettelheim, B. (1982). *On learning to read.* New York, NY: Vintage.

Index

A

abandonment, 103
abuse, 14, 159, 172, 175
Achenbach, 36, 49, 105, 144, 189
   Thomas M. Achenbach, x, 35
action understanding, 19
Adam, Jean-Michel, 30, 239
ADD - Attention Deficit Disorder, 34, 49,
   144, 190
ADHD, 34, 35, 105, 194, 195, 224, 239
   attention deficit, 37, 38
ADHD - Attention Deficit Disorder with
   Hyperactivity, vii, viii, 34
Adler, Alfred, vii
airplane, 106, 107, 118, 124, 133, 157, 158
alchemical vas, 212
alien, 224, 227
altar, 115, 116, 122, 171, 172, 198, 209,
   221, 229
anchor, 62, 106, 124, 205, 227
anger, 35, 49, 108, 110, 113, 116, 118, 119, 122,
   124, 134, 141, 144, 208, 210
anima, 226, 235. *See* animus; *See* animus
animals, 51, 52, 53, 54, 64, 66, 68, 72, 73, 81, 85,
   89, 90, 91, 93, 96, 102, 106, 108, 109, 120,
   122, 126, 127, 130, 131, 134, 136, 137, 140,
   150, 151, 157, 162, 163, 164, 165, 166, 167,
   168, 169, 171, 175, 178, 181, 183, 193, 198,
   214, 218, 239, 240
animus, 30, 69, 88, 90, 91, 94, 95, 96, 98, 99, 103,
   148, 151, 155, 159, 226, 235
anthropos, 55, 116, 122, 176
Antonio Damasio, 13
apprehension, 35
Arbib, 19, 20, 239, 243
   Michael A. Arbib, 19

archetype, 61, 65, 115, 116, 137, 155, 158, 171,
   176, 220, 235, 236, 237, 243
   archetypal, 24, 60, 66, 70, 84, 87, 90, 95, 98,
   104, 107, 119, 134, 146, 147, 148, 158,
   163, 165, 168, 181, 194, 197, 198, 204,
   205, 217, 218, 227
Arjuna, 87
Attention Deficit/ Hyperactivity Disorder
   Rating Scale, 35, 36

B

baptism, 66
bat, 51, 52, 54, 56
beach, 93, 94, 95
bear, 8, 21, 53, 80, 81, 85, 115, 116, 155, 165,
   168, 180, 181, 183, 237
Beck's Youth Inventories of Emotional and
   Social Impairment, 35
belief, 14, 23, 85, 147, 215
Bergström, 239
   Matti Bergström, 24, 25
Bettelheim, Bruno, vii
Bhagavad Gita, 87, 239
Bible
   Biblical, 131, 148
bird(s), 64, 66, 67, 72, 75, 77, 108, 112, 113, 115,
   120, 121, 127, 128, 132, 148, 156, 158, 166,
   171, 181, 209, 224
birth, 29, 70, 76, 82, 95, 121, 131, 132, 134, 141,
   155, 164, 165, 205, 209
black, 64, 87, 94, 121, 122, 127, 130, 133, 134,
   144, 146, 147, 157, 162, 163, 167, 172, 180,
   183, 186, 198, 209, 214
blades. *See* sword(s)
Blakeslee, S. & Blakeslee, M., 14
blood, 29, 85, 86, 108, 131, 163, 171, 184

blue, 6, 51, 54, 55, 56, 59, 83, 84, 85, 86, 112, 118, 144, 157, 161, 171, 172, 187, 193, 194, 201, 211
body map
    mental or mind map, ix, 11, 12, 16
Boleyn-Fitzgerald, 14, 15, 18, 240
    Miriam Boleyn-Fitzgerald, 12
bomb, 109, 118, 119, 124, 133, 135
bones, 54, 56, 64, 81, 115, 145, 147, 224
    skull, 106, 107, 110, 124
    vertebrae, 134
Book of Going Forth By Day, 147
books, ii, vii, viii, 1, 4, 5, 29, 37, 75, 76, 77, 106, 108, 109, 110, 111, 112, 113, 121, 130, 131, 133, 147, 153, 154, 155, 186, 234
bottle, 84, 88, 107, 123, 145, 146, 150, 151, 162, 171, 172, 187, 197, 198, 201, 205
Brahma, 56
brain stem, 25, 82
breast, 66
bridge, 106, 107, 112, 115, 118, 145, 146, 148, 162, 176, 193, 198, 204, 217, 221, 225, 226
Broca's area, 20
Brown
    Stuart Brown, 26, 240, 244
Buddha, 56, 62, 73, 81, 86, 95, 107, 108, 109, 110, 112, 113, 115, 121, 154, 156, 198, 209, 221, 239
Buddhism, 61, 244
Buddhist, 86, 95, 121, 244
butterflies
    butterfly, 102, 103, 104, 156
butterfly, 104, 156, 158, 166, 221

C

calculation. *See* Mathematics
camel, 123, 124
cats, 55, 68, 147, 151, 181, 187, 214, 242, 245
Cattanach, 240
    Ann Cattanach, 27
cave, 133, 135, 136, 150, 151, 153, 155, 186, 223, 224, 228
center, 52, 53, 55, 56, 61, 62, 66, 67, 69, 70, 74, 85, 86, 87, 88, 90, 91, 94, 99, 108, 110,

113, 116, 121, 134, 141, 161, 162, 168, 171, 183, 187, 194, 198, 201, 205, 209, 220, 221, 226, 227
center(ing), 88, 141, 160, 205, 224
center(s)
    central, 7, 15, 26, 29, 57, 59, 60, 61, 62, 65, 66, 70, 73, 83, 85, 87, 103, 110, 112, 113, 116, 128, 146, 147, 156, 160, 162, 169, 177, 181, 184, 198, 201, 202, 211, 214, 215, 217, 220, 221, 226, 235, 236, 237
cerebral cortex, 11, 25
chakra, 86
change. *See* transformation
Child Behavior Checklist, 35
    CBCL. *See* Achenbach; *See* Achenbach
China, 53, 128, 161, 162, 219, 220, 240
Christ, 61, 62, 74, 85
Christian, 61, 62, 74, 85, 214, 241, 243
Christmas, 76, 82
circle, 59, 61, 66, 113, 158, 161, 163, 177, 194, 204, 205, 221
    circular, 59, 66, 90, 152, 177, 205, 229
clock, 69, 102, 118, 119
collection, 4, 6, 8, 118, 134
collective unconscious, 23, 62, 146, 235
compensatory product. *See* transcendant function; *See* transcendant function
conflicts
    psychological conflicts, 8, 9, 81, 108, 113, 116, 217, 218, 220, 227, 243
confusing behavior, 35, 144
conscious, 7, 9, 12, 13, 15, 16, 18, 23, 24, 26, 27, 28, 56, 62, 82, 87, 91, 94, 95, 98, 102, 127, 128, 181, 198, 215, 217, 221, 224, 226, 227, 236, 237, 238, 240
conscious mind, 7, 15, 198, 224, 237
constellation of the Self, 61
cortical activity, 12
cowboy, 201, 202
creative thinking, 12, 26
creativity
    creative, 3, 5, 12, 16, 21, 22, 23, 24, 25, 26, 27, 30, 34, 49, 53, 57, 74, 81, 105, 159, 215, 224, 229, 243, 244

crocodile, 107, 109, 128, 140, 146, 147, 150, 151, 155, 156, 162, 169
crocodile(s), 105, 109, 126, 127, 128, 129, 130, 131, 134, 137, 141
cross, 16, 19, 57, 61, 110, 147, 193, 202, 221
cross hemispheric, 87
cross-hemispheric, 16
crown, 61, 85, 112, 152, 186

D

Damasio, 13, 15, 240
    Antonio Damasio, 13
darkness, 56, 62, 76, 86, 91, 95, 108, 131, 158, 163, 226
dark woman
    dark feminine, 166
da Vinci, 177
Da Vinci, 176, 177
dead
    death, 115
death, 29, 54, 61, 95, 121, 122, 124, 129, 131, 135, 209
depression, 26, 35, 38, 49, 144, 189
development
    of personality, 8
    personality, 9
developmental process
    change. *See* transformation
devil, 146, 148, 214, 244
devouring, 147, 151, 156, 159, 181, 209, 212
diagonal(s), 56, 57, 110, 193, 212
    diagonally, 56, 57, 110, 193, 212
Dieckmann
    Hans Dieckmann, 28
dinosaur, 53, 118, 119, 123, 124, 126, 127, 128, 133, 136, 137, 140, 168, 169, 194
directed thinking, 7, 24
direction of the healing, 53
Divine, 56
divorce, 105, 134, 141
divorce(d), 129
dog(s), 72, 93, 94, 102, 112, 113, 126, 127, 150, 151, 153, 154, 155, 164, 175, 176

Doidge
    Norman Doidge, 13
dolphin, 58, 59, 60, 61, 62, 103
Dora Kalff, 4, 5, 7, 28, 127, 148
Dreikurs, Rudolph, vii
duality, 56, 82, 134, 150
duck(s), 74, 153
dwarf(s), 60, 91, 103, 186
dyslexia, 45, 46, 143
    dyslexic, 34, 49, 54

E

earth, 52, 61, 66, 70, 74, 85, 88, 91, 102, 131, 132, 133, 136, 158, 163, 167, 171, 203, 221
educational deficits, 25
egg, 55, 90, 97, 98, 99, 107, 108, 112, 113, 115, 124, 128, 132, 136, 137, 140, 154, 155, 168, 170, 172, 176
ego, 26, 65, 77, 87, 90, 98, 99, 128, 154, 217, 221, 224, 235, 236, 237
elephant(s), 68, 69, 70, 84, 87, 130, 131, 158, 198, 214, 215
Elkind
    David Elkind, 25, 241
elves, 89, 90, 91, 93, 104, 164, 183, 184, 186
embodied cognition, 20
embodied semantics, 20
emotional, 1, 3, 18, 23, 26, 33, 34, 35, 38, 39, 46, 60, 144, 158, 165, 245
    emotions, 17, 24, 165
Estelle L. Weinrib, 1
executive function, 194, 239
extraterrestrial, 190, 223, 224

F

fairy tale(s)
    one-dimensionality, 29
    structure of fairy tales. *See* Lüthi; *See* Lüthi
fairy tales, 3, 23, 25, 28, 29, 86, 121, 243, 245
fantasy, 6, 23, 24, 25, 26, 27, 28, 29, 189, 210, 243
Father Christmas, 75, 76, 77
feather(s), 66, 97, 98, 99, 121, 122, 148, 156, 166, 171, 209, 229

feeding
  nourish, 74, 164, 211
feelings, 11, 13, 119, 132, 224
feminine, 52, 53, 54, 55, 56, 57, 59, 61, 65, 66,
  69, 70, 73, 74, 87, 90, 91, 94, 95, 96, 113, 146,
  147, 148, 151, 152, 155, 158, 162, 168, 181,
  183, 194, 198, 205, 212, 214, 226, 227, 235,
  236
  dark feminine, 52, 156, 163
figures. *See* Sanndplay figures
Finke
  Ronald Finke, 16, 21, 241
fire, 14, 52, 54, 61, 106, 159, 183, 243
fish, 74, 90, 115, 118, 130, 131, 161, 164, 175,
  214, 215
fisherman, 73, 74, 103, 157
five, 38, 44, 55, 56, 61, 66, 116, 120, 122, 132,
  133, 134, 144, 170, 175, 176, 177, 190, 215
Floor Games, 1, 5
flower, 160, 162, 163, 170, 171, 172, 181
food
  nourishment, 45, 72, 80, 93, 147, 157, 165,
    175, 180, 183, 228
forest, 84, 85, 86, 192, 211, 241
fountain, 66
four, 33, 35, 37, 38, 43, 46, 47, 51, 56, 66, 72, 76,
  82, 84, 86, 90, 102, 112, 121, 128, 165, 170,
  171, 193, 195, 197, 198, 209, 212, 235
four corners, 121, 171
Fox
  Carol Fox, 29
free and protected space, 7, 18, 28, 70, 137, 227
Freedom from Distractibility, 39
Freedom from Distraction, 40, 43, 44, 49, 144
Freud, 23, 24, 242
  Sigmund Freud, vii
frog(s), 55, 56, 64, 66, 75, 111, 112, 113, 115,
  122, 127, 128, 154, 161, 162
Full scale IQ, 39, 42

G

Gallese, 20, 241
Ganges, 62

gate
  gateway, 54, 60, 85, 87, 93, 95, 103
Gazzaniga, 14, 241
genome, 15
Glasser, William, vii
God, 56, 74, 85, 175, 220
god(s), 55, 67, 85, 86, 91, 119, 164, 192, 193, 194,
  205, 209, 211, 212, 215, 218, 240, 241
gold, 80, 107, 109, 111, 112, 113, 115, 116, 118,
  120, 121, 126, 127, 130, 131, 134, 175, 197,
  198, 208, 211, 214, 228
Golinkoff
  Roberta Michnik Golinkoff, 25, 26, 241, 244
Great Mother, 52, 67, 95, 151, 212
green, 55, 58, 59, 62, 65, 75, 76, 102, 103, 110,
  115, 126, 128, 135, 141, 151, 155, 158, 161,
  162, 181, 211, 224
greenery, 57
gun(s), 120

H

Haber
  Haber's, 16
  Ralph Haber, 12
habituated patterns, 15, 87
Hades, 148
hand, 14, 19, 20, 21, 24, 26, 35, 43, 65, 68, 69, 98,
  121, 151, 155, 246
handbag
  purse, 94
hand(s), 19, 20, 21, 64, 65, 69, 108, 150, 156,
  172, 177, 202
Hansel and Gretel, 86
healing, 9, 15, 28, 55, 62, 73, 103, 110, 116, 128,
  134, 181, 187, 194, 205, 212, 227, 239, 245
heart, 98, 108, 115, 128, 146, 147, 148, 154, 172,
  184, 209, 224
heaven(s), 61, 74, 91, 113, 132, 158, 171, 221
Henderson, 29, 242
  Joseph Henderson, 29
H.G. Wells, 1
Hindu, 74, 116, 198, 209
Hinduism, 61, 62, 193

hippopotamus, 64, 66, 130, 157, 168
Hirsh-Pasek
    Kathy Hirsh-Pasek, 25, 26, 241, 244
Homer, 86, 242
horizontal axis, 21
horse(s), 76, 181, 186, 187, 229
Howard, Japikse and Eden, 46
Huizinga, 25, 242
hyperactivity, 37, 38, 239. *See* ADHD

I

Iacoboni
    Marco Iacoboni, 11, 17, 18, 20, 21, 242
image, 7, 12, 15, 16, 20, 21, 22, 24, 33, 35, 46, 66,
    116, 128, 132, 143, 169, 220, 236, 237, 238
    images, 7, 8, 9, 12, 13, 15, 16, 17, 18, 21, 24,
        44, 46, 91, 165, 215, 238, 241
image, images, 1, 12, 235, 240, 246
imagination, 3, 16, 25, 81, 190, 217, 240
    activation of, 12
imaginative storytelling, 23, 33, 81
    storytelling, 23
implicit higher-order sequence learning, 46
implicit spatial context learning, 46
Inanna, 85
Indian, 68, 69, 70, 74, 118, 129, 197, 198, 201,
    202, 211, 216, 229
Indian(s)
    Native American(s), 70
Indians, 68, 69, 70, 133, 183, 186, 192, 193, 201,
    202, 206, 208, 209
individuation, 6, 23, 26, 65, 98, 99, 116, 236, 245
initiation, 29, 77, 86, 98
initiation rites, 29
    stages of, 29
instincts, 73, 87, 91, 112, 131, 132, 165, 181, 214,
    235
instinctual, 87, 90, 91, 94, 131, 132, 151
intelligence, 2, 20, 81, 83, 229
interdisciplinary studies, 2
International Society for Sandplay Therapy, 7
interpretation
    interpreting, 12

interpreter, 14
intersubjectivity, 18
intrapsychic conflict, 53, 108
island, 4, 89, 106, 107, 112, 113, 115, 118, 120,
    123, 134, 170, 197, 225, 228
I Think I Am, 35

J

jaguar, 55
Jesus, 56, 74
jewel, 54, 56, 76, 77, 115, 183, 184, 186
Jonah and the Whale, 131
Jung, 5, 6, 7, 15, 23, 24, 26, 28, 30, 56, 62, 98, 99,
    113, 129, 146, 147, 148, 211, 212, 217, 220,
    224, 226, 235, 240, 242, 244, 245
    Carl Gustav Jung, vii, 65, 232, 243
    Emma Jung, 5
Jungian analysis, 5, 6, 244
Jungian personality theory, 47, 128, 217, 220

K

Kalff
    Dora Kalff, 1, 5, 6, 8, 61, 65, 127, 134, 150,
        155, 158, 205, 220, 227, 242, 243
Kawato, 19, 20, 243
key, 15, 20, 98, 127, 145, 150, 153, 183, 186
key(s), 127
Konorski
    Jerzy Konorski, 13
Krishna, 87, 116, 156, 166, 209, 221

L

labyrinth, 97, 98, 99, 103
ladder, 91
ladybird
    ladybird, 53, 54
ladybug, 52, 53, 54, 68, 70, 146, 147, 150, 151,
    159, 162
Lakoff
    George Lakoff, 20, 241, 243
language, 19, 20, 21, 22, 24, 27, 28, 81, 181, 235,
    239, 244, 246

learning, 1, 2, 3, 15, 19, 21, 25, 31, 33, 34, 45, 46, 53, 64, 74, 81, 82, 202, 215, 244
    movement, 17, 20, 21, 25, 47, 56, 59, 66, 198, 204, 209
left hemisphere, 7, 9, 15, 16
left hemispheric, 9, 104, 236
leopard, 84, 87, 157, 159, 162, 163, 167, 180, 181
Lewin, 25, 243
life, 3, 6, 13, 14, 16, 29, 30, 52, 54, 56, 61, 62, 65, 73, 74, 81, 84, 85, 86, 87, 94, 95, 102, 103, 108, 115, 116, 119, 121, 124, 127, 129, 131, 133, 134, 144, 156, 159, 160, 163, 165, 168, 171, 172, 176, 181, 183, 184, 187, 193, 197, 198, 203, 205, 209, 235, 239, 244
lightening, 91
lighthouse, 52, 53, 57, 59, 69, 109, 110, 157, 158, 159, 172, 214
lightning, 90
limbic, 11, 17, 82, 194, 224
limbic system, 11, 194, 224
lion, 162, 186, 198, 214
literacy, 25. See learning; See learning
lobster, 148, 215
logic, 7, 24, 87, 236
losses
    loss, 9, 15, 28, 104, 110, 124, 129, 132, 134, 144, 158, 163, 172
love, 25, 53, 70, 76, 148, 160, 176
    loving, 53, 54, 60, 69, 94, 110, 115, 128, 172, 224, 229
Lowenfeld, 5, 6
Luria, 25, 243
Lüthi, 29, 243

M

macaque, 17
magic, 51, 54, 60, 80, 88, 91, 97, 98, 99, 106, 107, 108, 112, 130, 133, 145, 146, 151, 154, 155, 163, 172, 175, 176, 186, 190, 214, 220
magician, 73, 155
mandala, 61, 159, 181
manifestation of the Self, 52, 61, 220
Marco Iacoboni, 17
Martindale, 24, 243

masculine, 52, 53, 54, 57, 59, 61, 65, 66, 67, 69, 70, 73, 74, 84, 87, 91, 94, 96, 113, 116, 121, 146, 147, 148, 151, 155, 158, 160, 162, 163, 168, 172, 190, 194, 205, 214, 215, 226, 227, 235, 236
mathematics, 25, 35, 39, 49, 143, 190
Mayes, Clifford, vii
memory, 11, 12, 43, 214
mental image. See image
mental map. See body map or mind map
mental maps, 11, 12
metal, 61
mice, 127, 128, 198
mind, 7, 8, 12, 13, 20, 23, 24, 87, 159, 189, 198, 224, 239, 240, 241, 243
mind maps. See Body or Mental Maps
mirror, 17, 18, 19, 20, 56, 89, 90, 91, 239
mirror neuron(s)
    mirror neuron network(s), 17, 18, 19, 20
mirror neurons, 17, 18, 243, 244
mirror(s), 91, 95, 194, 209, 221
modes of thinking, 23, 24
    autistic and intelligent, 24
Mohammed, 56, 85
monkey, 17, 64, 65, 68, 69, 104, 145, 146, 148, 150, 152, 156, 166
Moomin, 98
Moominmamma, 94
Moomins, 94
mother-child, 127, 155, 158, 168
mother(ing), 54, 70, 94, 104, 147, 159, 160, 165, 168
mother(s), 53, 69, 127, 155, 165
motor cells, 17
motor movement(s), 19
mountain, 52, 72, 73, 80, 81, 82, 165, 181
mouse, 51, 54, 146, 150, 151, 198
movement, 11
Mulan, 76, 85, 88, 90, 162, 208, 240
Muslim, 85

N

Native American, 119, 162, 163
    Amerindian, 74
necklace, 150, 152, 201, 213

Neill, A.S., vii
neural
    growth, development, 11, 12, 13, 14, 15, 16,
        17, 18, 19, 20, 21, 22, 62, 81, 82, 87, 104,
        194, 224, 241
neural integration, 11, 87, 104, 224
neuroplasticity, 13
    neuroplastic, 15
Nidhogg, 131
No Child Left Behind, 25
nourishing, 53, 151, 211
    nourishment, 60, 156, 212
number, 1, 4, 56, 76, 82, 84, 102, 112, 116, 121,
    122, 124, 132, 150, 151, 171, 176, 197, 198,
    214
number two, 56
nurture(s)
    feed(s), 74
nurturing, 14, 27, 53, 54, 55, 74, 103, 104, 151,
    158, 212

O

object, 16, 21, 87, 112, 215
objects, 12, 21, 25, 27, 81, 144, 151, 171, 176,
    190, 215, 224
Odysseus, 86
one, 150
opposing energies, 61, 205
opposites, 134, 158, 202, 212, 218
opposition, 27, 50, 146, 205, 212, 218, 237
opposition(al), 26, 34, 99, 146, 202
Ouvinen, 35
owl, 108, 154, 162, 164, 221
owl(s), 198
Oztop, 19, 20, 243

P

panther
    jaguar, 130, 131, 214
parents separate
    divorce, 107
Parvati, 74
Penfield, Wilder, 11

Perception, 13, 44, 45, 46
Perceptional Organization, 43, 44
Perceptional Reasoning, 43, 44
Perceptual Organization, 20, 39, 40, 49, 144
Perceptual Reasoning, 39, 41, 42, 43
Performance IQ, 39
peripersonal space, 12
personality theory. *See* Jung; *See* Jung
Piaget, 24, 25, 244
pig(s), 70, 131, 164, 187
Pinker
    Steven Pinker, 14, 244
play, 1, 25, 26, 240, 241, 244
poison, 123, 144, 145, 146, 150, 151, 171, 172,
    187, 197, 198, 201, 202, 205, 209
poison(ed), 208, 209
polar opposition, 67, 237
    positive and negative poles, 26, 81, 218,
        237. *See* transcendent function; *See*
        transcendent function
pond, 55, 58, 61, 90, 103, 115, 129, 141, 215, 224
    pool, 59, 61, 62, 66
positive and negative, 98, 148
practice effects, 39
premotor cortex, 17, 19
primary and secondary process thinking, 24
primitive, 95, 108, 119, 122, 127, 134, 137, 212,
    218, 244
process. *See* sandplay process
Processing Speed, 39, 40, 41, 42, 44, 105, 144
projective identification, 18
psychic assets, 53, 148, 193
psychic change
    change. *See* development, transformation
psychic pressure, 27
    psychic tension, 19, 235
psychic stress, 18
psychopomp, 52, 61, 77
puzzle, 83, 84, 85

R

Ramachandran, 19
    V.S. Ramachandran, 244
rationality, 8, 21, 52, 57, 236

reading difficulties, 33, 39, 45, 46
reading difficulty, 46
reality, 14, 15, 16, 18, 19, 24, 56, 96, 102, 163, 171, 175, 189
red, 51, 52, 53, 56, 58, 62, 64, 65, 75, 76, 77, 94, 108, 112, 113, 126, 128, 137, 146, 148, 156, 157, 158, 159, 160, 161, 162, 163, 169, 171, 172, 183, 187, 209, 210, 214, 215, 217
Red Riding Hood, 86
repressed, 30, 65, 147, 237
　　repressed memory. *See* shadow; *See* shadow
right hemisphere, 7, 9, 11, 19, 22, 87
　　negative emotions, 19
　　pain, 19, 27, 28, 64, 73, 127, 152, 163, 165, 175
　　right brain, 19, 238
　　right hemispheric, 8, 13, 15, 235, 236, 238
Rizzolatti
　　Giacomo, 19
　　Giacomo Rizzolati, 20
Rizzolatti, Giacomo, 17, 244
Rogers
　　Carl Rogers, 27, 28, 244
rose(s), 85, 98, 147

S

Sacks
　　Oliver Sacks, 20, 244
sacred ritual(s), 95
sanctum sanctorum, 221
sandplay, 1, 2, 3, 4, 5, 6, 7, 9, 11, 12, 16, 18, 20, 21, 22, 23, 27, 28, 29, 31, 33, 35, 38, 44, 45, 46, 47, 49, 50, 53, 54, 55, 56, 57, 58, 59, 61, 69, 70, 81, 82, 83, 85, 103, 104, 105, 107, 108, 119, 124, 127, 128, 132, 133, 137, 141, 143, 144, 146, 147, 148, 149, 152, 155, 162, 165, 178, 181, 183, 184, 186, 187, 190, 193, 194, 205, 208, 211, 217, 220, 221, 224, 226, 227, 229, 240, 245, 246
　　sandplay procedure, 6
　　training to practice, 6
　　with adults, 6
　　with children, 6
Sandplay, 1, 3, 4, 5, 6, 7, 8, 11, 15, 18, 20, 21, 23, 47, 49, 105, 141, 143, 189, 240, 242, 243
sandplay case, 4, 18
sandplay process.　sandplay
Sandplay Therapists of America, 7
Sandplay therapy, 5, 7
sand tray
　　description, 6
sea, 52, 61, 64, 66, 74, 80, 81, 93, 94, 95, 96, 109, 113, 140, 147, 148, 157, 158, 159, 160, 181, 193, 197, 201, 203, 224, 228
seahorses, 110
sea urchin, 64, 66, 81, 224
seed(s), 128
selection. *See* Oliver Sacks
Self, 1, 4, 7, 15, 26, 30, 36, 55, 56, 62, 65, 66, 67, 69, 70, 74, 85, 86, 87, 88, 90, 91, 94, 98, 113, 115, 119, 124, 128, 132, 137, 147, 148, 152, 156, 158, 160, 171, 172, 184, 194, 205, 215, 217, 220, 221, 224, 226, 227, 235, 236, 237, 240
　　inner truth, 52, 70, 124, 194
self-image, 33, 35
self regulation, 28
self, sense of, 13
sense of self, 11, 13, 14, 17, 21, 141
sexuality, 152, 163
shadow, 30, 65, 113, 115, 128, 141, 147, 152, 236
shaman, 90, 128
shaman(s), 91
shell, 54, 83, 90, 93, 94, 95, 103, 107, 113, 146, 147, 151, 158, 167, 168, 175
　　conch, 93, 94, 95, 96
shells, 54, 56, 81, 85, 93, 94, 172
Shiva, 56
shoe(s), 80, 81, 82, 171
Shoes, 80
Singer
　　Dorothy G., 25, 26, 69, 241, 244
sky, 74
snail, 55, 68, 70, 127
snail(s), 128, 158